To Lawrence
with the
many due
excuses [...]
in pubs.

OPEN TO ALL

How Youth Hostels Changed
The World

Duncan M Simpson

Published in 2016 by FeedARead Publishing

A CIP catalogue record for this title is available from the British Library.

Duncan M Simpson Writing
www.duncanmsimpsonwriting.com

Contents

EPILOGUE

INTRODUCTION

Youth hostels changed the world. When travel was beyond the pockets of many and impossible for many young women, even if they could afford it, youth hostels opened the world.

Youth hostels taught us to travel. We used them to move from one place to another, to journey, not to have a holiday, not to tour but to travel using our own resources.

Youth hostels introduced independent travel for anyone. With a rucksack and guidebook, we travelled the world, met people, made friends and fell in love. Before the internet and budget hotels, youth hostels introduced us to ideas that resonate with travellers today, ideas like simplicity and sociability.

Youth hostels were the last of the big voluntary ventures that sprang from the 19th century's concern for improving lives. At the same time, they were forerunners of the many young peoples' movements of the 20th century, the sub cults of rockers, mods, hippies and punks.

Changing the world, youth hostels have grown up. Today's youth hostels boast bars, restaurants, en suites and free wifi. You can find them in all shapes, sizes and kinds. They are in cities, in towns, in the wilderness, in castles, mansions, mills and converted hotels. Architects design them too, plain with purpose and function.

Official youth hostels are no longer the only kind. Private individuals and chains, backed by venture capital, run hostels. In 2015 there were more than 56 hostels, official and independent, in London alone. Companies, like PGL, run adventure centres. Local authorities run their own centres for schools and groups.

In 2015 the official association of England and Wales, a charity, employed 1,200 people, owned 140 properties and had 1,200 volunteers. Anyone can stay in its youth hostels. You can hire a whole hostel for yourself, your family and friends, if you want.

Youth hostels have grown up. They're no longer the kids they once were. We all can travel independently now. We all can stay in youth hostels too. Mountain bikers use them. Marathon runners, charity riders and businessmen stay in them.

Mountaineers, Sir Chris Bonington and Alan Hinkes; David Bellamy, the naturalist; and former cabinet ministers Richard Caborn, John Prescott and Chris Smith stayed in them. So did Victoria Pendleton, the Olympic cyclist. Comedians Victoria Wood and Meera Syal lampooned them. George Orwell stayed in youth hostels while writing what became *The Road to Wigan Pier* and Patrick Leigh Fermor's diary was stolen from a youth hostel in Germany.

With so many different kinds of hostels doing so many different things with so many different people, you might ask what has become of youth hostels? What makes them special? What makes them different? They've almost become hotels. The things people used to think made them different, like membership, rules, curfews and chores, have all gone.

For those who don't know youth hostels, they can be a mystery. For others they are louche, seedy, a place to stay when there's nowhere else to go, where they have to take you in. They were part of childhood or teenage years, part of that first trip away from home.

Others, who know them, love them. They love the friendly, easy-going ways of youth hostels, their staff and the people who stay in them. They love their democratic attitude, the fact you can cook your own meal, have a meal cooked for you or buy a beer, all in the same place.

For a time, in the wake of the foot and mouth outbreak of 2001, youth hostels excited a great deal of passion. In March 2002 YHA in England and Wales - youth hostels in Scotland and Northern Ireland have their own associations - proposed selling some of its hostels. At the time I was working as YHA's Head of Corporate Affairs. I woke early in the morning and drove to Buxton in Derbyshire to meet the BBC's northern correspondent. It was early spring. The morning was dark. By dim light from inside the building, we set up the correspondent's broadcasting kit on a picnic table in front of the hostel.

People were waking up. Lights were coming on. The place was coming to life. One of the staff, Martin, was opening doors, laying tables and getting ready for the day, the way staff at the hostel had done since it first opened there in 1940, in the former quarry owner's house. Martin knew I was there as I waited with the correspondent for a signal that the *Today* programme, down in London, was ready. After his introduction, the correspondent interviewed Martin and button-holed guests on their way to breakfast.

When he had finished, I said goodbye to the correspondent and thanked Martin for his time. I went back to the office, down the road, in Matlock. The day became hectic. *The Guardian* newspaper and the BBC's *Working Lunch* also covered the story of youth hostel closures. YHA's chief executive, Roger Clarke, gave interviews. I arranged more. We took calls and answered questions. Through it all, I felt I had betrayed something or someone. The outrage of many people washed around me.

And yet, I knew the decision was right. It was the correct one. I believed YHA had too many youth hostels. Too few people stayed in too many of them. Many hostels made too little money whilst others were too busy and in need of money, to repair buildings and modernise facilities. We scraped and spread money too thin in a cycle from which youth hostels had been trying to escape for as long as I could remember.

Few people seemed to want to understand what was happening. People were simply angry. I grew weary eyed from reading irate letters and writing responses. We worked hard, explaining how necessary it was, to raise capital to invest in hostels. Youth hostels were their only assets.

When I finished work in 2013, after 37 years working for youth hostels, I began the explorations that led to this book. I wanted to find out more about youth hostels. Why did they excite such passion? How had they got in the position they were in? Where had they come from? How did they happen? What did they mean and what were they meant to be?

I knew a German school teacher had begun youth hostels. Caught in a thunderstorm when walking with his pupils in 1909, they sheltered in a school. While his pupils slept, Richard Schirrmann lay awake, listening to the storm. He dreamed of a chain of simple places spread across the countryside where young people might stay. Travelling between these youth hostels, children would be out in the fresh air. They would walk and exercise and stretch their limbs. The idea excited him. He opened the first youth hostel in his own school and others caught his excitement. His idea spread throughout Germany before and after the first world war.

I discovered others were doing the same thing, around the same time, in many different places. In Britain the first youth hostel opened in 1930. Then I found chains of hostels had opened in Scotland and Northumberland before that.

The Holiday Fellowship also had a chain of simple huts in the Lake District in 1929 and another in Snowdonia. Youth hostels had been an idea waiting to happen, part of the thinking of many different people in many different places. They were the idea of many, a shared dream and a mass flowering, a growing movement that emerged from the growing leisure of the many and their desire to travel and explore the world beyond their homes.

Everywhere I looked were myths and illusions. Youth hostels were more different and more complicated than I had expected.

The story of youth hostels has two faces. One is the romance of a world wide movement, descended from young people in Germany who had wandered the countryside, with guitars and flags, around 1890. They had been determined to recapture a better life an older generation had betrayed.

Youth hostels inherited their genes. They were forerunners of the great social movements that flowered in the 20th century, the mods and rockers, teddy boys, hippies and punks. Slightly anarchic, ascetic and abstemious, in favour of freedom, youth hostels were a grass roots movement, anti-materialist, pacifist and populist, in love with the pastoral and rural retreats, escapist.

The other face of youth hostels is one that belongs with the last of the big voluntary ventures, emerging from the 19th century's drive to improve people's lives. Descended from the Scouts, the Guides, the Boys Brigade and others, part of the force to preserve the countryside, linked to the National Trust, youth hostels were idealistic, charitable, conservative, worthy and paternal.

By the 1960s youth hostels showed another face. They had become an institution, part of the social life of the country. They settled into a kind of complacency. They forgot their radical roots. They clung to rules and achieved a reputation for being old and out of date when the 1970s caught them.

The next 30 years became a struggle for survival as first one then another event fell upon them. Soaring inflation, rising prices, the demands of their own staff for better conditions, industrial action by teachers, accidents involving children on school trips, each forced change on youth hostels while successive generations demanded more comfort, more privacy and more freedom. Other organisations, institutions and political parties and all of us in our own lives faced that same struggle to modernise.

Finally the foot and mouth outbreak and the internet disrupted youth hostels. Youth hostels had no choice but to change themselves to meet the changes they had created in the world. They changed themselves to meet the demand of a new generation for the kind of footloose independent travel youth hostels had done so much to create.

The story of youth hostels traces the development of travel through the last century to the contemporary world of the internet, of Trip Advisor and Airbnb. It is the story of the outdoors in the 20th century, from the 'back to the land' movement, through national parks, to consumerism. It is also the story of voluntary organisations, of their development into modern, centralised bureaucracies, managed by paid staff.

It became a biography of the people who made youth hostels happen. And it became a bit of my own biography. I've included that too, to emphasise that this is my view of how youth hostels changed the world, not an official history.

Duncan M Simpson
Derbyshire
24 March 2016

PART 1

A PIONEERING SPIRIT

-1-

From Germany to Liverpool

In the summer of 1929, in July, seven young friends from Liverpool
went to Germany. They travelled by train down to London and on to
Harwich for the cross-channel ferry to the Low Countries, Holland and
Belgium. The route was one of the few, before air travel, hovercraft and
tunnel, of crossing to Europe.

The journey they took changed the world of travel for young people.
That summer, when share prices were up and the City of London full of
confidence, there were many reasons for going to Germany. Throughout
the period, mountains, music, culture and rest cures drew people to
Germany. Winifred Holtby, John Maynard Keynes, Wyndham Lewis,
Harold Nicolson, Vera Brittain, WH Auden and Stephen Spender all went.
Christopher Isherwood, the poet, writer and friend of Auden, went too,
for the young men and sex of Berlin. The novel he wrote about his visits
became a play which became a film, *Cabaret*. He left a view of Germany;
lush, decadent and shameless. Others, like Unity Mitford, went to see
Hitler, to witness National Socialism rising from the divisions of a broken
country in the wake of a terrible war.

For slim, boyish and curly headed Tom Fairclough and his friends
another revolution had begun in Germany. That revolution had nothing to

do with Hitler and everything to do with new ways of living. At its heart were healthy living, tramping and walking in footloose freedom over the countryside. Small groups carrying pennants and banners, singing, playing guitars and whistles and other musical instruments had started it. These young people, called *Wandervögel*, wandering birds, opened the countryside beyond the dirt, squalor and poverty of teeming industrial cities. They released young people into fresh air, into nature and the beauty of the countryside. They set off a new style of accommodation, especially for young people.

These new places to stay, *Jugendherbergen* or youth hostels as the British came to call them, proliferated in Germany in the early years of the 20th century. Richard Schirrmann, a young school teacher invented them. Schirrmann loved the outdoors and walking. He believed that children learned best in the outdoors and he took his pupils walking whenever he could. On a walking tour in 1909, when their accommodation for the night fell through and a thunderstorm caught them, they sheltered in a school. While his pupils slept, Schirrmann imagined schools throughout the country providing shelter for young people.

He lost no time bringing his dream to life. Each night, with the help of the school caretaker and his wife, he converted his classroom to a shelter for young people tramping the countryside. He talked to people in his local walking group. He wrote articles for newspapers and journals. Despite the opposition of teachers and colleagues, word of his experiment spread. Success swamped him. Not only children, but young people and adults arrived to stay and not just in summer when he had expected. They began arriving throughout the year. He moved his shelter from the school to a castle which became the first permanent youth hostel in 1912 in Altena, the town where he lived. Others followed. By the 1920s Germany had more than 2,000 youth hostels.

For the first time young people travelled with ease, knowing there would be somewhere for them to stay at the end of the day. Schirrmann wondered if there were youth hostels in Britain. Early in 1928, he wrote to the Anglo-German Academic Bureau in London. He asked if young Germans travelling to Britain would find youth hostels available there. The bureau replied on 1 May that in Britain it was unlikely "that the near future will bring the establishment of youth hostels. It is not customary for young people to go on tours... English young people normally go out into the country in groups and stay at one fixed point in a camp, using their own or hired tents."

But rumours of Schirrmann's *Jugendherbergen* drifted back to Britain. People studying or visiting Germany stayed in youth hostels and experienced them. Coming back they told others about the friendliness and relaxed informality of *Jugendherbergen*. They wished for something similar in Britain. They began agitating for youth hostels at home.

In Liverpool Fairclough heard about them and determined to find out more. He was an office clerk and fortunate to have a job that gave him a modest, steady income. He had served in the first world war and returned from the trenches with a zest for the outdoors. In his leisure time he was the catering secretary for his local walking group.

Germany offered the hope of something new for Fairclough and his friends from "the great lower-middle-class backbone of Liverpool's city life," working in shipping firms as clerks and secretaries. They and others like them were great ramblers and walkers. They called themselves trampers and they were following a new fashion for hiking. They left the cities to walk in the countryside. Whenever they could they swapped the smell, noise and confusion of cities for the peace of the countryside and the pleasure of exercise, if only for a few hours. They could have stayed out longer but they couldn't afford expensive hotels and inns and in any case they were not welcome in those kind of places. They might have slept in hedgerows or camped but Fairclough disliked sleeping out. It was too like life in the trenches and the comfort of having a roof over his head appealed more.

Their trips to the countryside were brief. The distance they could cover in a day limited where they could travel. They wanted to go further. They wanted to see more. They wanted to stay out for one night or longer, walking the hills of Snowdonia or the Lake District. The author, JB Priestley, writing in *John O'London's Weekly* in 1930, highlighted the lack of youth hostels in Britain and what it meant for young people. "All this miserable business at the end of the day," Priestley complained, "this sneaking into hotels and perhaps out again, this searching for a bed at anything like a reasonable price, going round almost cap-in-hand when you ought to have been resting. Many a youth has cut short his walking tour simply because he disliked ending a day in this wretched fashion…"

Fairclough had heard of "the remarkable welcome that awaits trampers at the Youth Shelters in Germany." He wrote to a Mr Walter Simon in Berlin, who put them in touch with a local leader in the Rhineland. In Germany, they made every effort to sell the idea of youth hostels to pioneering enthusiasts from other countries. They made all the arrangements for Fairclough to tour the beautiful Rhineland countryside. They organised leaders, travel and accommodation in hostels and in private homes where needed.

Six others took part in the trip. He went with Connie Alexander, Miss C Banks, Miss JA Shepherd, Miss CD Hall, Dr D Beilenson, and Mr MC Lowenthall. The hostels in Germany required membership of their organisation so all seven took membership of what Fairclough called the '*Verbands fur Deutsch Jugend-herberge*' at 5/- each.

No hint of excitement survives in the accounts they left. No one mentions how many of them had travelled out of England before. No one mentions the excitement of being young and travelling. No one left descriptions of the scents, the change of light crossing the sea, the new languages, the smell of different cooking and the taste of wider landscapes on the continent as they left the sea behind. But it must have been exciting.

They took the cheapest way to Germany, leaving by train from Liverpool at noon on a Saturday. They arrived 36 hours later in Cologne on the Rhine. They stayed in Deutz, on the right bank of the Rhine. The youth hostel, an old converted cavalry barracks in the inner city, could accommodate 300 and was busy most of the summer. Fairclough and his friends paid charges up-front and took their beds for the night in dormitories shared with others of the same sex. They made up their beds with light weight sheets which they hired. Others carried their own. It all kept the costs down and made youth hostels cheap places to stay. Choice extended to the food too. The youth hostel kitchen sold meals or they could prepare their own in kitchens provided for self-catering. Meals were simple and cheap. Those cooking for themselves might have only had sausage and bread.

After eating, people gathered in the common room. They met other boys and girls, young men and women from different towns, cities and countries. They sang together and entertained themselves. They went to bed early and woke the next morning early too. After washing in cold water, breakfast followed. Directed by the house-parents they swept, cleaned and prepared the hostel for that night's guests. In youth hostels receptionists didn't greet guests. Boot boys didn't carry bags. Domestics weren't there to clean and clear. The simple, distinctive style of youth hostels made a special atmosphere of camaraderie, of working together and common ownership. And it kept down costs.

Fairclough and his friends travelled on to Bonen, which Fairclough called Bannen, for the next two nights. They visited a silk factory. They tramped with their hosts. They joined in folk singing and found their hosts eager to learn their songs too. On the Wednesday they watched a play about William Tell in the open air as part of a huge gathering before travelling on to Hagen for the night. They thought Hagen was a poor hostel compared with others they had seen.

From there they went to Weilberg in the Lahn valley, between Westerwald and the Taunus mountains. A new leader joined them. They swam in the river. They sun bathed and toured a historic castle. At Hofheim, close to Frankfurt on the south of the mountain range, they stopped for two nights. The scenery captivated them. They wandered in the woods and heard old folk stories below Grosser Feldberg, the highest mountain in the Taunus.

They spent their last Sunday in Frankfurt and went tramping in the low mountains of the Odenwald, "a vast tract of gloriously wooded country." They stayed in Jugenheim and then in the old city of Heidelberg. Its university and castle impressed them. Heidelberg's youth hostel was one of the most up to date and comfortable they experienced. From there they returned to Frankfurt where they spent an afternoon in bathing costumes becoming sun-baked. They were at an apple-wine-house for the evening. From Frankfurt they went to Wiesbaden and to Rudesheim where they took a steamer through magnificent Rhine scenery. In Cologne their journey ended, back where they had begun.

Fairclough was pleased. They had managed the entire trip of a fortnight for £12. Their adventure had fostered international friendship and had shown them that German people were a great and hospitable nation. "The warmth of the welcome we received was one of the most pleasing features," he reflected. He hoped to support efforts to build youth hostels "not only to take our own Youth out into the beautiful places but also to foster this wonderful international movement so well established in Germany."

Connie Alexander stood with Fairclough on the deck of the ferry coming back to England. Later she recalled it was a bright summer Sunday morning as they approached the English coast. Their thoughts and conversation turned to all that they had heard and seen. "I remember saying pessimistically "Isn't it a pity there are no youth hostels in England?" To which Tom replied, "There is no reason why there shouldn't be.""

She didn't agree. English traditions were different to those in Germany. Parents kept a watchful eye on sons and daughters, limiting their freedom. Her mother and father had only allowed her to go walking in a mixed sex group with reluctance. She couldn't imagine parents allowing their young people to roam the countryside on their own, as they did in Germany. But in answer to all her doubts Fairclough replied "What Germany can do England can do."

His optimism never left him. "He lost no time in gathering together all the forces he could, to bring the idea to the notice of all his rambler friends and influential people." In Liverpool he enlisted Alf Embleton, secretary for the Liverpool and District Ramblers' Federation, in his plans. Since the 1880s walkers had been banding together to go walking. An early group was the Sunday Tramps, a small group of friends in London including the writer Virginia Woolf's father. Walkers in Liverpool had founded their federation in 1922. Federations were social, for those who liked walking in groups, but they also campaigned and fought to preserve footpaths and were part of the drive to give more access to the countryside for ordinary people.

Fairclough proposed that the federation in Liverpool should sound out views and opinions for his radical scheme. They should discover what support there was for youth hostels in Britain. The federation responded in the way organisations often do. They set up a committee and passed the problem back to him. They put Fairclough and Embleton on the committee with another, Ingram Knowles. He was from the British Youth Council that had already been organising tours to Germany using youth hostels. The three of them wrote to clubs, societies, schools and local people. They invited help and support for "Youth Hostels on simple lines, first in North Wales and then elsewhere, where lovers of the open air will be able to obtain accommodation at a price within their means…"

Bertha Gough, a friend of Connie Alexander, kept a diary of the early days of youth hostels in Liverpool. She and Alexander worked at the

African & Eastern shipping line before the firm transferred to London in 1931. In her spare time Gough was secretary for the Holiday Fellowship's clubroom on Lord Street where Fairclough was also a member. The Holiday Fellowship (HF) organised holidays with an emphasis on low cost and sociability for young working class men and women. Fairclough also drew the HF into his plans. On 14 November 1929, Fairclough and Embleton invited people to come and talk things over at the HF Clubroom. Gough helped prepare and serve tea.

Fairclough and Embleton arranged a second meeting, on 12 December 1929. They thought the Reverend HH Symonds should be chairman. He was headmaster of the Liverpool Institute, a local grammar school for boys. They reckoned from the way he spoke that Symonds was a forceful character with all the zeal needed for the job. Symonds, in his forties, was a keen walker. Educated at Rugby and Oriel College, Oxford, he had taught at Clifton College, Bristol, before moving to teach classics at his old school, Rugby, in 1912. After a short time as headmaster at Kings School, Chester, he became headmaster at the Liverpool Institute for Boys where he could create the first-class modern school he wanted.

His views about teaching echoed those of Richard Schirrmann. He also believed that young people learned and developed best by experiencing the world outside the classroom. Symonds encouraged his pupils to take up walking. He set up summer camps for them in the Lake District, at Borrowdale and in the Duddon Valley. With his interests he was an obvious supporter for youth hostels. He accepted an invitation to chair a meeting. But only to get things off the ground. He wrote that he would not accept the post of chairman.

The meeting was a success. 46 people present resolved to form a local Youth Hostels Association. The next day the *Liverpool Post and Mercury* reported the meeting. The new association would provide youth hostels in North Wales "for holiday sojourns on the lines of those already existing, on the Continent." For the first time in English the compound noun 'youth hostel', to describe the kind of accommodation they wanted, appeared in writing. They described themselves as the Merseyside Centre of the British Youth Hostels Association. They had begun.

Symonds, after saying he would not, became chairman. His book *Walking in the Lake District* would become a classic in its day. When the rambling federations banded together to form the Ramblers' Association in 1932 he became editor of their magazine. In 1935, when a relative left him an inheritance, he would give up teaching and retire to the Lake District where he became an active campaigner for national parks and for preserving the Lake District. He would also found the Friends of the Lake District.

The new group held their first council meeting on December 19. They declared the British Youth Hostels Association to be "a movement to establish a chain of hostels, first in North Wales and then in other districts, where young people on walking tours can stay for the nominal charge of 1/- per night." Their object would be "the provision of Hostels and other facilities for enabling young people to visit and enjoy the countryside, either alone or in small parties, and with a preference always to those on foot; so providing for the healthy enjoyment of leisure, for the encouragement of out-door life, and for raising the standard of health, intelligence and general well-being."

T Lloyd Jones represented the Ramblers on the council. ER Jones, a hard headed businessman, also joined them and offered a field as a site for a youth hostel. They invited TA Leonard, who had founded the HF, to be their president. Leonard and Fairclough were friends. Leonard had founded the HF but he was becoming dissatisfied with it. It was becoming too middle-class and conservative for his tastes. He wanted a new organisation with international links to provide young people's camps and mountain huts. Not for the first time Leonard was shifting his allegiances from one organisation to another. He was an inveterate founder of organisations and would become known as the father of social tourism in Britain.

In 1890 he had been a congregational minister at Colne in Lancashire where he loved the wild upland moors on his doorstep. But the habits of his congregation dismayed him. When the mills closed for maintenance once a year, workers and their families fled to the seaside. They went to Blackpool, Morecambe and, if they could afford, to Douglas on the Isle of Man. Their holidays, in Leonard's opinion, "led to thoughtless spending of money, the inane type of amusement and unhealthy overcrowding in lodging houses, moreover it made for vitiated conceptions of life and conduct and produced permanent effects on character."

Leonard dreamed of something better, of fresh air, exercise and companionship, especially for young people. In 1891 he formed a rambling club and took 30 young men for a four-night break to Ambleside in the Lake District. The trip was a revelation. "Long after our return we talked about our experiences and the scenes we had gazed upon, of the gems of wit from certain members of the party and of the jolly songs we sang as we tramped over many a dusty mile," one of the participants on Leonard's first trip remembered.

They went to Caernarfon in North Wales in 1892. A year later they went back to Keswick in the Lake District. Leonard expanded his holiday programme and founded the Co-operative Holidays Association (CHA). He gave up work as a minister to run the CHA full time "to provide recreative and educational holidays." Leonard was an inspiring general secretary. As the CHA expanded he moved around the centres. He lived in different centres at different times. He stamped them with his personality, creating a strong link with the organisation he inspired. By 1913, thirteen British centres catered for over 13,000 guests.

Despite success, Leonard became disillusioned. Disagreements grew within CHA. Some guest houses, such as Ardenconnel with sweeping lawns and mountain views, were too comfortable. The centres were becoming middle class. They attracted the wrong kind of guest. In 1913 Leonard resigned from the CHA. In May that year, in a CHA centre overlooking Masson Mill near Matlock Bath in Derbyshire, Leonard and 13 friends founded the HF.

The falling out was amicable. The Central Committee of the CHA supported his new venture. Some of its members joined him. Leonard was adamant that they were not breaking away from the CHA. They were developing the work begun twenty years before and carrying it further. They had a vision of a simple type of centre, a camp with as little comfort as possible. The goal of the HF was to be "holiday making, to promote the healthy enjoyment of leisure, to encourage the love of the outdoors and to promote social and international friendship". By the end of the 1920s, the HF had 23 houses in the UK and 30,000 guests.

Again, growth brought problems. Once again the wrong kind of people went to the centres; "a frivolous crowd that does not want to think." Too much centralisation was leading to too much bureaucracy. Workers were becoming paid officials and petty bureaucrats. Leonard tried to change the HF. They set up a small chain of mountain huts in the Lake District and North Wales, but before these ideas developed, he turned to youth hostels.

He joined the new committee on Merseyside and went to their meetings and though he had not founded their new movement, he played a leading role in its beginnings. He hoped once again that the new organisation would attract working-class people. He, and others like Fairclough, Alexander and Gough who had been part of the HF, brought to youth hostels an emphasis on low cost and simplicity. They also brought an emphasis on sociability.

They had taken the first step to radical change in Britain. Before youth hostels there were few ways young people could tramp from one place to another. When they did there were no places for them to stay. Since the end of the first world war an increasing jumble of organisations, from the Scouts to the Young Communists, had been venturing into the countryside. They arranged camps and competed with one another. At home in the cities Scouts mocked the Boys Brigade and vice versa. John Hargrave had broken away from the Scouts in 1920 and created the Kindred of the Kibbo Kift, an eccentric less militaristic version of the Scouts. The Kift in turn had given rise to the Woodcraft Folk.

None of them encouraged young people roaming the countryside. Before youth hostels little freedom for the individual or small group to set their own itinerary and to make their own way in the countryside existed. There was little history of wandering from place to place in Britain. Those who did so were likely to be vagabonds, tramps or thieves, except rare individuals, like the poet and writer, Edward Thomas, who wandered the countryside, sleeping in hedgerows or woods. But he was a depressive eccentric, who befriended tramps.

There was no tradition of wandering in Britain and large areas of the countryside were closed, never visited by anyone but the people who owned the land or who lived there. Farmers and landowners resented the invasion of their property by townspeople, who knew nothing of the countryside, who caused damage to crops, left gates open and left litter in their wake. Events on Kinder Scout in Derbyshire, when walkers battled with the police and estate workers for the right to walk on open moorland, and which ended with five men jailed, were two years away.

The group on Merseyside were intent on encouraging young people to wander the countryside in mixed sex groups. Critics would see their vision as dangerous, unhealthy and immoral. The idea that young people, boys and girls, should spend the night together, in the same building, caused disgust. Church groups wanted people in church on Sunday, not wandering about the countryside, and inn-keepers would resist the arrival of competition on their doorsteps.

Youth hostels in Britain were distinctive for other reasons too. Youth hostels in Germany had Richard Schirrmann. The Scouts had Lord Baden-Powell. The Boys Brigade had Sir William Alexander Smith. HF and CHA had TA Leonard. Embleton, Fairclough and Symonds worked together with others. Leonard supported them. But youth hostels had no single leader.

They began when young people seized their own opportunity and created their own freedom. They had no leader and no politics. They were open to anyone and anyone could become a member. Anyone would be able to stay in the radical new style of accommodation they hoped to offer.

Other meetings followed. A Manchester region held its inaugural meeting on 7 February 1930. It would concentrate on youth hostels in the Peak District. But success required something bigger. People would want to go to North Wales from Birmingham, not just from Liverpool. From London people would want to go to the Lake District and Wales as well as the South Downs and the New Forest. As holidays and time off expanded, people would want to travel further. The Merseyside centre of the British Youth Hostels Association could not achieve this on its own. Its success required an organised national movement and a nation wide network of youth hostels.

Notes and references

Oliver Coburn covers the beginnings of youth hostels in England and Wales in his book *Youth Hostel Story*. Tom Fairclough wrote about his trip to Germany for the Ramblers' Association and Reg Taylor included a transcript of the article in *The Pioneering Years*, a history of the early days of youth hostels on Merseyside. Connie Alexander wrote about her early memories of Tom Fairclough and the trip to Germany in *The Youth Hosteller* magazine in July 1965. Ian Shaw, YHA Vice Chairman from 1990-93, with Bertha Gough's permission, copied her diary and made it available to a wider audience, retyped and augmented with images. Graham Heath's biography of Richard Schirrmann was invaluable for this chapter and others. A copy of TA Leonard's *Adventures in Holiday Making* founds its way to me courtesy of Helen Maurice-Jones, who wrote two invaluable histories of youth hostels with Lindsey Porter. TA Leonard tells the story of CHA and HF up to the time when youth hostels started.

"that the near future..." Grassl, Heath, *The Magic Triangle*, p40

"the great lower middle class..." Taylor, *The Pioneering Years*, p2

"All this miserable business..." Coburn, *Youth Hostel Story*, p7

"The remarkable welcome..." Taylor, *The Pioneering Years*, Appendix 1

"a vast tract..." Ibid

"The warmth of the welcome..." Ibid

"not only to take..." Ibid

"I remember saying..." *The Youth Hosteller*, July 1965

"What Germany can..." Ibid

"He lost no time..." Ibid

"a movement to establish..." Taylor, *the Pioneering Years*, p8

"led to thoughtless..." Leonard, *Adventures in Holiday Making*, p19

"Long after our return..." Ibid, p20

First night

My sister told me about youth hostels. She began the journey that brought me to writing this, about youth hostels, after 37 years of staying and working in them. Without her advice, I may never have stepped inside one. Marketing and advertising were crude and unsophisticated in 1976. We learned by word of mouth.

She had been to Europe. For almost a year she had lived and worked in London. She was sophisticated and smart, this sister of mine. She had toured Europe and camped and stayed in youth hostels too. I had seen her photos of Paris, of Switzerland, Venice and Rome, and one of a bus on the side of an Alpine pass. A crowd of smiling young people stood beside it.

While I was packing, getting ready to leave, we talked about my lack of plans. I had little idea of what to do or where to go. She told me if I was looking for somewhere to stay, wherever I went, youth hostels might be right for me. Young people stayed in them and they were cheap. I tucked the idea of youth hostels at the back of my mind, an address I didn't expect to use, an insurance I hoped would never matter.

From the window of the hotel where my family had come to see me, the ranked buildings and geometry of Johannesburg and its streets surrounded me. My family had come all this way to say goodbye to their son and brother.

I was eager to get away, out of a city that stank of petrol, sweet in the hot African sun. I was keen to abandon home. The northern hemisphere, Europe, Britain and England were my dream. A trip round Europe and a job in London was, for many colonial boys and girls, our coming of age, our escape into the metropolitan, the world of city lights and life, where life happened. Where we lived was the periphery, where nothing happened, where we went back and grew old, like our parents, settled for life in the back of beyond, in Africa.

For me, a Rhodesian as we called ourselves then, escape became more serious when the army called me for military service. I had no wish to join the war that was kicking off along the border. Brutality, bloodshed and murder would only delay inevitable change. As soon as I could see where injustice, inequality and poverty were leading us, I had known Rhodesia was no place for me. My home had a limited future and I wanted to be gone before its days ended. I bought a one-way ticket, to my father's and mother's dismay, knowing that once I made that escape I would not be coming home. Breaking the law, I became a draft dodger, beyond the pale and, for many of my parents' friends, beyond the acceptable.

A gang of my friends drove me, full of illicit smoke and cheap red wine, to the airport. I was unprepared for nerve wracking moments of waiting. Anxiety clogged my tongue and dried my mouth as if it was stuffed full of cotton waste. An official, in a short sleeved shirt and wearing a tie, ran his finger down a list I could not see, checking my name against records. The state police had arrested friends and acquaintances and held them in jail, under arbitrary detention laws. At South Africa's borders officials had stopped and held others like me when our visas were nearly expired. They returned draft dodgers to Rhodesia before they could escape. But I was not. With a glance of an eye and a nod, the official passed me towards the exit, towards my flight. I was free.

Mid-winter in Luxembourg, courtesy of budget airline, Luxair, ice on the steps and snow on the ground, shocked me. My fellow passengers groaned and hurried from the plane, eager to get indoors while I stared at gleaming wet tarmac and a low fogged-up sky. I had seen nothing like this before. I had felt no wet cold wind like this. The damp air clung to my suede coat. Damp seeped inside its sheepskin lining in ways I could not comprehend.

A bus took me to Amsterdam, through snowfalls blown about the grey landscape like feathers from plucked birds. When the coach stopped for refreshment breaks, I stamped and slipped on frozen mud in empty car parks. Everywhere seemed strange, empty and remote. Snow flakes, I learned, melted and were wet, something I'd never guessed from all the films of every Arctic landscape I'd ever seen.

Dark came down like a fist on Amsterdam, on inky canals and bridges furred in frost. How it was possible for a day to be so short or for dark to arrive so early I could not understand. Bare trees glistened with frost as if loaded with jewellery.

Loss and impending loneliness, in late-night, empty streets, when everyone was hurrying home from the cold, enveloped me with rising panic. I could find no sign of these youth hostels my sister had told me about and, worse, I had no idea where to look, or even what I sought.

After 36 hours without sleep, after swapping the dry heat of the African high veld for the depths of a Dutch winter, out of desperation and exhaustion, I slept that night in a room that was smaller than a cupboard but which cost more money than I could spare. The receptionist at that quaint hotel on a wide main street must have guessed how little I could afford their high prices. Breakfast was cold meats, bread and coffee. I ate all I could and vowed I would find a youth hostel.

In Vondel Park children on bicycles, sweeping in circles about the bench where I sat, called me a hippy, their voices stirring crows from trees into awkward flight. Elation I had gained from van Gogh's sunflowers in the bright light of a big-windowed, modern museum, where a pianist gave a recital, slipped away. I was adrift in a crowded continent, miles from the familiar smell of heat and dust. When the midday sun finally shouldered the fog aside, I couldn't recognise it for what it was. Caught in the bare branches of a tree the surprise of a disc of dull sun so low in a sky shook me.

I resolved to leave Amsterdam. I took the train to Hook of Holland. A ferry drummed across the sea to Harwich. I arrived among tall cranes on enormous docks in an overwhelming blaze of lights. Six in the morning and beyond the lights it was still dark, still cold and still damp. I steeled myself and found a way to a waiting train where I sat in an empty compartment. Doors down all the empty carriages banged shut and a whistle blew for our departure. The train flew over frozen fields ridged in snow, passing hedges and clumps of trees and dark towns with their lights still on, over Essex to London's Liverpool Street Station. We must have gathered commuters on that journey I now know but I remember none. I remember nothing but grey light.

In London I felt at home. London excited me. A grandmother had been born here. She called the city home and talked about the smell of coal and steam trains. My universe fixed on London. I found a way among landmarks familiar from childhood books. Near Charing Cross station I bought a youth hostel membership card.

Youth hostels required membership and without one nobody stayed. I should have had it before I left home. Because I was not a resident of England or Wales, I wasn't entitled to one. But the people in the office who sold memberships were friendly and neither my ignorance, nor my appearance, age and accent, caused comment. They gave me a pink slip of paper, a temporary pass to last until I had an address and somewhere to live.

The youth hostel at Earls Court was a tall building, set back from the street behind a low wall and up a couple of stone steps. It might once have been a family home. A crowd of people about my age stood or sat outside the front door, down the steps and on the pavement, waiting for the hostel to open. That would be at five o'clock, someone explained. We chatted, laughed and shared cigarettes in a cold, happy idle way, with nothing to do until the big door, painted black, opened. An easy camaraderie enveloped me.

In a lounge, like a doctor's waiting room, we waited again while the pale officious man who admitted us stepped outside and told the less fortunate left outside that the hostel now was full. They would have to find other places to stay about which he made vague suggestions. We lucky ones stepped, one by one, to a big reception desk. I handed over my pink slip of paper, signed a big book and heard the rules of the place, the hours of opening and closing, which would bind my stay. The ritualised welcome ended, I took a small piece of wood on which someone had painted two numbers. One was the number of the room I would share with others, reached up wide linoleum covered stairs. The other was the number of the top bunk in which I would sleep that night.

The hostel only opened in the evening and again the next morning. Between you slept and by ten o'clock in the morning departed. The rules for the place were quaint and the house itself a little as I thought an orphanage or some other charitable institution might be. It reminded me, too, of my college at university which also had tricky-to-fathom rules. The house was domestic in scale, walls shining with fresh paint, smelling of disinfectant in a not unpleasant way. The room in which I would sleep was airy and spacious at the top of the house, with a small window looking over roofs at a glowing night sky. The bare floor, iron beds, thin mattresses and old grey blankets gave the room a spartan look, like a well worn, well scrubbed, dormitory at a boarding school. A night cost £1.25 so my £70 might last for some time I hoped.

I felt at home. At last I had arrived. I lay on the bed and stared at the ceiling and chatted to others who came and went in the room talking, not about Michelangelo, but about places like Rome and Athens. Some of the boys were from Argentina and they shared their beers with me. I went with an Australian for a celebratory burger at a greasy shop on the Earls Court Road. He was like me, full of plans and excitement and anticipation of all that lay around us.

I slept a deep sleep, untroubled by dreams. I gave no thought to the old building creaking into silence around me as we all fell into sleep. I didn't wonder how youth hostels came about or who might have started them. The place was familiar and comfortable and old, as if it had been there forever. On the gatepost an old, green, metal sign proclaimed that this youth hostel was one of many, in this country and abroad, where people of any age could spend the night, irrespective of race or creed. I liked that any one of any age could stay, irrespective of race or creed. After the divisions of apartheid South Africa, its park benches reserved for people of particular race, where people went to jail or killed for the colour of their skin, I loved the big liberality of that sign. If this and the friendliness of those I met was what youth hostels were all about, I was happy to be there.

-3-

A national beginning

Captain Ellis, of the National Council of Social Service, took the decisive step that started youth hostels in Britain. He invited 22 organisations to meet in March 1930. He brought different groups together around the idea of youth hostels and supplied the ingredient that until then had been missing.

Different people in different places were trying to start youth hostels in Britain. Fairclough and the others on Merseyside aimed to establish youth hostels in North Wales. Others in Scotland and Northumberland had been doing something similar. These efforts were local or focused on single centres. None of them were creating a distinctive national network of places where people could stay until Captain Ellis supplied the missing ingredient. He made youth hostels a national initiative.

The Cyclists' Touring Club, which started in 1878 as the Bicycle Touring Club and changed its name in 1883 when it admitted tandem cyclists, had promoted places to stay as well as tearooms, pubs and inns for their members for many years. Distinctive plaques adorned these recommended places. Some of them are still in place today.

Members of another more socialist cycling club, the Clarion Cycling Club, began creating clubhouses in 1895. Members could stay in these clubhouses when they were away for a weekend in the country. The first was a caravan at Tabley Brook, near Knutsford, in 1895. A permanent clubhouse in an old house opened in June 1897 at Bucklow Hill.

The Young Mens Christian Association (YMCA) opened their first holiday centre on the Isle of Wight in 1873. They aimed to improve the spiritual condition of young men by providing for their learning, leisure and relaxation. From 1855 young women had their own association to support their social and spiritual welfare. Both organisations spread throughout the world. Their distinctive triangular badges may have influenced the youth hostels' own triangular badge and there are suggestions that they brought the word 'hostel' back into use to describe their centres.

HF and CHA also offered accommodation in centres across the countryside but their members had not walked from one centre to another until HF took hold of that idea in 1928. They began running tramping tours using a chain of huts in the Lake District and another in Wales. Their simple shelters were small but used elements that emerged in youth hostels. Huts offered equipment and trampers cooked their own meals. Each single-sex group of eight cleaned up before they moved on, leaving the camp prepared for the next group's arrival. Like all the HF's holidays, tours were pre-booked with a set itinerary. An organiser led the walks and made the arrangements.

Before HF, the Scottish Young Men's Holiday Fellowship set up a chain of lodges in 1926. In co-operation with the Scottish National Council of the Young Mens' Christian Association (YMCA), the Rover Scouts and the Young Men's Guild of the Scottish Churches, they ran holiday lodges in the Scottish Borders and Highlands. Only fellowship members could use the lodges, paying a membership subscription of 2/6 a year. The lodges provided paliasses and blankets and usually people spent only one night at a lodge before moving on.

Another small group were active across the border in Northumberland. 46 walkers, cyclists, and climbers, from holiday associations and young peoples' organisations in Newcastle, formed the Northumbrian Trampers Guild towards the end of 1928. They took as their president the local MP, Sir Charles Trevelyan, a keen walker and supporter of causes for young people. Sir Charles and his brother, the historian George Macaulay Trevelyan, would in the later story of youth hostels be influential forces. The guild opened six shelters, one in Durham, one on the Cumberland border, and three in Northumberland. Sir Charles Trevelyan provided another for men only in a stone-built barn at the north-west corner of Wallington Hall, his family home, in Northumberland.

The British Youth Council (BYC) was also pushing for youth hostels. The council arranged tours to Germany using youth hostels and they knew young Germans were looking for tours and cheap places to stay in Britain. In June 1929 the council appointed three people to a small committee to look into establishing youth hostels in Britain. The committee's secretary, Henry Ecroyd, wrote to anyone who might have or know of "a loft, shed or room which could be used as a shelter." Tom Fairclough later disparaged his efforts. "The British Youth Council would dearly have liked to claim credit for starting youth hostels, but all they did was write about them in their literature. They didn't do anything," he observed.

In late 1929 another group of young men in London set up the Wayfarers' Hostels Association. One of those was Barclay Baron who knew about youth hostels from visits to Germany.

Different people in different places, through the winter of 1929 / 1930 were trying to start youth hostels. None was making progress until the National Council of Social Service (NCSS) took a hand. They "offered, not to organise our effort in any way, but to sponsor it," Barclay Baron recalled.

The NCSS was the ideal sponsor for the new venture. Today, it's the National Council of Voluntary Organisations. Beginning in March 1919, it aimed to avoid too many voluntary services working in the same areas. By better co-ordination, it reduced waste, confusion and overlap. It was an initiating body. It pointed out tasks that needed doing and helped to create organisations to meet needs. Sometimes it administered organisations as they began until they could manage their own work. It had helped start, among others, the National Association of Boys' Clubs and the Council for the Preservation of Rural England.

The NCSS solved exactly the problems youth hostels faced. It had no ability to start youth hostels; that kind of practical work lay outside its remit. But it could bring all the interested groups together. It could cajole them into doing what it couldn't. It could get a national organisation started.

In early 1930 a coalition of six organisations prompted the NCSS into action. The National Council of YMCAs, the National Adult School Union, the Workers' Travel Association, the Holiday Fellowship, the Co-operative Holidays Association and the British Youth Council asked the NCSS to call a conference. They wanted national bodies to consider launching a movement to provide inexpensive sleeping accommodation at suitable places for young people spending week-ends and holidays walking through the country.

Captain Ellis called a meeting on Thursday 13 March at 11am. 28 people met at the council's offices on the north side of Bedford Square, around the corner from the British Museum. Ronald Norman, vice chairman of the NCSS and chairman of the London County Council, started the meeting. He reminded those present of the steps leading up to the meeting.

He then invited Barclay Baron to speak. Baron described the *Jugendherbergen* of Germany with their 2,500 hostels and 3,000,000 overnight stays. "The effect of this provision of hostels on the youth of the country is remarkable," he declared. "In place of the heel-clicking mechanical type of character, a healthy, clean youth is springing up, whose dominant note is a self disciplined freedom. The shallow attractions of city amusements are abandoned in favour of open air life. Intelligent interest is taken in the many aspects of nature, a love is developed for the simple folk song and dance. The violin, the guitar, and the lute replace the ukelele, and pride in bodily fitness, moral uprightness, and a friendly spirit to all, are the dominant principle."

The conference decided to explore providing something similar in Britain. They didn't wish to slavishly follow the German system. They wanted a scheme suited to British conditions and they immediately appointed a provisional executive committee. The first committee members were HW Barter, School Journey Association; Clifford Hall, YMCA; Ingram Knowles, Merseyside Youth Hostels; Ralph Nun May, National Union of Students; Henry Stone, HF; Henry P. Weston, CHA; Nevill Whall, CTC; and Ernest Wimble, the Workers Travel Association.

Others joined later, from a Birmingham Regional Council and a Bristol Regional Council, when they formed, and from the British Youth Council, recognising the work they had done in investigating youth hostels. JJ Mallon, warden of Toynbee hall, an educational settlement in the East End of London, also joined the committee. Lady Dorothy Meynell, from the National Federation of Women's Institutes was on the first executive too.

They appointed Barclay Baron as chairman. He later claimed that asking a simple question at the meeting caused "seven years of hard labour." In his 40s, a strong social conscience and concern for others dominated his life. He was "a genial soul... devoid of vanity... an artist in words as well as in paint," a "lively, invigorating man," interested in people of all sorts and from all backgrounds. He was a gifted speaker and a colleague claimed "to hear him speak was sheer joy."

Born in 1884, into a Quaker family in Bristol, Baron was the eldest and only son among four children. His father was mayor of Bristol and founded an ear, nose and throat department at Bristol General Hospital. After University College, Oxford, and art studies in Germany, Barclay was a freelance journalist in London, then a private secretary in the Home Office. When war broke out in 1914, unfit for military service, he volunteered with the YMCA. In Flanders, a chance meeting with Rev. 'Tubby' Clayton changed the direction of his life.

In 1915 Clayton, an army chaplain, had set up a rest house in Poperinge in Belgium for troops behind the war front in Flanders. The rest house was, unusually at that time, open to all ranks, both officers and men. Clayton called the house Talbot House in honour of a colleague's dead brother. Users abbreviated the name to TH or, in the language of radio signalmen, Toc H.

Toc H aimed to ease the burden of service on others and to promote reconciliation. Baron involved himself in its work in France and later in peacetime. He became one of Toc H's pioneers, credited with designing Toc H's badge. He wrote hymns and edited the Toc H journal.

His role as one of the pioneers of youth hostels would be influential. With HP Weston and George Wright he drew up the new youth hostel organisation's draft constitution. Weston was Secretary General of the CHA and Wright, like Baron, was a member of the Wayfarers' Hostels Association.

The meeting gave them some of the elements for a constitution. Regional councils would have local authority while a central co-ordinating council provided national headquarters. They set out who would make up the regions and the central council, and discussed fees for accommodation and membership. Regional councils would decide their own procedures.

They would arrange accommodation, recruit members and issue badges, membership cards and literature in their own area.

They organised another meeting at the NCSS offices a month later. On 10 April a diverse range of national organisations with an interest in youth hostels attended. The existing regional youth hostel groups in Liverpool and Manchester sent representatives with the Wayfarers' Hostels Association. Others at the meeting came from broad groupings of organisations. Despite differences, they had in common an interest in improving the lives of young people through encouraging them into the countryside. Youth hostels united them.

Germany owed its youth hostels to a teacher who believed that children learned best out of the classroom. Before Schirrmann invented youth hostels, he began what he called wandering schools. He took his pupils walking in the outdoors to learn. They saw real fish in real rivers and studied nature first hand.

Appropriately teachers and people from the wider world of British education came to the meeting: the National Union of Teachers, the School Journeys Association, the Association of Headmistresses, the National Adult School Union, the Education Settlements Association and the London Association of Old Scholars Clubs.

Organisations working to improve the lives of young people took part: the Boy Scouts, the British Youth Council, the YWCA, the National Council of YMCAs, the National Association of Boys Clubs, and the National Union of Students. The Workers Travel Association, the Holiday Fellowship and the Co-operative Holidays Association, already providing low cost holidays and breaks for young people, also joined the meeting.

Concern about unsupervised and ignorant young people wandering in the countryside, causing a nuisance and creating damage, might have prompted a group with broad interests in the countryside to attend the meeting: the Federation of Rambling Clubs, the Council for the Protection of Rural England, the National Trust and the Society for the Protection of Ancient Buildings.

The CTC represented cyclists. A wider group, the Rotary Club from Hendon, the World Alliance for Promoting Friendship through the Churches, the Catholic Social Guild, the Theosophical Order of Service and the Sunlight League, made up the rest. The Carnegie United Kingdom Trust, with offices in the building where the meeting was held, came too.

All together, guided by the NCSS, they "pushed the boat out" and set up a national association for youth hostels. They were off, without funds, without buildings, and without resources.

When it came to choosing a name for the new organisation they ran into controversy. Several didn't want an organisation on Continental lines. Some wanted a title linked to Wayfarers. The Merseyside delegates wanted a name focused on youth hostels. That best described their aims, they argued. Youth hostels linked them with the movement in Europe which they hoped to join. They had already been publicising the name. They won the debate by a single vote and the conference adopted the name 'the Youth Hostels Association (of Great Britain)'.

The new association would have a regional structure. An elected national council would be the supreme body for youth hostels. Regional groups, like those in Liverpool and Manchester, and societies and organisations, like the Scouts and the National Trust, would sit on the national council. Societies and organisations would pay a small fee to affiliate to the youth hostels organisation. The national council would meet once a year to review the year and appoint honorary officers. Its own auditors would check the accounts. The council would elect an executive committee to conduct its business during the year.

On 9 May *The Times* reported that the NCSS had started a British version of the youth hostels' movement of Germany.

Barclay Baron chaired his first executive committee meeting on 28 May 1930 at the NCSS offices. He and his committee faced an enormous task. They had to set up regional groups and decide standards for the hostels they would have. They needed to publicise the new movement and to co-ordinate the work of regional groups as they began.

Baron saw that their bold venture's success or failure depended on finding the right man for secretary. He had more than one candidate in mind when one of the committee suggested Jack Catchpool. He and Baron met in the basement of the NCSS offices and Baron made a snap decision. He had found a 'winner'.

Egerton St John Catchpool's family pronounced their name as *Catchpole.* Jack, or Catch as Catchpool was often known, was a practical energetic man. He ran to keep fit. Long before jogging was a fashion he ran in his shorts through London causing amusement as he went. He had boundless enthusiasm and believed his father had passed him the virtues of tenacity, or obstinacy, whilst his mother taught him patience.

He worked for the benefit of others. He had shared poverty and hardship and seen suffering at first hand. A conscientious objector in the first world war, after volunteering in the Friends Ambulance Unit, he went halfway round the world for the Friends War Victims Relief Committee. In Russia, Armenia, China, Japan and Palestine he worked on behalf of refugees and the homeless for peace.

Before the war, he had studied at the Quaker college, Woodbrooke, in Birmingham. He had longed for a career in social work but his father decided otherwise. Sent to work in an export house in London, Catchpool continued his social work in the East End of London in his spare time. He lived in rooms where he fought with bed bugs, which meant he better understood the plight of young mothers in the flats around him. With a fresh understanding of poverty, against his father's wishes, but with support from his mother, who paid his fees from her personal allowance, he returned to college.

After college and returning from war, he continued his battle to improve lives. He married Ruth Wilson, a Birmingham girl he had known at college. When she qualified as a doctor, they lived in a tenement flat on Gunthorpe Street in Whitechapel. He supervised boys' and girls' clubs, scouts, cubs and neighbours clubs and lobbied successfully to open school yards out of hours as places where children could play.

He was a founder of the Workers Travel Association. The association provided holidays so that workers, in even the lowest paid industries, could get away for a short time, to the Continent or the seaside.

He arranged for families from the East End to visit Cambridge and Oxford. They met students, punted on the river and took tea in the colleges. The visits were fun and educational too. Students, for the first time, met people from very deprived backgrounds, socially and on an equal footing.

He organised visits by the YMCA from the USA and Canada. He provided accommodation for these visits by furnishing rooms in nearby schools with beds, just as Richard Schirrmann had done at his first youth hostel.

He took families and children walking in Epping Forest. At the end of a long day walking they faced a long journey home. Catchpool realised how badly they needed cheap places where they could spend the night so that they could extend their visits.

He had all the enthusiasm he needed for youth hostels when Baron invited him to join the committee. Catchpool's appointment as secretary was only temporary and part time. He continued his adult education work for the Welwyn Garden City education association. He and Ruth had been living in Welwyn since 1926.

As secretary he brought persistence. He brought an organisational flair, an ability to get on with people from all sorts of social and cultural backgrounds. More than any of these, he brought an emphasis on social work. He believed in education in its widest form as a way of improving people and building better lives.

The executive committee gave Catchpool the job of organising an open council meeting to formally establish youth hostels as a national movement. The conference met on June 26 and 27, 1930 at Digswell Park in Hertfordshire.

The choice of date and venue caused resentment. They met on a Thursday and Friday because many of the committee had speaking and other engagements for the weekend and could only find time during the week. But some of the delegates would have preferred a weekend meeting. They wanted ordinary working people running the new organisation and taking time off work in the week for ordinary working people was difficult. A weekend would have been better. The Merseyside delegation detected a bias in favour of those from the south of England when notice of the meeting gave directions to Digswell Park from London, as if all the delegates were coming from there.

The council had to balance power between conflicting demands, between regional groups and national societies. They agreed national societies would pay a small fee to affiliate themselves to the new organisation. In return they attended council and elected members to the executive committee.

Regional delegates saw things differently. They wanted a strong, locally based organisation. They expected the regional groups would effectively pay for youth hostels, as they would recruit members and run the youth hostels. In return they wanted a majority for regional groups on the executive committee and they argued for delay. The conference should wait for more regional organisations before finalising a national constitution.

Regional delegates from Merseyside and Manchester could not see the movement getting off the ground nationally unless local initiative held power. The conference finally agreed a constitution giving the balance of power to regional groups. They would have two more places than the affiliated societies.

Delegates from Merseyside wanted the new association to give preference to young people. They wanted young people under 25 years of age to have priority and to pay lower fees. Young children were the essence of the youth hostel model in Germany. But the idea of unruly young children using youth hostels in large numbers frightened some at the conference. They feared large groups of children would drive away older walkers and cyclists. The conference agreed no lower fee for young people staying at youth hostels.

No one argued about the principle of membership. Youth hostels would only be open to members. Membership was a key feature of the German model. Anyone staying in youth hostels in Germany had found that they had to pay and join the German association. Many wanted a British youth hostels association and their own membership scheme so that they could use youth hostels in Germany.

Whether membership should be open to anyone was more contentious. Some regarded youth hostels as the precious preserve of those who loved the countryside. They considered that if "all and sundry were admitted, there would be ignorant intruders and, worse still, vandals, who got the Association a bad name." Some wanted youth hostels restricted to walkers and cyclists, for those travelling under their own steam.

Baron and Catchpool were firm. Membership should not exclude anyone. The new association had to be open to all to succeed. They argued against any test. They believed "YHA could become the finest out-of-school educational movement in the country; that it was especially designed for boys and girls living in congested city areas, who would learn not only the beauty of the countryside and the exhilaration of healthy open air exercise, but a sense of responsibility and comradeship."

The majority of the executive committee supported Catchpool and Baron who won the debate. "So, it was resolved that when someone applied for membership, there would be no means test, no questions of his past history; everyone should be given a chance to prove himself worthy…"

Barclay Baron saw the new organisation's goal very clearly. He knew of no time "which has cried louder for the kind of service our movement tries to give." He and Catchpool came down firmly on the side of youth hostels providing a social service and a contribution to the nation. They aimed to encourage a sense of responsibility and comradeship among young people.

Their vision today seems imperialistic. The idea of building better people for a better country put youth hostels in line with other movements to improve the lives of young people, like the Scouts and Guides, the YMCA and the Boys Brigade.

The view of the regions may have been less idealistic. For the regional groups youth hostels would be the realisation of a long held dream to have cheap places where they could stay, so that they could go walking, climbing and cycling. The meeting over, they departed. They had pushed the boat out and started youth hostels as a national organisation. The hard work lay ahead. The decision to create a national organisation was critical for the future of youth hostels. They now set out to create a national network for the first time.

The conference at Digswell Park revealed the tensions and divisions inherent in creating a national organisation. The national organisations that affiliated themselves with youth hostels held different motives for wanting youth hostels. A social service ethos clashed with the regional groups who wanted youth hostels for themselves. Different organisations defined young people differently and saw them with varying degrees of benevolence or fear.

Debate about the degree of preference to be given to young people in youth hostels emerged. An intention to restrict youth hostels to those travelling under their own steam also emerged. The Digswell Park conference gave no formal preference to walkers or cyclists but the desire was there at the outset for some.

The debate about giving preference to young people did not go away. Fairclough and the others from Merseyside continued to lobby for young people. After the meeting they succeeded by showing that Germany and others in Europe were doing the same. The executive committee agreed and those under 25 paid 2/6 for their membership, half the 5/- those over 25 paid. Youth hostels though would charge everyone the same for a night's stay. Irrespective of age, everyone would pay one shilling a night to stay, a shilling that bought a bed, blankets and a pillow. Members came to call the price of a night's stay the magic shilling.

Differences on matters of policy would continue, sometimes sharp. Baron as chairman recalled that personalities of opposite qualities had to be welcomed into a working team and the executive meetings, once a month, often lasted late, almost to the point of exhaustion.

Tensions were resolved in a spirit of openness. Youth hostels would be open to all. Youth hostels were not going to be the preserve of one group or another. Their aim would be 'to help all, but especially young people, to a greater knowledge, use and love of the countryside, particularly by providing hostels or other simple accommodation and educational and recreational facilities.'

The constitution enshrined democracy in what historian GM Trevelyan later described as the best British tradition. No single leader or group could impose views on the rest. The regions had considerable autonomy but they would all have to work together, to broker agreements, to ensure that all points of view were taken into account. Democracy would resolve their differences.

The first council at Digswell Park had agreed a price for a night's stay without opening a single youth hostel. They had agreed that regions would hold the balance of power when only two regions were established. Having set up an organisation for hostels they still had no hostels, no money and little influence.

The boldness of their decision is baffling. Today we are more cautious. We are more cynical. We have business plans and kick start funding. Finance comes first. We don't move, without certainty or capital, and our efforts are individualistic and monetarist, not communal or benevolent. Our heroes are individuals like Alan Sugar, Richard Branson, Steve Jobs, Jeff Bezos, and Mark Zuckerberg. Our myths are about those who start in a garage and, by buying and selling, end up owning a part of the world.

People like Catchpool and Baron had survived the horrors of the first world war and the trenches. They were familiar with ventures like the Friends Ambulance Unit. The first 43 men of the unit left London on Friday, 30 October, 1914, heading to the front in France. They had no idea of what work they would do or where. They only knew that there was a shortage of ambulances. The unit grew to more than 600 men with a guiding principle to "Find work that wants doing; take it; regularise it later, if you can."

Baron, Catchpool, Fairclough and all of those involved in the start applied the same spirit to youth hostels. They had no idea where they were going to find youth hostels, or what they would have to do to build them, but they were going to do it. The determination of them all working together around the undefined idea of youth hostels would open the world of independent travel for young people.

Notes and references

This chapter emerged from research in archives, reading papers and hunting down hints from books like Oliver Coburn's *Youth Hostel Story*. Sometimes it required detective work. Coburn intriguingly mentioned six organisations pushed the NCSS to call a first meeting but YHA's papers seemed to hold no record of that first meeting until I found papers in the London Metropolitan archives. Others contributed information. I am grateful to Douglas Hope for information on HF's chain of huts in the Lake District and Wales.

"a loft, shed or room…" Coburn, *Youth Hostel Story*, p16
"The British Youth Council…" Taylor, *The Pioneering Years*, p5
"offered, not to organise …" *The Rucksack*, June-July 1950, p8
"The effect of of this provision…" Report of a conference convened by the NCSS, 13 March 1930
"pushed the boat out" *The Rucksack*, June-July 1950, p8
"seven years of hard labour…" *The Rucksack*, June-July 1950, p8
"a genial soul…" and following, *The Youth Hosteller*, August 1964
"all and sundry were admitted…" Catchpool, *Candles in the Darkness*, p141
"YHA could become the finest…" ibid
"So, it was resolved…" ibid
"which has cried louder…" *YHA Rucksack*, Winter 1932
"Find work that wants doing…" Tatham, Meaburn, and Miles, *The Friends Ambulance Unit 1914 - 1919, A Record*

-4-

Windermere

Youth hostels had their own guide, a booklet, light and easy to carry. Mine became bent and scarred from journeys, stuffed in a pocket, the pages rubbed with use. It was the kind of book I read to pass the time, while I waited for a bus in Coventry or sat on the steps of a youth hostel, waiting for it to open.

The Queen was the patron of youth hostels. They had a president, called Cadbury, like the chocolate bar. The little book of hostels told me all that. There was late news, advice and a section of the book for people like me, new to something called hostelling. I learned that youth hostels were there to encourage me to explore the countryside, hoping that I would come to love and care for the countryside. That seemed to imply I didn't already, that I would behave without common sense, with no courtesy or consideration and that, until I was a member behaving in the proper way, I would most likely cause damage to property and livestock. It was a bit presumptuous.

The handbook told me the best way of getting to know the countryside was by "travelling under my own steam," by walking, cycling, climbing or travelling by canoe. A store at each hostel would sell "sufficient foodstuffs... to prepare a meal". Youth hostels supplied cutlery and crockery. Page after page listed the places youth hostels were, when they were open, with clear little maps, directions and brief descriptions. The youth hostel at Whitby was at the top of 199 steps and another was two hours walk from Church Stretton. Their names were poetry, full of romance and future journeys anyone might take to Tanners Hatch or Wilderhope, to Clun, Rock Hall, Bryn Gwynant or Inglesham.

The names gave me more ideas than I would ever have time to fulfil. But at the youth hostel shop, in John Adam Street near Charing Cross, they showed me a route. I made bookings and bought a ticket from London Victoria to Windermere in Cumbria. A day later the bus, edging out of London traffic, carried me into a country bruised purple, brown and yellow, of muddy fields and bare trees. But I knew where I was going. I was excited to be going, getting out of London at last.

I remember little of the journey. I was too excited to care about the places I passed. I was going to the Lake District where Wordsworth wrote his poetry. The Lakes were the heart of so many lessons and lectures from school and university. I was going to the origin of words dissected and analysed through so many years of study. Wordsworth's vision, the places of his childhood, Brotherswater, Ullswater and daffodils, gave me a way of seeing. They instilled hunger in me for the natural world. I had read and studied, and read and reread his poetry for more years than I could remember. Now I was going to the places where he wrote and the places that made him

"A lover of the meadows and the woods
And mountains; and of all that we behold
From this green earth…"

Youth hostels were for people who wanted to discover these "beauteous forms." Their "tranquil restoration" was for people who walked or cycled, who travelled under their own steam. Wordsworth was the original. He travelled under his own steam. He walked mind boggling distances, of twenty miles or more, over mountains, for a chat with Southey. He walked to visit Coleridge for an evening and came home by moonlight.

The coach dropped me on the side of a narrow road, in darkness. Somewhere water rushed and the cold air smelled damp. It was one of those nights in February without frost, with just a chill in the air, like a fridge door opening. Someone left the coach with me. A voice asked if I was going to the youth hostel. I couldn't see who I was talking to but she knew where she was going. She led the way and explained that she was here for a weekend of walking. She strode up the steep hill, threatening to outdistance me, showing the way in the swinging beam of her torch. Streams and constant water rushed and the road gleamed wetly.

The youth hostel was down a short drive, through dark trees, a pale ghost of a place. In the morning I would discover "a strange concrete edifice [built] as a guest-house for clergy by an eccentric." Electric light inside blinded me for a moment. The warden knew my companion. He explained to her which room she had for the night. While I was still blinking, before I had time to thank her for her kindliness, for showing me the way, she was gone. The walls were bare, the furniture spartan, I noticed, as the warden greeted me. He was short, bearded, and welcoming, friendly and easy-going, exactly as a youth hostel warden should be.

The next morning, after a breakfast cooked by Dave - we were on first name terms by now - and toast and tea, with a borrowed map, I followed the route he had picked for me. I walked to Ambleside. I probably sang. I might have skipped and danced, along the muddy path that shone when the sun emerged from low ragged cloud. I saw the distant hills, yellow, bronze and red, and further away, washed the blue of watercolour. On the edge of a crag, looking down through trees at the shining water of Windermere, I was Keats on his walking tour of the Lakes, seeing the lake and mountains of Winander. He could not describe them. They passed his expectations, "beautiful water-shores and islands green to the marge - mountains all round up to the clouds..."

I loved the colours. I loved being there. I loved everything I remembered about the Lake District. I remembered Beatrix Potter and my mother reading to me when I was a child. Arthur Ransome had Windermere in mind when he wrote Swallows and Amazons as well as another lake not far away at Coniston. Where I stood might have been the peak in Darien where the children received the telegram, telling them that they could sail out to Wild Cat Island where all their adventures began. If they were duffers, they were better drowned. If they weren't duffers they wouldn't drown. The place where I had arrived was more real because it had been written about. It was part of my childhood memories. Swallows and Amazons was the first book I remembered reading. If I felt like a stranger I didn't care.

Back at the hostel that evening I felt I had arrived. My walk to Ambleside and back had tired me. Along the way I had climbed Wansfell and seen other hills in waves. Dave welcomed me back and cooked my meal. The youth hostel was exactly as I had hoped. It stays in my mind, after all these years, as a place of true hospitality, the epitome of natural service and generosity.

Notes and references

The quote about the youth hostel at Windermere comes from the Lake District Annual Report of 1979.

The first youth hostel

"We could not have chosen a more difficult time for the start of a movement," Barclay Baron, the Youth Hostels Association's first chairman declared.

The 1929 stock market crash set off economic shock waves. British exports, already falling in the 1920s, fell further and unemployment rose causing widespread poverty. In January 1929, 1,433,000 people were out of work. By March 1930, the figure was 1,731,000. In June it reached 1,946,000 and by the end of the year reached a staggering 2,725,000.

The first open council meeting at Digswell Park in June 1930 secured a future for youth hostels. But Jack Catchpool, the first youth hostel secretary, admitted it was a miracle they survived. They had no money and few of the regional groups needed to sign up members and do the work. They had to wait until the end of 1930 for the first youth hostel to open and the first listing of hostels would not appear until the following year. Even those like the Northumbrian Trampers Guild who had hostels at their disposal didn't join the new organisation until a year after it formed.

Youth hostels survived with support from influential people. Prime

Minister, Ramsay MacDonald, and two ministers in his government, George Lansbury and Sir Charles Trevelyan, offered encouragement. Others "too numerous to mention" brought influence, finance and an ideology to youth hostels so that they not only survived but grew and endured.

The first regional group on Merseyside had made TA Leonard, founder of the CHA and HF, their president. The national executive committee followed and made Leonard their first vice president. He had better knowledge and credentials for how to launch youth hostels than anyone else. He had dreamed the dreams and believed the ideals which fired youth hostels. He thought youth hostels would be closer to the ideals which started both the CHA and the HF. The holiday centres of CHA and HF were becoming conventional. The more simple, out of the way places, that Leonard loved and thought should be at the heart of both organisations, were less popular. Leonard hoped that youth hostels would be the new organisation they all needed.

Barclay Baron asked the Most Reverend William Temple, Archbishop of Canterbury, to be their second vice president. The two men had been at university together and Baron described Temple as "a keen debater, a brilliant speaker, a thought provoking writer, a most amusing and stimulating companion." He became an outstanding vice president, according to Baron." In spite of his stout figure, he was a redoubtable walker and a great lover of the British countryside, above all of Lakeland."

In the summer of 1930 Catchpool travelled north. He went to see Leonard, in the Lake District, planning a tour of the Lakes and North Wales, using Leonard's extensive knowledge of the areas. On the trip he hoped to meet Clough Williams-Ellis, the influential architect, who owned extensive property in North Wales. Williams-Ellis also chaired the Council for the Preservation of Rural Wales. He hoped for support and perhaps property from the influential man.

Catchpool left no record of his trip or meetings but back in London, in September, he reported to the executive committee he had found a president. He had secured the support of the historian and writer of bestselling history books, George Macaulay Trevelyan.

Catchpool might have chosen Trevelyan's elder brother, Sir Charles, the politician and minister for education. His was the more romantic figure. He was the socialist who loved walking and the Northumberland hills. A tall rangy man, he had been a keen supporter of early efforts to create more access to the countryside. He had moved the second reading of the Access to Mountains and Moorland Bill in Parliament in 1908. Though the bill failed, it was an early attempt at legislating for access to the countryside.

Sir Charles was a controversial figure. He was a civil servant in Ireland for a time and then, bored, returned to England. He won election as the Liberal MP for Elland, Yorkshire, in 1899 and joined Asquith's government as education minister from 1908.

A committed pacifist, he opposed war. In protest against the declaration of war in 1914 he resigned from the government. He left the Liberals and joined the Labour Party, believing that Labour offered new hope. As the Labour candidate he lost his parliamentary seat in the 1918 General Election. But his political career did not end. Four years later, he won election as a Labour MP in the Newcastle upon Tyne Central constituency in 1922.

Ramsay MacDonald led the first, short lived, Labour government in 1924. He appointed Trevelyan to his old post as minister at the Board of Education. Trevelyan returned to the post of education minister when Labour was back in government again in 1929.

He was a popular minister. In 1924 he reversed the cuts in education spending imposed in 1922. He fought to break down religious barriers in education, to raise the school leaving age and to make universities accessible to all young people of ability, irrespective of their wealth. He increased the number of free places at grammar schools and encouraged local authorities to raise the school leaving age to fifteen.

He had inherited the family estate at Wallington, along with his father's baronetcy, in 1928. The house and estate had been neglected, but with his wife, Mary, he began restoring the hall and its garden and grounds. He improved his tenants' properties and opened the estate, allowing tenants to borrow books from the hall's library.

He helped the Northumbrian Trampers Guild set up its hostels in 1929, giving the guild a building in the hall's grounds as one of its hostels. He had sent his good wishes to the first youth hostels' council at Digswell Park and expressed his interest in the new association, watching already from the wings.

But when they were looking for a president, despite his support for the cause of youth hostels, Catchpool and the executive turned to his younger brother.

George Macaulay was a famous Cambridge historian with a bestselling list of history books to his name. He was also Regius Professor of Modern History at Cambridge, appointed by the king on the recommendation of the prime minister. Catchpool told the executive committee that the younger Trevelyan wanted to help and was willing and ready to be their new president. Trevelyan believed they asked him to be president because "walking across country has been and still is the chief recreation and passion of my life." He saw himself as a figurehead. He was always keen for everyone to know that Barclay Baron and Jack Catchpool were the ones doing the real work.

Born in 1876 he had developed his love of history from studying his family's illustrious past. Ancestors included a long line of Whig politicians and the historian Macaulay, author of a history of Britain. From the family home in the Northumberland moors he developed his love of the countryside and walking. At Cambridge he linked with the Bloomsbury group and intellectuals like Keynes, Bertrand Russell and EM Forster. Unlike his brother, he supported war in 1914. He believed that he had to oppose the tyranny of the German Kaiser. Poor eyesight made him unfit for military service and instead he served with distinguished bravery, commanding the British Red Cross Ambulance brigade in Italy. He shared conditions with the ambulance drivers and the Italian government decorated him for his service.

After the war he returned to writing. He involved himself in a battle to save the Ashridge Estate in the Chilterns near where he lived in Berkhamstead. Many families, in the aftermath of the war, sold their estates and big old houses. Many had lost their heirs. Houses became expensive to run and servants difficult to find. Families had to pay death duties and often faced little alternative but selling off property to pay taxes.

Builders and speculators bought the old country houses. They stripped, gutted and demolished them. New owners in the USA, like media magnate William Randolph Hearst, offered a ready market for antique English furniture and fittings. For a historian like Trevelyan the loss of a country house heritage built over centuries was devastating.

He and others intervened when the estate at Ashridge faced a similar fate. They feared speculators would buy the beautiful hills, woods, commons and parkland and parcel the land into building plots. He played a leading part in the National Trust's appeal to save estate. He organised and addressed public meetings. He published a letter in *The Times* signed by the Conservative prime minister, Stanley Baldwin, the previous Labour prime minister, Ramsay MacDonald, and a clutch of well connected peers.

The battle to save Ashridge brought Trevelyan to the National Trust. The trust elected him to its council in 1926 and immediately appointed him to its estates and executive committees. As chairman of the Estates Committee he was responsible for the management of all National Trust properties. Appointed as YHA president, he and Catchpool started discussions about ways the trust could help youth hostels.

With men like Leonard, Temple and the Trevelyans supporting them, the youth hostel organisation moved ahead. In the winter of 1930/31 regions established themselves in Birmingham, Bristol, London and in the West Riding of Yorkshire. But nobody had opened a youth hostel.

On Merseyside, Fairclough, Embleton and Symonds had an idea of the kind of hostels they wanted. They proposed two kinds of hostel, a single building, for 25 people, and a double, with accommodation for 50. A youth hostel might be in an old converted building, or a new one, built for the purpose; they did not mind which at that time. They expected it would cost between £300 and £500 to set up, according to the size and equipment needed.

They would provide only the simplest accommodation. The sexes would sleep and wash apart, with a common room for meals and for socialising. They would provide three blankets for each bed, showers and/or foot-baths where a water supply permitted, and a room for cooking, separate from the common room.

As in Germany, those using youth hostels would attend to their own beds and be responsible for cleaning the building. The Merseyside council expected that its youth hostels would be in or near North Wales. They had the idea of a chain of youth hostels approximately 15 miles walking distance from each other. Wherever possible hostels would provide for hikers carrying their own tents. Campers would be able to use hostel kitchens, the common room and washrooms.

First, the Merseyside group had to find and convert property. If they built the hostels themselves, they needed land. They proposed a list of youth hostels for North Wales, at Nerquis, near Mold; Llanfairtalhaiarn;

Pont Wgan, in the Conwy Valley; Llanfairfechan; Nant Francon; Maentwrog; Llanfihangl; Yspyty Ifan and at Gyffylliog, near Ruthin. The Ramblers offered to build the hostel at Nerquis.

Summer was ending and they still had not found a site. Bertha Gough recalled that on Sunday 28 September 1930, Embleton organised a bus party to look at possible sites. They went to Nerquis. Mr. Emrys Jones had presented a site there where they could build the first hostel. They walked via Moel Fammau, Moel Arthur, and Moel Etty to Newmarket, where they proposed a second hostel. On a fine day the party walked 21 miles, full of enthusiasm for youth hostels.

The next day, back in Liverpool, the Mayor, Lawrence Holt, from the Blue Funnel Shipping Line, launched an appeal for £5,000. The Blue Funnel Shipping Line company, A Holt & Co; A Earle of Puddington Hall; an anonymous donor and the CHA all promised to pay for one hostel each at a cost of £300 per hostel. A local architect, PJ Clarke, offered professional support and a cheque for £300.

The CHA provided a site for a youth hostel and the Liverpool and District Ramblers Federation were trying to provide another. Through November and December 1930 they carried on raising funds. Gough and her friends sold stamps. They addressed and stuffed hundreds of envelopes with appeals. On 3 December Gough helped raise more funds with a whist drive at the HF clubroom. The evenings were so successful they ran two more, adding to the growing fund. They only needed a youth hostel.

By October they had dropped the Nerquis site and found another site at Maeshafn. They developed ambitious plans for a purpose built youth hostel there. They secured an old school at Gyffylliog. TA Leonard and former prime minister, David Lloyd George, supported their efforts to secure the tenancy for an old mill at Pont Wgan. As Christmas 1930 aproached the proposed youth hostel at Pont Wgan fell through and their plans changed.

On a bright December day Bertha Gough's friend, Connie Alexander, was walking down Lord Street in Liverpool. She was happy and carefree. Christmas was coming and bright days in December can be few. On a street corner she bumped into Tom Fairclough and Alf Embleton in the middle of an animated discussion. Her chance appearance pleased them. She was just the person they were looking for. There was a little job they wanted doing. They had found their first youth hostel. They were going to open Pennant Hall for Christmas and they wanted her to get a group of people together, as many as possible. They wanted the new youth hostel to be a success.

"For the last few months I had been in the habit of taking orders from these two" Alexander recalled, but this seemed a bit too thick. "I murmured vague excuses, but they were of no use and, with a promise to do what I could, I went on my way a sadder and less confident creature."

She may have been less confident but Alexander sold the proposal for Christmas at Pennant Hall to her friends. She had never seen the place but, she assured the others, they would have a wonderful time. Their surroundings would be glorious and the whole visit would cost little.

On the day before Christmas Eve an advance party of six in two carloads with boxes and cases set off for the hall. More people would follow. When she arrived Alexander found the hall and its glorious surroundings as good as she had expected. The hall, near Eglwysfach in the Conwy Valley, was a large house high on the Denbigh Moors near Llanrwst. Bertha Gough visited two months later and described the hall in her diary. "It had a beautiful entrance hall, with very shallow stairs, large lofty rooms and queer underground passages, which we explored with torches."

The pioneering party set to work. They lit fires in the big empty rooms, unpacked equipment and set up beds. They worked hard, creating a dormitory and washroom for each sex. They furnished a common room and equipped the kitchen with an oil stove and pressurised kerosene cookers, the primus cookers that became widespread in youth hostel kitchens. They ate sausages, the instant packaged food of the time, all that Alexander had been able to provide for their first meal. She had no experience of cooking, something Fairclough and Embleton had overlooked. The rest of the party decorated the youth hostel on Christmas Eve while Alexander went in search of food. She returned with a good fat goose, eggs, bacon, more sausage and lots of other food she thought necessary. She also brought back a cookery book.

30 people spent Christmas at Pennant Hall. Embleton organised them all to explore the surrounding countryside on Christmas Day. They cooked dinner on the complicated oil stove and primus cookers and sat down to eat at tables set for the occasion. Afterwards they all sat around a huge log

fire telling tales. They relaxed with contentment.

But their first night in a British youth hostel was uncomfortable. They were all so cold in their camp beds that few of them slept much. Alexander's friends, Bertha Gough and Tom Fairclough, missed the occasion. They went camping instead leaving Alexander to record the occasion and to become warden of the first British youth hostel.

In the New Year a meeting in Westminster agreed that a regional council should form in London. Barclay Baron spoke at the meeting on 20 January 1931 and *The Times* reported the event the next day. Baron announced that people were reacting against the machine-made age. Youth hostels would help young people get out into the countryside. He had a vision of an ideal world that youth hostels were creating.

A day later GM Trevelyan gave a talk on the new British Broadcasting Corporation. The BBC had begun broadcasting a little over a year earlier, in 1929. Trevelyan declared "the young folk of today, whether men or women, get glimpses afar off of the promised land, the lovely rural England which is theirs by heritage, of which they read and are taught at school, but which they are never allowed to enjoy in actuality. That is not the way to breed good citizens or good patriots." Youth hostels would "meet this deficiency."

Trevelyan, by giving his talk on the radio, affirmed that youth hostels were part of a wider revolution. Youth hostels were as new as radio broadcasts. YHA saw the speech as important enough to print.

Trevelyan explained how youth hostels had come about. The wealthy had kept the great open spaces of the country for themselves for too long he declared. Those who could afford to, had only to get in their cars and soon they could reach the most beautiful places. Hundreds and thousands of others felt that same powerful hunger. But they could not afford a car of their own.

Trevelyan attacked the way cars were spoiling the countryside. Roads were becoming like towns and cities were spreading because no one controlled their development. Too many people were building alongside roads. Advertising on the roadside was spoiling the countryside too. Trevelyan aligned youth hostels with the drive to control the spread of towns and cities into the countryside.

To be at one with nature you had to leave the roads, Trevelyan declared. You had to tramp across fields and moors. For this reason walking had grown up. Thousands of young men and women were going out walking at week-ends and on holidays. He described their walks as 'tramps'. Sometimes they went alone. Sometimes they went in parties great or small. But few of them could afford to stay out for the night. Hotels and inns were for motorists and charged prices young people could seldom pay. A lack of places to stay, a lack of money and a lack of cars cut young people from large parts of the countryside. Youth hostels met and corrected this great deficiency in Trevelyan's eyes.

During his talk Trevelyan reassured his listeners. Youth hostels were responsibly managed. They were working with other responsible people and some of the most important organisations connected with youthful recreation. The YMCA, YWCA, The Boy Scouts, Toc H, the HF, the CHA, the School Masters and Mistresses, all supported youth hostels. The upstart organisation was trustworthy and reputable. Neither were they cranks.

Trevelyan explained what youth hostels would be like. He expected they would be of different sizes but the normal hostel would have from 15 to 25 beds. Men and women would sleep in separate dormitories.

They would build youth hostels from scratch or they would use existing buildings. Trevelyan expected that they would avoid putting up new buildings as much as possible, adapting wherever possible. For anyone who feared that youth hostels would be in jerry built constructions cluttering the countryside Trevelyan offered reassurance. Youth hostels would not be like that. The Council for the Preservation of Rural England would advise on converting buildings. Architects would give expert guidance if they needed a new building.

A responsible manager would supervise every hostel wherever it was open. Trevelyan emphasised the supervision. He would have wished to reassure that youth hostels would be run with propriety despite the young unmarried people staying in them. On Merseyside they had already determined to abandon the German term of house-parents. They didn't expect children staying in youth hostels. They used the term wardens in Britain. The term is harsher than house parent, maybe with connotations of lock-ups today, though it might have been more familiar, then, to anyone who had experienced a college or residential school.

As he spoke to an audience across the country, Trevelyan emphasised that youth hostels were a federation, not a centralised bureaucracy. The true life of the association would be in regional groups. Each of these groups were developing youth hostels in its territory. He had a vision of youth hostels fifteen miles apart from one another, spreading in chains. He hoped to see a chain linking Merseyside with Kent, from Dover to Anglesey.

These were the kind of youth hostels they were going to create. They were not going to be slavish copies of German youth hostels. The youth hostels they aimed for would be smaller. In Germany 200 or 300 bed youth hostels were common. They had abandoned converted buildings. As far as possible youth hostels in Germany were purpose designed and built for youth. The German association had abandoned the idea of youth hostels in chains. Instead they focused on having youth hostels in popular areas.

Together, men like Leonard, Trevelyan and Baron set out the ideas behind youth hostels to a wider audience, reaching out beyond those already involved. They sought to reassure that youth hostels were not the idea of cranks. Their thoughts gave youth hostels an ideology, the basis of action and the beliefs that guided the conduct of youth hostels. They were the great spokespeople for youth hostels and espoused ideas that became key parts of the youth hostels of the future.

Youth hostels would charge as low a price as possible. They would not be for the privileged or wealthy. They would bring the opportunity to travel to the countryside to young people and would end the exclusion of young people from the countryside. Baron and Trevelyan firmly stood against their own privileged backgrounds.

They took an enlightened approach in a society which had only allowed all women to vote two years before, in 1929. Youth hostels would be for men and for women. A young woman organised and ran the first youth hostel. Women played an active part in the development of youth hostels on Merseyside. The search for and setting up of hostels in North Wales involved Bertha Gough heavily as for a while she had time on her hands and no job.

When Richard Schirrmann opened the first youth hostel he intended it for children. In Britain youth hostels would be for young people. Neither Trevelyan nor anyone else was ever clear about what age group they intended to use youth hostels. Sometimes they might have been for children. Sometimes they might have been for students. Connie Alexander and Bertha Gough were young working women. Young people under 25 years of age could buy membership for half the price anyone over 25 paid. Perhaps youth hostels would be for young unmarried people rather than any particular age group.

Trevelyan expressed ideas that set youth hostels against the car. He opposed the car because it was ruining the countryside and because it was a symbol of privilege. This idea more than any other came to epitomise youth hostels.

Support from Trevelyan and others helped assure others that this new organisation was not run by or for cranks. They were responsible people with a valid and responsible vision to help young people.

Trevelyan and his brother played their part in the physical creation of youth hostels. They gave generous gifts of land and money to adapt buildings. But once erected Trevelyan expected to make youth hostels self-supporting. Youth hostels would pay their way from the small fees they charged for a night's lodging.

The first youth hostel wasn't self sufficient at all. Neither was it long lasting. By February they discovered that drainage from the nearby farm was running into the river. Bertha Gough wrote in her diary "the sanitation was most primitive, the drainage running into the river from which we got our drinking water…" Symonds, the chairman of the group on Merseyside, recalled how the cow dung flowed from the farm, as it does in rain on British farms. The hostel soon closed setting a trend whereby youth hostels opened and closed. Sometimes, closure swiftly followed opening.

For a shilling a night people grasped their heritage as Trevelyan had wanted. For Trevelyan these youth hostels would help breed better citizens. It is less clear whether Bertha Gough, Tom Fairclough or Alf Embleton held those ideals. They may simply have wanted their share of the heritage Trevelyan had outlined and from which they had been excluded. Youth hostels were self sufficient and for those who helped themselves.

Despite the difficult times, youth hostels started more quickly than anyone might have expected. None of them waited for anyone else to give the order. Connie Alexander opened the first youth hostel less than 18 months after she came back from Germany. They did it with no money, no staff, and against her expectations. Early plans changed or were dropped. Friends and supporters like the Trevelyans. Temple, Leonard,

Lawrence Holt and others were ready to help. But more than anything in the coming months they needed financial help.

Notes and references

YHA printed Trevelyan's broadcast in a small booklet, a mark of its importance as it was one of three publications released in the first months of YHA, before it published a handbook and before *The Rucksack* magazine. The main source for the first Christmas at a youth hostel is Connie Alexander's personal account included as an appendix in Taylor's history of Merseyside Youth Hostels.

"We could not have chosen…" *The Rucksack*, June-July 1950, p8

"a keen debater…" *The Rucksack*, New Year 1945, p2

"walking across country…" *Address by Prof GM Trevelyan, 21 January 1931*, p8

"For the last few months…" Taylor, *The Pioneering Years*, Appendix 3

"It had a beautiful entrance hall…" Gough, *A Diary of Seven Years with YHA*, 7/8 February 1931

"the young folk of today…" Address by Prof. G.M.Trevelyan, 21 January 1931, p4

-6-

Cambridge

I found work in a youth hostel through an Australian. Lying on a top bunk in the youth hostel off Holland Park, I overheard him talking about work in youth hostels. He had a job, starting the next day. But other jobs were going, in other places. Youth hostels were recruiting for the summer.

We gossiped about the job, what it might or might not involve, the hours and rates of pay. It didn't seem like much of a job, for not much money, but jobs in youth hostels came with somewhere to live. Travelling can get wearying. Both of us liked the idea of somewhere to live, somewhere to settle, if only for a while. And we'd be working with other people like us, meeting people, having fun. A summer might get me on my feet.

Youth hostels had their headquarters in St Albans, a little town in the countryside beyond London, in an old house, up a hill, away from the centre, in a green and muddy garden of trees and soaked lawns. I would come back there to work as YHA's Head of Corporate Affairs 25 years later but then I was only looking for a seasonal job, to tide me over until I found work on a newspaper, as the journalist I had trained to be. In an empty hallway, people came and went, while I completed an application, before heading to watch a film, with music by Pink Floyd, in a backstreet cinema.

A couple of weeks later, I was sleeping on the floor of a friend's flat in Edinburgh, running out of money, increasingly desperate for work, when a letter arrived from the youth hostel at Cambridge. They were looking for staff. I called from a phone box at the bottom of the stairs, shovelling coins, pushing buttons. I talked the job over with Betty, who was 'the warden's wife'. In a soft Scottish accent she asked me to come down to Cambridge for an interview. I went down on the overnight coach and, dropped at a bus shelter in winter darkness, off the A1, a bus full of children on their way to school, took me to Cambridge, through muddy fields clamped in early morning fog. I loved the city. It was just of a size to suit me, low scale and down beat, with a medieval air of stone and leaded glass, especially on a foggy morning.

I took the job I was offered. I was worn out and grateful for work that promised plenty of cleaning, some decorating, and little responsibility. The job came with a bed, a room, my own bathroom and a small staff lounge with a television. I earned £15 a week. The hostel was big, by English standards, its long rooms stacked with beds. Through summer people like me, on short journeys and longer tours, packed its dormitories. Aussies, Kiwis, South Africans, Americans, Germans, Dutch, Danes, Norwegians, every and any nationality could and did turn up on any night. They came on bicycles, by train, or coach. They hitch hiked or, rarely, travelled by private car. They were my own age or younger, a generation discovering easy travel, with long hair, jeans and no thoughts of careers.

The hostel was a bay-windowed Victorian home, with ugly modern extensions, all glass and grey brick, on a street full of lodgings and bed and breakfast accommodation. Dark narrow stairs, up and down the cramped older house, emerged into bright modern rooms, stairs and steps at confusing levels.

The wardens, Graham and Betty, ran the place to a strict routine. By seven thirty, downstairs, we were preparing breakfast. We stopped for our breakfast, eaten in a rush around a table in the kitchen, before opening the dining room and serving breakfast to guests whom we called "the members." Cornflakes, Weetabix, boiled eggs, salami, jam, marmalade, toast and tea; we didn't serve the traditional cooked English breakfast of bacon and eggs. This approach to breakfast was a sign of the radical ways of the hostel where I had come to work.

Graham and Betty ran the youth hostel in a modern professional manner. They had worked in the Lake District where they met and married. The youth hostel was now their profession and one about which they were passionate. Graham, with a dark thatch of hair, a broad face and provocative manner, walked with a swagger, learned in the hard trades of Salford. Theirs was no vocation. They were not amateurs. They had trained at the job for years. Their forthright approach and professional manner set them at odds with their colleagues and the volunteer regional management. But no one could fault the cleanliness, efficiency and profitability of the hostel.

Routine was strict and anyone late for breakfast risked getting none. Guests did their own washing up or swept the rooms and folded blankets before they could reclaim their membership cards, before 10am when everyone was expected to be gone. If they had not already departed, Graham reminded them, in a loud voice, all youth hostels closed between the hours of ten and five. When the hostel was empty and the front door locked, we sat down to coffee and biscuits in the lounge. Graham read the paper and entertained us with outrageously conservative views to Betty's embarrassment and dismay, before we hurried back to scrubbing, tidying, shaking and cleaning.

Three of us ran the hostel with Graham and Betty. Mick, with red hair and a beard, came from Newcastle. Jane, from Romford in Essex, had left school that summer and was taking a year out before going to university. Jenny, an A-level student, came in the afternoons to scrub showers and wash down walls. She introduced me to Cambridge pubs and life.

Graham and Betty waged war on a daily basis against youth hostels' general reputation for scruffiness. Years of not much money and work supposedly done by the guests had run down many hostels and left them scruffy or plain dirty. The true professional, the capable warden, took pride in the job.

Graham kept the building well maintained, well oiled, every door hung with precision on its hinges. Every wall, every stretch of wood was freshly painted whilst Betty made sure not a door was marked by dirty fingers, not a skirting board scuffed by a clumsy shoe. We scrubbed the toilets and showers. We swept and mopped floors. We carried dirty bedding in piles downstairs and hung sheets to dry in the warm clammy air of a drying room in the cellar.

By midday when we stopped we were weary. With the youth hostel closed and its rooms empty, I was free until 5pm when the doors reopened and a crowd pushed its way in a line to the desk where Graham checked them in. We worked in the kitchen at his back with Betty. We laid tables in the dining room or made packed lunches for the next day. The food was simple and cheap, without pretension.

We worked in a cheerful family atmosphere, with jokes and ribbing and minor disagreements. The whole world of youth hostels seemed to be a big family. I was lent to a nearby hostel for a few nights while the warden there took time off for a wedding. She left me in charge of a creaking, dusty mill on the glassy edge of a still pond sweltering through the long summer drought of that year.

On days off or holidays, I stayed in other youth hostels. People knew Graham and Betty and, from that, knew me. They made me welcome. I went to the New Forest, down to Cornwall and, at the end of a year, I moved to the Lake District, to the youth hostel in Ambleside. What had started as a job for a summer was proving to be more than that. I loved the constant travel. I loved being surrounded by people on the move. Though the routine grew tedious, there was always something new, someone new, some fresh girl wanting to chat and late night assignations that were always against the rules.

I was learning my way, finding my routes through the network of youth hostels that had grown up in Britain and through the world. In Carlisle, after a short spell working at the youth hostel there, I went back to the youth hostel in Ambleside where my bedroom overlooked Windermere and I could see the blue hills of Lakeland on a clear day. I forgot ideas of work as a journalist.

Paying the way

Youth hostel affairs reached a turning point in 1931. After the Digswell conference of 1930 momentum for youth hostels grew. People had begun joining the new organisation. Public figures, politicians and organisations gave support.

Journalists wrote about youth hostels in the left wing *Daily Herald*, in *The Daily News* and *The Times*. More than a thousand people joined an association with no hostels because they had waited long enough. They determined that they would have youth hostels. Their subscriptions provided £241 in the first year.

Plans for youth hostels were ambitious. First president, GM Trevelyan, talked about a chain of youth hostels covering the countryside, stretching from Kent to Wales. Youth hostels would be in walking distance of one another, 15 to 20 miles apart. They expected a youth hostel would cost between £300 and £500. To run regional groups throughout Britain would take stationery, travel, postage and time. Their plans all required money and they had precious little of that.

The CHA and HF, the Workers Travel Association, the CTC, the

World Alliance, the National Union of Students and the Wayfarers Travel Agency made donations. The regions raised funds too. Merseyside ran an appeal, the Blue Funnel line and others pledged funds, and the Reckitt Trust granted £100 towards youth hostels in the north of England.

But by the beginning of 1931, of the regional groups, only Merseyside had opened a youth hostel that lasted only a short time. Other regional groups were establishing themselves but without youth hostels they risked losing any support they had. Without youth hostels they would not change the world.

Jack Catchpool worked part time as honorary secretary. While he looked for a permanent office, he secured an office for the first few months at Toynbee Hall, the Educational Settlement in London where he had once been sub-warden. He found the first permanent YHA national office in a redundant army hut in Welwyn Garden City. He leased the vacant hut from the Welwyn Garden City Company and employed Margaret Porteous as the first member of staff. Even without a salary for Catchpool, running a national organisation in its infancy cost money. YHA paid more for postage, printing and stationery in the first year than it did for salaries.

Catchpool, Baron and others on the executive committee travelled tirelessly. They supported groups setting up in the regions. They hunted for youth hostels. They met with others sharing an interest in youth hostels. Catchpool went to Scotland to meet those thinking of forming a group north of the border. Terry Trench, a young Irishman studying modern languages at Sidney Sussex College, called on GM Trevelyan in Cambridge. Trench had heard that a Youth Hostels Association of Great Britain planned to extend to Ireland.

The 22 year-old had studied for a year in Germany and was keen to see something like the German *Jugendherbergen* in Ireland. Trevelyan told him YHA had no plans to extend its youth hostels into Ireland. He encouraged Trench to set up an organisation for youth hostels there. Trench's father was the Professor of English Literature at Trinity College in Dublin. Trench wrote to his father asking him to arrange a meeting with some representative people with a view to starting youth hostels in Ireland.

It was a hectic time for Catchpool. He addressed meetings, met possible secretaries for regional groups and advised on the organisation of regional councils using a pamphlet he had written. He searched for buildings that might make youth hostels. He and Trevelyan had been talking about ways the National Trust might work with youth hostels since Trevelyan first agreed to become president.

The National Trust was a small organisation. In 1930 its membership reached 1000, a figure that the new youth hostels achieved in less than a year. The trust concentrated on protecting landscapes and was less interested in protecting property, unless it was of particular historic interest and on the verge of ruin. Knowing that the trust was sometimes given property it could not use, Catchpool suggested that, if the YHA was responsible for the upkeep of some of these buildings, it could help the National Trust protect buildings they might otherwise have had to turn down.

Discussions between Catchpool and Trevelyan paid off when a group in Winchester bought the city's old mill. It had been empty for more than thirty years. The group passed the building to the National Trust. The trust had no use for the mill, spanning the River Itchen on a main road into the city. But from Catchpool's point of view, it was ideal for his pet project. He wanted to open a chain of hostels down the Pilgrims' Way, an ancient pathway stretching from Winchester to Canterbury. The City Mill could be the first hostel in the chain. When they heard there was a chance of getting the mill, Catchpool and Barclay Baron drove down to look over the building. They took with them Dorothy Tomkins, an unemployed architectural student.

Arriving in the afternoon Tomkins described the mill's great gable of red brick glowing in the afternoon sun. They crept along a dark passage with the echo of tumbling water rushing to meet them and climbed up to a long wooden room, floored with rough wide planks of sold oak, with a wall of the pleasing red bricks. Diamond encasements lit the room's proportions on either side. "Everywhere was thick with dust and cobwebs. We viewed the loft among the beams, the two little rooms which were earmarked for the girls' dormitories, and the colder, more forbidding stable accommodation for the men. We admired the walled garden projecting into the river which is perhaps the most beautiful and unexpected part of the Mill."

On their journey back to London, Catchpool and Tomkins agreed that he would provide £50 of his own money to buy furniture and equipment. The hostel was his baby but Tomkins carried out the work of furnishing and opening the new youth hostel. She worked hard. She improvised a table from a notice board and trestles. She creosoted old wood and drafted visitors into the backbreaking work. Success rewarded her efforts when the youth hostel opened for Easter 1931. The hostel was soon heavily booked and Catchpool's loan repaid.

The old mill was the first hostel leased from the National Trust. By Easter 1931 about a dozen youth hostels had opened, including the youth hostels at Idwal Cottage in Snowdonia and at Street in Somerset, both still open today. By the end of April, 31 youth hostels were open.

The National Trust provided more youth hostels over time but they would never be able to meet every need for a youth hostel. Generous donations and grants might help provide a few more but YHA urgently needed more funds for the kind of organisation they wanted to create. An enthusiastic and rapidly growing membership demanded more youth hostels.

The group on Merseyside turned to the Carnegie Trust, one of the biggest donors in Britain. But the trust turned down their application. It only supported national organisations, so Catchpool picked up the challenge, on behalf of the national YHA. Early in 1931, he applied to the Carnegie Trust for funds.

Multi-millionaire, Andrew Carnegie, was born in Dunfermline in Scotland in 1835. After his family emigrated to the USA and growing up there he made a fortune in American railways and steel. To some, he was the most ruthless of a ruthless band of 19th century money-makers. Underhand practices and union busting mired his name and associated him with the excesses of corporate greed. To others, he was an outstanding benefactor. When he had made his money he used the bulk to finance philanthropy. He gave to libraries, to education, to the pursuit of peace and scientific research.

He never forgot his roots in Scotland. He created a Carnegie Trust for the United Kingdom in 1913. He gave it a wide and flexible brief for the "improvement of the well-being of the masses of the people of Great Britain and Ireland." The shrewd capitalist encouraged trustees to continually support new causes. He prevented them from linking to a narrow purpose that might diminish and decline in time or hold them from supporting other, more beneficial causes.

The Carnegie Trust funded wide ranging causes. It helped build village halls and supported marriage guidance and citizens' advice bureaux. In 1927 the Carnegie Trust allocated £200,000 (around £10 million today) to the National Playing Fields Association. The fund helped develop more than 900 playing fields sites between 1927 and 1935. The Carnegie Trust helped the Workers' Education Association (WEA) to extend from cities into rural parts of England.

Carnegie trustees made every effort to support the long term development of the bodies they backed. They were determined that the funds they gave should leave an organisation better equipped for the future. They didn't want dependant organisations returning, year after year, for more and more funding. They supported better administration and extensions to work and they made their grants with shrewd care.

The trust shared offices with the National Council of Social Services in Bedford Square, London. The NCSS was the organisation that prompted the national beginning of youth hostels in 1930 and a Carnegie trustee, Elizabeth Haldane, attended that first meeting in April 1930. Haldane was a trusted and active advocate for the trust. After witnessing squalor, dirt and overcrowding in Edinburgh Haldane dedicated her life to social service. When Carnegie founded his trust he made Haldane the first woman member of its board.

Catchpool, supported by the executive and Trevelyan, applied to the trust for an ambitious £30,000 (£1.5 million today) over three years. The trust's Social Service Sub-committee, including Elizabeth Haldane, reviewed his application on Friday 8 May 1931. He told the committee youth hostels would provide good accommodation for young men and women walkers and cyclists. Prices would be low and youth hostels would be 'under proper supervision'.

During the first year funds would help six regional councils: Manchester and Derbyshire covering the Peak District; Birmingham for the Shropshire-Worcestershire area; Bristol and the Mendips for the Quantocks and Exmoor; Merseyside for North Wales; Cardiff for South Wales and London for south-east England. Trustees would fund a model youth hostel in each area. These youth hostels would demonstrate the new style accommodation to potential supporters. Finally, trustees would stimulate local fund raising. Catchpool proposed they reward each area with £1 for every £2 they raised.

At the end of their discussion, the committee agreed that they were interested in and sympathetic towards the youth hostel project. But £30,000, even over three years, was more than they would recommend. They realised youth hostels were just beginning and their structure and administration was weak. They wanted more detail and asked for a modified scheme by July.

On Monday 8 June 1931, *The Times* reported the Carnegie trust were going to grant £10,000 to the Youth Hostels Association of Great Britain for the provision of hostels. Barclay Baron claimed in *The Times* report that there were no conditions for spending the money, except that it should be used to further the association's objects.

Funding went to all the established regions for completing existing work and for developing new schemes. No one any longer expected them to double any funds from Carnegie. The trust would simply match what they raised £1 for £1. Funding covered central expenses too, increasing what could be done centrally and nationally.

Catchpool dropped plans for a specific number of model hostels in favour of creating model hostels in selected parts of the country at a total cost of £4,000. Carnegie trustees suggested these hostels should be within easy reach of well wishers who might contribute to funds. The trustees were keen that youth hostels, and especially these, should be self-sustaining and not dependent on the trust for funds in the future. The trust's money was a 'seed fund' to help youth hostels start. Money was available immediately. YHA was able to call down funds as and when they needed.

Catchpool and the executive had much to celebrate. £10,000, nearly half a million in today's money, was twenty times what the association made centrally in its first year.

Carnegie trustees were right when they observed that the structure and administration of youth hostels was weak. In the midst of hectic activity the executive committee were caught up in misunderstandings and embarrassments.

Relationships with cyclists were tricky at the outset. Cyclists and walkers viewed each other with some suspicion. The National Cyclists' Union had requested representation on YHA's council. The executive committee believed that the union was concerned with 'stunt' racing. They reluctantly accepted the union to the YHA council because they had no legitimate reason to refuse but word of what of the executive's discussion filtered back to the union. The cyclists felt insulted by the description of them as stunt cyclists. The executive committee dispatched Catchpool to smooth feathers.

More embarrassment with cyclists followed. A member of the Merseyside group said that youth hostels would always give preference to walkers over cyclists. His views found their way into the press just when the CTC was finalising funding to support youth hostels. The CTC only released their funds after receiving apologies, assurances and clarification.

Terry Trench went home from Cambridge for the Easter vacation that year. He met with a small group in the Trench family home in Palmerston Park, Dublin in April. Representatives of the Scouts and other outdoor organisations attended. They decided to start youth hostels in Ireland and immediately afterwards Ruth Patten, a lecturer in zoology at Trinity College, began searching for possible sites. For most of the search she rode pillion on the motorbike of another Trinity College scientist. A meeting at University College Dublin on 7 May 1931 brought *An Óige*, Youth, into existence. Before the end of May 1931 they opened the first youth hostel in Ireland.

The founding of a Scottish Youth Hostels Association caused further embarrassment. In late 1930 Catchpool had travelled to Edinburgh. After his meeting there he hoped that Scotland would form a regional group within the British movement. But he had not convinced the Scots and they began their own organisation. They believed a society based in Welwyn Garden City could neither appreciate their needs or possibilities nor fire their imagination. In February 1931 a meeting in Edinburgh set up the Scottish Youth Hostels Association (SYHA) with a district committee in Edinburgh. A Glasgow committee followed and Scotland opened its first youth hostels in May.

In June 1931, an angry Dr Alan Fothergill, chairman of the new Scottish association, supported by Mr Beith, attended an executive committee meeting of the Youth Hostels Association of Great Britain in London. Fothergill made a lengthy speech. Their title was misleading, he informed them. Scotland in no way regarded YHA as the parent body. An offer from Catchpool to spend £450 on the erection of a hostel in Scotland was not enough, now Fothergill and Beith knew the money would come from the huge Carnegie funds. Having made their case, the pair withdrew, leaving the committee to ponder their response.

The executive had little choice. They dropped Great Britain from their

title. They would confine themselves to England and Wales. Their youth
hostels would accept memberships from Scotland and they would submit
to the Carnegie trustees that £2,000 of the funds granted should go to
youth hostels in Scotland. They communicated the climbdown to
Forthergill and Beith "who repeated a good deal of what they had said
previously and abruptly withdrew."

Funds from the Carnegie trust drove change to strengthen the
organisation and its administration of youth hostels. The executive
committee appointed John Simpson as manager for the office in Welwyn
Garden City. He and Catchpool made an ideal combination. Simpson
spent most of his time in the office doing all in his power to see that every
penny was well spent. He freed Catchpool to spend time away, promoting
youth hostels, finding property and the money to buy it. He watched his
boss with care and subjected even Catchpool's schemes to a dose of close
scrutiny. The executive appointed Mary Lander as shorthand typist. A BSc
graduate of London University, she spoke fluent German and French and
she had experience of youth hostels in Germany. She supported
Catchpool, attending international meetings with him.

The executive strengthened their own resources. WH Washington,
manager of Barclays Bank in Welwyn Garden City, had been acting
treasurer. In 1932, they appointed Sir Percy Jackson, a manufacturer from
Huddersfield in Yorkshire, to join them as honorary treasurer.

Sir Percy came from the Carnegie trust. Like Elizabeth Haldane, he
had been at the trust's meetings which discussed youth hostels. Knighted
in 1925, he was involved in the development of national education policy.
He was chairman of the West Riding Education Committee. At the height
of the depression, he set up the Land Settlement Association, to get
unemployed families from industrial cities onto small holdings where they
could work again. Land gave them the chance to become successful,
producing food for themselves and for sale.

Jackson was influential and persuasive, known as a capable
administrator, with sound judgement. His arrival on the YHA Executive
Committee looks in many ways as if it was creating a conflict of interest
but the Carnegie trustees may not have seen the appointment in that way.
They may have been reassuring themselves that one of their own was there
to guide the new organisation.

All over the country people established regional groups. Catchpool had laid out careful guidance on how to form a regional council which sheds light on how these groups first established themselves. Catchpool suggested writing to the local newspaper to encourage support. After meeting informally in a private house anyone could set up an unofficial group. They could then call a meeting of representatives from local branches of large organisations. He offered a list of organisations to invite including the Association of Headmistresses, the CTC and the National Union of Students. Others included the Brotherhood Movement, the Institute of Industrial Welfare Workers and Christian Endeavour.

Catchpool advised great care over the choice of chairman for the initial meeting. "Someone who is much respected in the locality, and who is therefore likely to produce a feeling of business confidence in the minds of intending subscribers, is a great asset to the meeting." He suggested an agenda for the public meeting including the election of a provisional committee. A further meeting would 'regularise' the work of the provisional committee and prepare a scheme for publicity and raising money.

Catchpool based his advice on his own experience but events didn't always work out that way. Local efforts sometimes went before a regional group was in place. A schoolmaster from Kirkby Stephen, FW Parrott, suggested the Friends Meeting House in Kirkby Stephen as a youth hostel. One opened there on 28 June, 1931, six months before a regional group constituted itself in the area.

TA Leonard's ideals, Trevelyan's vision and Catchpool's energy mingling with lessons from youth hostels in Germany, were creating something special in England and Wales. When they first discussed youth hostels in March 1930, those at the meeting were determined that they would not slavishly copy the German system. They wanted a scheme "suited to British conditions and temperament."

But they were no longer a British association suited to British conditions and temperament. They were a Scottish association and an English and Welsh association. Youth hostels in Ireland united for a time. In November 1931 *An Óige* formed a northern branch in much the same way as Catchpool had hoped for Scotland. The branch had complete autonomy from the headquarters in Dublin. They opened the first hostel in Northern Ireland in December 1931 at Dromara, County Down. By Easter 1932 they had opened two more but it was becoming clear that if they wanted public support they would have to go it alone. They broke away and formed a Youth Hostel Association of Northern Ireland (YHANI). The association in England and Wales renamed itself as the Youth Hostels Association (England and Wales), more popularly known as YHA (England and Wales) or simply YHA.

The move ended ideas of unity for Britain or Ireland. Ever since, the four organisations for the Irish Republic, for Northern Ireland, for Scotland and for England and Wales have maintained cordial relations, attending each other's national councils and holding regular joint meetings. At brief times they shared space in each other's magazines.

Two years after the first regional group started on Merseyside in December 1929, 17 regional groups were in place in England and Wales. Birmingham, Cambridge, Gloucester and Somerset, Lakeland, London, Manchester, the North Midlands, Northumberland and Tyneside, Oxford, Plymouth, Portsmouth, South Wales, Teeside and Eskdale, Warwickshire and Northants, and the West Riding of Yorkshire had joined the first group on Merseyside.

Numbers joining and staying in youth hostels soared. 100 youth hostels were open by March 1932, 15 months after the failed attempt to open a youth hostel at Pennant Hall. Devolved structure and a lack of organisation was also a strength. Youth hostel numbers rocketed on the back of local enthusiasm and energy.

The Carnegie trust took a more critical view. In 1932, trustees considered a report on youth hostels and the work done so far and a request for more funds. Trustees were uneasy at the pace at which YHA was moving, at the lack of funds and clear plans. They saw no organisation behind Jack Catchpool. They considered he was working practically single-handed.

Before they agreed proposals for acquiring buildings as youth hostels they wanted more information. They wanted to know the intentions for properties. They would not give any kind of general approval for building, buying or leasing property as youth hostels. Maintenance and repair would be costly, perhaps more than anyone involved in youth hostels at the time understood. In a businesslike way, Carnegie trustees repeated that the takings of each hostel should cover maintenance and repair as well as ordinary current costs including the warden's salary.

Carnegie trustees saw the organisation growing beyond its means.

They wanted to prevent problems occurring in the coming years. A steady stream of income had to pay for publicity and supervision. Trustees were nervous that YHA members were taking all the benefit from youth hostels. They wanted individual members contributing more than they did to the hostels they were using. Youth hostels after all benefitted members and they should be paying more towards them. The Carnegie trustees agreed they would give no further assistance.

The decision prompted YHA's executive committee to finally form a trust to hold YHA's property in 1933. Carnegie trustees had sought assurances since 1931 that youth hostel properties were properly owned and managed. Members of the executive and regional groups had also been reluctant to take on the risks and responsibilities of negotiating for and owning property. As leaseholders they faced personal loss. A separate trust with limited liability to own property was long overdue. Regional groups could now transfer their properties to the Youth Hostels Trust and the trust could now receive legacies of property or money.

Formation of the Youth Hostels Trust came too late for the Merseyside group. They had already set up as an incorporated body, Merseyside Youth Hostels Ltd, with limited liability, against the wishes of the national executive committee. That decision would return and cause problems more than fifty years later when the national executive wished to wind up the affairs of the Merseyside group. They found they had none of the powers they had over other regional groups.

That the Carnegie trustees saw a lack of organisation behind Catchpool was not surprising. He was working as a part time volunteer, paid an honorarium of £250 whilst he reduced his other commitments. He had support from Baron and a few others on the executive but mostly it was Catchpool on his own. If something needed doing he did it. He found new hostels. He helped set up regional groups. He lent his own money and found funds. He dealt with the media and arranged publicity. He and Baron were designing badges and metal signs while the group on Merseyside designed the first membership card. Catchpool only became full time secretary with pay in 1934.

The Carnegie trust contributed vital funds at just the right moment. They lifted the new movement to its feet. As well as material help, youth hostels gained prestige and publicity. The Carnegie trust's careful investment encouraged others to give and support youth hostels. But no one seemed to pay much heed to the trustees' concerns. Growth hid problems for the future. The issue of ensuring that youth hostels funded themselves would be ignored or brushed aside during the coming decades.

Despite their concerns and their decision, Carnegie trustees continued to support youth hostels for many more years. They were proud of the part they had played in setting up youth hostels throughout Britain. The first years of youth hostels became a story of pride. A sense of purpose and triumph became overwhelming. GM Trevelyan wrote a foreword for the first issue of the brand new youth hostel magazine, *YHA Rucksack*, in late 1932. Booted and kitted, he declared, they were on their way. Young people of the day were at last enjoying the heritage that was theirs. They had read and learned about that heritage at school. Now it was theirs to enjoy. Youth hostels were changing the world.

Notes and references

I made wide use of the National Executive Committee's minutes. John Martin pointed me towards Catchpool's guidance to regional councils *How to Form a Regional Council*. Dorothy Tomkins' account of the discovery of the old City Mill at Winchester is included in Coburn's book. Terry Trench told the story of the beginning of *An Óige* in his book *Fifty Years Young*. I read extensively in the Carnegie UK Trust's minutes and records, available on line. The trust continues to set an example by making its archive records so widely and easily available.

"Everywhere was thick with dust…" Coburn, *Youth Hostel Story*, p53
"who repeated…" *Minutes 1930-1933*, June 1931
"suited to British conditions and temperament." *Report of a conference convened by the National Council of Social Service, Executive Committee, 1930-1933*

8

Ambleside

Ambleside youth hostel was on the edge of Windermere where ferries came and went among piers and jetties bustling with crowds. Holiday makers shopped, drank in pubs, ate fish and chips and slept in the sun on park benches.

The youth hostel fronted the lake in two old hotels knocked together. Lake views, a lounge with enormous picture windows and a self service restaurant, with queues and trays, gave children a glimpse of sophistication their age more usually denied.

The youth hostel was a giant experiment, just as growing up should be. Some moments the children were adult, full of cool reserve, until giggles and excitement overwhelmed them and they collapsed. Teenagers in twos, threes and fours and sometimes more came and went throughout the summer making the youth hostel with its 240 beds the busiest outside London.

After a night at Ambleside, buying sweets from the hostel shop, talking in whispers in the dark, homesick or on the edge of teenage love, they left. They went by foot, from hostel to hostel. They tramped the roads and low paths, overladen with rucksacks bought from army surplus stores.

They wore old shoes. Their waterproofs were anything but waterproof. They were like a travelling caravan, like the old *Wandervögel* of Germany, along the roads and paths of the Lake District. But they carried no flags. They sang pop songs not folk songs. They queued for the pay phone each night to call home, to reassure parents that they were alive, not lost in the wilds and not out, getting drunk, pregnant or kidnapped. At the end of a few days or a week of freedom, they went home, by bus or train.

Youth hostels were safe, like the overcrowded homes where they lived with parents and siblings. Anyone wanting trouble would have gone elsewhere. Adults opened the door and admitted them. Adults served meals and demanded they keep the place tidy and clean. Each morning they helped with the cleaning. They dragged vacuum cleaners down corridors. They scrubbed sinks and washed baths and tidied beds.

They shared crowded bedrooms and washrooms with others of the same sex. There was no privacy and little chance for anyone to be on their own. With a friend or two there was little chance of anyone kidnapping a teenager and there was no reason for that to happen, no reason for any danger to befall a child. If you misbehaved, as a final sanction, a warden could send you home.

I was one of those wardens. I loved the work with a crowd of others about the same age, runners and cyclists and walkers, outdoor people who worked there to be close to the hills. We worked for free time, to get out in the afternoons or on the long evenings. Pay was low. I earned cash and all the food I could eat. I lived in a small room at the top of the hostel. Early in the morning the view stretching into the distant hills took my breath away. A man in a canoe went like a spider over the glassy water most mornings.

I went climbing in Langdale and on Dove Crag, climbing in ice and hail and rain and in sunshine too. Once on a long evening of sunshine on Dow Crag the blue of Goats Water below was a jewel. I camped in a tent or slept in a sleeping bag and woke in the morning with mist like candy floss in my companion's hair.

I visited nearby youth hostels where I stayed for free. That was part of the job too. Staff at other hostels made me welcome. We met in pubs. We drank and played darts, part of a network of news and gossip. The rain sometimes came down too much and too often. But the sun, when it shone, made the Lake District more of an England than I ever dreamed England could be.

When summer ended, schools came to the youth hostel. Enthusiastic teachers brought their classes with parents and friends to help them. They took children into the hills. They took them walking. They studied maps. They taught geography. They taught the lucky ones to be self sufficient and free. They gave them an introduction to the countryside that would stay with them for the rest of their lives.

Some might never have been out of the city or the town in which they were born. Some might have been to the seaside for a day or a week. Many had never seen the open countryside or gone walking anywhere other than down to the shops.

Many of my friends first went to the countryside with their school, stayed in a youth hostel and never wanted to go home again. A youth hostel trip to the countryside, a week in the summer was a rite at the time. Some were following in the footsteps of a mother or father. The previous generation had escaped to the countryside during or after the war and now they did the same. Children when they went home began planning to come back again, the next summer, when they were done with exams and teachers and schools. They were always excited when they learned they could stay in youth hostels on their own.

Some of them took up walking or climbing. Travel and adventure bit some. Youth hostels changed their lives. That was the point of youth hostels. That was what they were there for.

9

Architects and buildings

Youth hostels proliferated in Britain as they had in Germany. They spread on the back of widespread enthusiasm and rampant demand. Increasing opportunities for leisure and a desire to explore the countryside fuelled phenomenal growth.

Simple ideas change the world. Richard Schirrmann's idea was simple. Youth hostels would be in school classrooms during the holiday season. "Two classrooms will suffice," he wrote. "One for boys and one for girls. Some of the benches will be stacked up. That will make room for fifteen beds. Each bed will consist of a tightly stuffed straw sack and pillow, two sheets and a blanket. Each child will be required to keep his own sleeping place clean and tidy."

His design for a hostel was rudimentary, without ornamentation. His idea was practical and inexpensive. It needed only the least effort and expenditure, using buildings and rooms already in every city, town and village.

Schirrmann never anticipated how demand for youth hostels would explode. Using schools and taking groups in holidays wasn't enough. His idea required a more permanent solution, a building open all year round, with staff doing no other work, dedicated to the welfare of their young guests. In 1912, in the castle in Altena, in what is now North Rhine-Westphalia, the first permanent youth hostel opened. Schirrmann designed it with two dormitories, a kitchen and washrooms.

Schirrmann and his colleagues adapted buildings as youth hostels. They equipped dormitories with bunks, double or triple tiered in wood or metal. They created a kitchen, separate washing and toilet facilities for the two sexes and a common room. Youth hostels won support from the army and the army made barracks available for hostels while youth hostels in fairy tale castles, like the one at Altena, stirred and caught the imagination of visitors from abroad. They became the best kind of advertising for Schirrmann's idea.

But the reality of converted castles and barracks was impractical. Putting youth hostels in buildings never meant to be accommodation made youth hostels difficult to run and expensive to keep. By 1926 Schirrmann and others realised that they needed youth hostels built for purpose. Youth hostels should be dedicated to being one thing, not a classroom with add-ons, not a castle.

By then, Schirrmann was adamant. "We don't want to build any gloomy medieval fortress, any miniature castles from an over-romantic age with mock turrets and lighthouse-like towers, any barracks, any sheep-pens. Buildings must be constructed to accommodate youth, the rising generation; simple and functional, light, easily ventilated, yet retaining the warmth, pleasant to live in, beautiful…"

Schirrmann and his colleagues began building youth hostels from scratch. Public authorities supported them with funds and sites. Such hostels were a completely new field of architecture. Big numbers of lively children and young people required heavy, robust equipment. A hostel in Munich opened in 1927 for up to 300 guests with a classroom attached to each dormitory and a kitchen where groups and classes could cook their own food and another where they could buy meals. The hostel recorded 45,000 overnight stays in its first year.

In less than twenty years the concept of youth hostels had leaped from ad-hoc and temporary accommodation in classrooms to purpose built, architect-designed youth hostels with a single, simple purpose of accommodating large numbers of young people.

After visiting Germany in the summer of 1929, Fairclough and his friends formed the first regional group in Liverpool. They grasped the need for purpose built, architect-designed youth hostels they had seen in Germany. They also wanted expert advice. They realised their own enthusiasm and dedication would not be enough. They were walkers. They worked as clerks, teachers and secretaries. They knew nothing about the buildings they needed for youth hostels.

They involved builders and architects to give them essential, specialist advice. A Liverpool architect, PJ Clarke, offered professional support and a cheque for £300 to the group. Rev HH Symonds, chairman of the group, pulled Clarke into youth hostel affairs. Symonds also knew Patrick Abercrombie, Professor of Civic Design at Liverpool University's School of Architecture. Symonds invited him to join their new House and Sites Committee.

Abercrombie began his long career in town planning in 1907 as a junior lecturer and studio instructor at the architecture school in Liverpool. He's best known for planning London after the second world war. He suggested decentralising the city into four rings with a suburban ring and a green belt of countryside surrounding the inner core of city. Outside he planned new towns like traditional country towns. Two of these new towns, Harlow and Crawley, were built on sites Abercrombie proposed.

Abercrombie would have found the enthusiastic members of the Merseyside group attractive. They, like him, loved traditional landscapes and country towns. Their aim of encouraging a love of the countryside placed them with men like him. They were the heart of a movement to protect the countryside. The founders of youth hostels believed they could be of "great service to all lovers of the English countryside by maintaining the freedom of footpaths, by preventing the destruction and disfiguration of natural beauties..."

People wanted escape. Many men sought peace in the countryside after the mud and death of the first world war. Some believed that they had fought for an ideal countryside. A rural dream fired them, not towns and cities. For some land was an appropriate reward for all they had suffered. Memories of the countryside had inspired and consoled them in the trenches. They longed to escape the dirt, poor housing and overcrowding of metropolitan Britain, if only for a weekend. People were also rediscovering the places of Britain, of England and Wales. Popular books by JB Priestley and HV Morton and Trevelyan's histories encouraged them to get out of the metropolitan landscapes that confined them.

Not all who dreamed of a countryside, open to all, were walkers. Speculators built suburbs in countryside on the edge of towns and cities. A growing network of roads chewed up rural peace. Towns and cities lurched into the countryside. Small factories, petrol stations, roadside cafes and tea rooms sprang up. Pylons and advertising hoardings littered the way.

Walkers and others like Abercrombie viewed this erosion of the countryside with dismay and some snobbishness. Poor and ordinary people believed they too were entitled to a patch of British countryside. Speculators parcelled land into cheap small plots and sold them on to the poor of London and other cities who planted trams and railways carriages as their own country retreats and weekend homes and camped on the land without drains or supplies, horrifying many. They built townships like Peacehaven and Jaywick Sands. They fled the squalor of cities, at least at the weekend, as the wealthy did.

Youth hostels also offered ordinary people a weekend retreat or a temporary home in the countryside. Involving Abercrombie, a well known opponent of the destruction of the countryside, added credibility to the new venture of youth hostels. They reassured anyone that youth hostels and their users would not damage the countryside. The founding youth hostel members, at their first conference at Digswell Park in 1930, earnestly implored the new organisation to do all it could "to foster... a proper regard for the amenities of the countryside." It should take steps "to prevent the disfiguration of places of natural beauty by the erection of unsightly buildings."

The uglification and destruction of the countryside was not inevitable. Little restricted the expansion of cities into the countryside. Abercrombie was one of the growing band demanding greater efforts to preserve and protect the countryside. Planning regulation could limit, control and even improve the spreading ugliness.

An English-born Welsh architect and colleague of Abercrombie, Clough Williams-Ellis, also opposed the trashing of the countryside. His book, *England and the Octopus*, cried against the urbanisation of the countryside and the destruction of traditional villages. Williams-Ellis saw youth hostels as a sign of hope in dismal times. Thousands of young people tramping into the countryside and seeking knowledge of beauty in nature encouraged him.

Abercrombie became the first secretary of the Council for the Preservation of Rural England (CPRE) in 1926. CPRE dedicated itself to preserving landscape particularly against urban sprawl and ribbon development. He founded the Welsh equivalent of the council with Williams-Ellis.

Clough Williams-Ellis was a fashionable architect. He was more than a protectionist. He was reacting not only against the unsightly. His vision was positive. He believed people were meant to live in happy beautiful surroundings. He wanted a new architecture that enhanced surroundings. He wanted colourful, beautiful buildings that blended with the landscape. He fulfilled his dream by building the village of Portmeirion on land he owned in North Wales. He had already begun this work when he designed a small youth hostel for a site two miles from the main Mold-Ruthin road, at Maeshafn in Wales.

The simple wooden structure of unusual design made an immediate statement. It aligned youth hostels with modern architecture, in a colourful style, linked to the arts and crafts movement. The building was Italianate and Mediterranean. Blue doors in the yellow walls of a central common room opened into two dormitories, one for men on the south side and one for women, on the north side. He divided each dormitory into four cubicles for cosiness and suspended stout canvas bunks in the cubicles.

His design was as far from the large purpose built hostels of Germany as it was possible to be. It was small where those of Germany were big. The building cost £900, far more than anyone expected though at £45-55,000 in today's money, it does not seem that expensive today. Private money, from the Liverpool shipowners, A Holt and Co, paid for the building, not the public authorities that were building youth hostels in Germany.

The youth hostel opened at Whit 1931 and an official opening followed in July when Williams-Ellis was there. In her diary Bertha Gough recorded that 52 people stayed afterwards and, although it was a warm June night, they were all cold in the bunks. Some slept two in a bed for warmth. Symonds later bought five acres of land around the hostel, gifting it in memory of his wife who died in 1937. The youth hostel at Maeshafn was, over time, messed around with and altered, had a balcony added and taken away. Its windows were replaced and its shutters removed. A room was added as the hostel struggled to adapt to change and demand until it closed and was sold in 2006.

Colwyn Ffoulkes, another of Abercrombie's colleagues, designed a second structure for the Merseyside group. He planned a simple wooden building, like a plain, little chapel, to provide more beds for a youth hostel in the church rooms at Llanfihangel Glyn Myfyr on the Denbighshire / Merionethshire border. But an innkeeper protested that the youth hostel was incompatible with rural life. The vicar refused continued use of the church rooms and the youth hostel closed. The Merseyside group dismantled the wooden dormitory, which would sleep 15 in triple tiered bunks, and moved it by lorry to Idwal Cottage. Since then the youth hostel has used it as a dormitory, wet weather refuge, cycle shed and store. Restored to use as a sleeping shelter for seven, it still stands in woodland opposite the hostel.

The Carnegie trust spurred another two architect designed youth hostels. £4,000 of the trust's funding was for demonstration hostels, to show users and enquirers a well-organised hostel and the purposes it could serve. The national executive invited proposals from regional groups. The executive reckoned they had enough for three or four of these new hostels and expected one each in the north, the midlands and the south of England. They wanted these hostels in centres "much frequented by visitors or within easy reach of a large population." Each hostel would have separate dormitories, bath or shower rooms, a common-room and dining-room. Members would have a kitchen where they could cook their own meals, a drying room for wet clothes and a cycle shed.

The first of the new breed opened in Thorney Howe, outside Grasmere village, in the Lake District. A converted Lakeland farmhouse, an architect did not design it. Across the Pennines, the Nothumberland regional group, formed out of the old trampers guild, was opening a chain of hostels along Hadrian's Wall. Architect F Austin Childs designed another demonstration hostel to complete the chain, at East Bog Farm on the Military Road, near Bardon Mill.

The hostel was a Trevelyan family affair. GM Trevelyan, the first YHA president, added his own money to the Carnegie trust's grant to get the hostel built on land owned by his brother, Sir Charles, whose wife, Lady Mary, opened the hostel in 1934. Hearing the nearby pub called the "Twice

Brewed" Inn, Lady Mary claimed that, as the hostel only served tea, it should be called "Once Brewed." The name stuck.

A 26 year-old architect and member of the newly formed London regional council designed another demonstration hostel at Holmbury St Mary in Surrey. Woodland surrounded Howard Lobb's red brick hostel in its idyllic setting. Its long low lines faced east and west among broad and gently sloping hills. Lobb designed everything for simplicity, with men downstairs, women above. He broke the two large bedrooms for 24 into cubicles to give a sense of privacy. Each cubicle slept four in two bunks. Under each window, between each pair of bunks, built-in lockers provided seats. The common room opened on a sun terrace with space outside for camping and games. In the common room, with windows on three sides, was a cheerful painted frieze and a low open fire. Miss Prunella Potts painted the frieze of country scenes, youth hostel members and a satyr. She included the builder, the architect, Lobb, and herself in the design.

Lobb designed a second youth hostel at Ewhurst Green in brick and timber. He used local hand-made roof tiles and untreated Western Red Cedar. Intended to be all brick, like the hostel at Holmbury St Mary, he introduced wood to save money. Timber work was in British Columbia Pine, stained and polished with beeswax and turpentine. Potts painted a second frieze direct on to the wood with preliminary sizing only. Sir Philip Gibbs, gifted reporter and war correspondent, knighted for his reporting of the first world war, donated the site. He used his own money, with funds from the Imperial College of Science, for the building. A user described the youth hostel as "super modern" with showers, electric cookers and bright painted furniture. YHA sold it in 1983 and, demolished, it made way for a new house.

Lobb designed no further hostels, but his practice flourished. During the second world war he was architect to various ministries and built many schools for county authorities. He drew big public works in his later career. They included the Hunterston A nuclear power station in Ayrshire, the motorway service areas at Frankley on the M5 and Leicester Forest on the M1. He designed racecourse buildings at Newcastle, Newmarket, Goodwood and Doncaster.

The influence of art and artistic touches showed in other places. Friezes and murals appeared on the walls of other youth hostels. Eleanor Farjeon, a protégé of the poet Edward Thomas, wrote a poem for the 1933 *Youth*

Hostel Handbook. Novelist Sir Hugh Walpole contributed a foreword to that handbook. Woodcuts decorated the covers of handbooks, annual reports and magazines. Youth hostels were striving to be more than functional. They demonstrated an open colourful spirit, an air of freshness and health.

But no one expected purpose built and architect designed hostels would be so expensive. In view of the high and unexpected costs of Maeshafn, the Merseyside group decided they would not design and build again. They would wherever possible lease or rent. Holmbury St Mary cost an estimated £2,500. Bertha Gough visited there and noted in her diary "a very beautiful hostel, but rather overdone. So much money had been spent on it!"

The national executive was coming to the same conclusion. They told the Carnegie trust in 1932 they believed it was wiser to get or rent existing buildings. They would adapt them to their purpose, rather than erect new buildings which might be out of keeping with their surroundings.

After Maeshafn, Once Brewed, Holmbury St Mary, Ewhurst Green and another at Chelwood Gate, near Haywards Heath in Surrey, architects designed youth hostels less frequently. John Dower, Sir Charles Trevelyan's son-in-law, designed youth hostels at Bellingham, Northumberland; at Eskdale, Cumbria; at Malham, West Yorkshire; and at Langdon Beck, County Durham. His designs are tidy and neat. Committees keeping an eye on costs may have constrained him. The Lakeland regional group built a last architect-designed youth hostel in Borrowdale in the Lake District. The hostel in red cedar opened in 1939. After that none were built until the 1950s.

They ditched the lessons learned by Schirrmann in Germany. Youth hostels in Britain retreated from the purpose built and the big. Youth hostels were small, in adapted buildings, rarely "constructed to accommodate youth, the rising generation" and very often not "simple and functional, light, easily ventilated, yet retaining the warmth, pleasant to live in, beautiful…"

Other factors as well as cost drove change. Property was abundantly available, especially in rural areas where an agricultural depression was driving workers off the land. They left cottages empty, for sale or rent, for demolition or to fall into ruin. Authorities allowed the building of new houses with little restriction. Low interest rates made building new homes in sprawling suburbs affordable and attractive. The boom in new house building left older homes ignored and empty. Farmers, desperate for income, threw derelict cottages, outbuildings and barns to those searching for youth hostel sites. Of the approximately 80 youth hostels opened in 1931, a quarter were in farms or farm buildings.

Agricultural depression, inflation, taxation and the rising cost of servants threatened old country houses. The first world war killed many owners and their heirs. Attitudes to wealth and property changed. Inheritance tax rose to 50%. The crash of 1929 and the Labour government of 1929-31 struck a further blow. Cash strapped families sold large estates and country houses. Ornaments, panelling and fire places crossed the Atlantic and adorned homes in a country that welcomed the old. Clough Williams-Ellis wrote that there were more country houses in England than rich men to inhabit them.

YHA's regional, grass roots structure also pushed youth hostels from the purpose built and designed. Enthusiasts, out walking or cycling, found or stumbled upon empty property, some of it derelict, some of it being demolished. They had flexibility to snap up properties or make deals. A youth hostel could open almost overnight, on the basis of a handshake with a willing owner. The number of youth hostels grew as a consequence of the grassroots structure.

John Cadbury, a Quaker and one of the family of chocolate manufacturers, found the youth hostel at Bridges in Shropshire while out walking with Barclay Baron. Cadbury also found Wilderhope Manor while walking on the Long Mynd. A local farmer was using the Elizabethan manor with its enormous hall and moulded ceilings as a farm store and stable. Cadbury, a member of the Birmingham regional group, bought the manor and its estate. He passed it to the National Trust with the manor house to be a youth hostel.

Organisations with a social conscience also opened youth hostels. Toc H opened the first youth hostel in London, in a house used by Tubby Clayton, and in Canterbury. Youth hostels came into being through the Quakers in Street and at St Athan in Wales. The Rowntree family of York, like the Cadburys in Birmingham, supported youth hostels including one at Cloughton, near Scarborough in Yorkshire. Others contributed to hostels. Lord Trent, a local benefactor, paid for the beds when the youth hostel at Eastwell Lodge on the Leicestershire Wolds, close to the Vale of Belvoir, opened.

Old buildings offered immediate advantage. They were an established part of the landscape. A new, purpose built hostel had to be carefully placed in the landscape and might offend traditionalists. Buying, converting and saving an old building offered an easier option.

Sir Robert MacDougall, who made his fortune milling flour, created the opportunity for Ilam Hall in Derbyshire to become a youth hostel. He bought the hall and its estate and presented it to the National Trust in 1934. The trust took the estate as part of its plans to protect the Dove Valley. The hall in its Victorian Gothic Revival style must have been seen as being of little value to both the trust and YHA. YHA took it on lease from the trust and demolished most the building to fund conversion of the rest to a youth hostel.

Trevelyan assured listeners to his radio broadcast in January 1931 that where it was "necessary to alter an old building, such alterations will only be carried out under the expert guidance of the Council for the Preservation of Rural England." Catchpool echoed the advice to new regional groups. "Any structural alterations or additions to old buildings which may be found desirable, should only be undertaken after consultation with the Council for the Preservation of Rural England."

Increasing demand for new youth hostels, with more and more members joining, and more and more staying in youth hostels, focused early enthusiasts on finding youth hostels quickly. By 1934 membership had risen to 37,285 and 221,271 overnight stays were recorded. They used whatever buildings came their way. They had no time for lengthy construction. Opportunism ruled the way. The military abandoned the fort at Cawsand Battery on the Rame Peninsular and another at Laira, near Plymouth, in a five sided Palmerston fort. Youth hostels ran at both briefly in 1931.

Catchpool sensibly advised regional groups "until such time as experience has indicated the probable demand for accommodation" temporary arrangements would be prudent. "It is often possible to make use of barns, old windmills, disused railway stations and schools, warehouses and other similar buildings. On many routes it will be possible to discover existing Guest Houses where the host or hostess may be found willing to offer accommodation to members of the YHA at 1/- a night on the understanding that their Guest House will receive the advantage of the wide publicity of the YHA Handbook. Such an arrangement offers a very important saving in expenditure and in many cases will solve the difficulty of supervision. The use of these Guest Houses is not intended as a permanent arrangement, but as being a valuable temporary expedient whilst experience is being gained."

In its first decade YHA took on less than 70 youth hostels in purchases, leases and gifts. At the same time 200 youth hostels, which YHA did not own, opened and closed. Most of these came to be called adopted hostels. Owners ran them in the kind of arrangement Catchpool recommended for guest houses. The London region listed 36 youth hostels in 1935 as it struggled to find a way forward. 30 of those were adopted hostels. The approach was cheap. Regions with very little money relied on adopted youth hostels for their needs. But owners often struggled to make the arrangements pay. Many closed as easily as they had opened. The London regional group culled their adopted hostels around 1935. The group closed them because the owners relied on selling meals for their profits and discouraged or would not provide rudimentary members' cooking spaces.

Using any available property, from shepherd's huts to a Duke's mansion, YHA grew. The hunger of people to explore their hinterland, to travel and experience new places and to meet with others was growing at a phenomenal pace. By 1936 a membership of 59,000 had 262 youth hostels available to them.

Richard Schirrmann had learned over time to build youth hostels as a unique architecture. Even if architects and builders had been available, the early regional groups in England and Wales did not have the funds. Neither did they have the support of local authorities as Schirrmann did in the 1920s in Germany.

Practicality pushed them toward whatever property they could find. They abandoned professionals like architects and builders. They encouraged individual owners to create their own youth hostels and shared the limited profits from running youth hostels with them. Amateurs and volunteers embedded themselves in the ethos of youth hostels.

Opportunism and the ability to create youth hostels as cheaply as possible became fundamental ways of working. Youth hostels shifted from the simple to the spartan. An ethos that welcomed discomfort established itself along with voluntarism and amateurism. If no other bed was available, they could make a bed from a cartwheel and wire. If no building was available, they could create one using bell tents. Armed with enthusiasm and optimism they could achieve anything. There was no time to waste. Young people were in a hurry to experience the wider world.

Notes and References

I made wide use of John Martin's invaluable historical listing of youth hostels in writing this chapter. Christopher Cross guided me to the RIBA library and much of the background on Lobb. In 2015 the manager at Ilam Hall discovered copies of documents that overturned my previous understanding of the discovery of Ilam Hall and its subsequent demolition. More work will need to be done to verify these documents. They show YHA, with agreement from the National Trust and Sir Robert MacDougall, instructing the builder who demolished the building and using the proceeds from demolition to pay for converting the remaining building to a youth hostel.

"Two classrooms will suffice…" Heath, *Richard Schirrmann, A Biographical Sketch*, p17
"We don't want to build any gloomy medieval fortress…" Ibid p33
"great service to all…" Report of the first meeting of the council of the British Youth Hostels Association, Thursday 10 April 1930
"to foster…" ibid
"much frequented by visitors…" *YHA Annual Report 1932*
"super modern" the quote comes from an anonymous account of a hostel stay in April 1940
"necessary to alter…" *Address by Prof GM Trevelyan, 21 January 1931*, p8
"Any structural alterations…" Catchpool, *How to Form a Regional Council*
"it will probably be necessary…" Ibid

PART 2

THE TRUE SPIRIT

-10-

Black Sail

Black Sail is a legend among youth hostels. The magic of coming over a pass in the hills and seeing below a small hut, where you will spend the night, is not forgotten.

I heard about Black Sail before I worked in the Lake District. I had seen photos and posters, heard talk and read descriptions but nothing prepared me for the remoteness of Black Sail. At the head of a scoop of valley, staring at the great hills around it, the hut seemed less built, more washed up and anchored like a tiny boat. I had not expected anywhere could be this remote and still be in England.

To reach Black Sail I walked, with two friends, over the hills from Eskdale. Martin, a Northern Soul veteran of Wigan all-nighters, lead us from Eskdale. We stopped for a beer at Wasdale Head and then climbed over the pass from which the hostel takes its name. No one quite explains the name. It's Norse and has nothing to do with Vikings or their boats.

Black Sail is a legend because of its location and because everyone shares the same experience getting there. Everyone walks to get there. It is as simple as that. No bus, no car and a track, not a road, goes there. We walked, putting one foot in front of another. We could have walked up the valley from Gillerthwaite. We could have climbed over Scarth Gap, from Buttermere. We could have come from the east through the highest hills in England. But, from wherever you came, you walked, unless you were especially adventurous and cycled, or unless you were a cheat and drove up the ruinous track. There's no other way to get there.

Black Sail was also a legend because of its simplicity. Its only facilities were two rooms, one for men and one for women, a shared common room, a low kitchen built at the back and two toilets, for eighteen or more people. Coal and wood kept the place warm and hurricane lamps lit it. The warden carried everything and anything needed on his back up the track. Willing farmers or neighbours helped deliver coal at the start or end of a season.

It was little more than the hut at Walden Pond in Massachusetts where the writer and philosopher Thoreau lived for a year, keeping the diary that became an inspiration because of its stand against unnecessary luxury. Black Sail was similarly pared back, without luxury. It opened on Good Friday, 1933. No one knows much about its origins. It was a simple shepherd's hut. The Lakeland regional group leased it from the Forestry Commission and GM Trevelyan paid for its conversion. Low roofed with three rooms when it opened, people washed in the stream. In 1954 an international working group dug out the hillside behind the hostel for an extension and better facilities. The stone built extensions, at the side and back, housed two outside toilets, a kitchen for guests and one for the warden along with her or his bedroom.

Black Sail is a legend because of the friendliness it creates amongst those staying the night. On my first visit, in that bowl of hills with mist shutting down on the hills, the cramped interior of the hut shocked me. Coming in, stooping to get through the low doorway, people greeted us. It was hard to tell who was the warden and who was the guest.

The hostel was fully booked and every bed taken. Brian, the warden, appeared amongst the crush. Too tall for the low ceiling of the hut, in his soft wry voice he told us where we could leave our bags. Two of us could sleep on the floor in the dormitory. One could sleep in the common room where the first warden had bedded down for the night beside the stove.

Everyone made us welcome with tea, biscuits, chocolate and

questions. I thought we had arrived in the midst of a gathering of friends. It was only later I realised that it was just a Black Sail gathering, a regular night at the hostel. At Black Sail you couldn't escape your fellow guests. You could ignore them or try being rude to them but close proximity brought strangers together. There was always something to talk about. A question prompted a conversation. Which way you came to get there or whether you had been before?

Everyone ate at the two tables. They praised Brian's food. It was plain, from tins and packets but earned praise as if it were from the kitchens of a Michelin starred restaurant. Tired, cold from walking, from being outdoors, the Michelin star wasn't necessary. Simple food tasted best. Afterwards when everyone had lent a hand in clearing tables and washing up, we played cards, read or talked about hills, mountains and other countries. They were a well travelled lot and Brian the most well travelled. He was a South African. He thought his family originated from a nearby valley. He had climbed in the Alps, in the Himalayas and in North America and years later, he died on one of his many adventures, in Santiago in Chile.

People drifted to their beds in the dormitories, having to go outdoors to reach them and the toilets. There was no escaping the weather at Black Sail. Disconnected from the modern world, you were always reminded about the weather. You saw the stars if the night was clear and understood what darkness meant if it wasn't. Popping out to the toilet in the night, kept anyone informed of what the world was doing.

When everyone was gone to the dormitories, I bedded down by the stove on a low bench seat. A board kept my feet from the heat and I woke in the morning when Brian produced a big tea pot and asked for help laying tables for breakfast. Outside it was raining. People ate breakfast with grim concentration, amending plans, considering what, more than a soaking, they could achieve on such a wet day. No one delayed. We had a bus in the next valley to catch, to get us back in time for work that evening. We abandoned our plans and trudged up the beck and over to Honister.

When we were gone, I wouldn't forget. Something would draw me back. The quality of air, light on a crystal clear morning or the way the overwhelming hills soaked up sound, drew me back. We camped in winter, when the hostel was shut, once, almost ending in disaster when snow came down. We took our daughter there, carried over the hills on my back. Wood smoke and coal fires, the resinous tang of pine woods reminds me of Black Sail. A glimpse of hills through a gap in the cloud, companionship or simplicity, as little as that takes me back.

-11-

Simplicity

Simplicity was fundamental to youth hostels. The YHA constitution enshrined simple accommodation. It was an ideology that underlay fellowship and democracy. It gave youth hostels values and set them apart from hotels and inns. In their simplicity, youth hostels encouraged people to mix together and to rediscover social and personal as well as physical landscapes. Simplicity encouraged personal discovery.

At the first meetings in 1930 the founders argued. They argued about the name, whether they should be an organisation of wayfarers hostels, country hostels or youth hostels. They disagreed over favouring young people. They refused to give priority to those who walked, cycled, or otherwise travelled under their own steam. But they did not debate their chosen simple style. Youth hostels aimed to provide hostels and other simple accommodation for everyone and especially young people.

The founders, not arguing about the term, never defined it. The word has many layers of meaning. From the *Oxford English Dictionary*, meanings include having or being composed of only one thing; not involved or complicated; not elaborate, elegant, or luxurious; humble or lowly in condition or rank; ordinary or common.

The architects who designed youth hostels meant to achieve a designed and considered version of simplicity. An architectural journal described Howard Lobb's plan for the youth hostel at Hombury St Mary as simple. Clough William-Ellis' youth hostel at Maeshafn was a simple wooden structure. Their buildings were not involved or complicated. John Dower's youth hostel at Malham echoed the cottages and homes of the surrounding Yorkshire village. But when youth hostels were just beginning in Britain no one regarded hostels as ordinary or common. They were new and radical.

Simplicity can have a spiritual dimension, one that may have arrived from the Quakers. Many prominent people at the start of youth hostels were Quakers, including Jack Catchpool, the first honorary secretary. YHA vice president, TA Leonard, became one. The Friends lent buildings and property as some early youth hostels including Kirkby Stephen in Cumbria, Street in Somerset and Jordans in Buckinghamshire.

Simplicity is important to the Friends. The testimony to simplicity is integral to their faith. They believe that spiritual responsiveness demands that they be as free as possible from dependence on material security. They resist defining themselves through material possessions and their acquisition. Their simplicity avoids luxury, is unassuming and unpretentious.

TA Leonard expressed this dimension in his aims for starting the CHA and HF. "With a civilisation in which materialistic conceptions of life and conduct are rapidly becoming dominant... we are making an honest attempt towards the better use of people's holidays. We offer them the healthful ways of an out-or-door life among the hills, instead of the rowdy pleasures of popular holiday resorts. We provide a simple, homely life in our guest-houses, and whilst discouraging extravagance in both food and dress, help people to find joy..."

Leonard set up the HF because CHA centres were attracting dressy, more middle class people, used to comfort and service, not at all the kind of guest he wanted. His book *Adventures in Holiday Making* is nostalgic. He reminisced about early CHA centres, amongst them the centre at Keld, which closed soon after it opened. That decision still rankled.

His regret was stark. "Keld lived but three short seasons. It was "too simple," some said, "not quite proper" according to others, and certainly .. was rough on those who cooked our dinners. So the domestic committee decreed that it should be closed, and though many of us have since wandered disconsolately over the old haunts the way has never opened for a return." Leonard turned his desire and hopes for simplicity towards youth hostels.

Simple accommodation gave an advantage to youth hostels. Simplicity kept down costs and brought youth hostels within reach of less wealthy people. Simplicity created fellowship in youth hostels, an atmosphere that was the opposite of snobbery and an antidote to glaring class divisions. "There were no privileges, boys from richer and poorer homes cleaned and cooked and slept side by side." Simple youth hostels encouraged equality, sharing and a hearty robust democracy. With one washroom for boys and one for girls there was little privacy and no privilege.

Everyone mucked in. Everyone was treated just the same. No one chose their rooms and those were allocated on arrival. They were all the same any way, bare with bare floorboards and crammed with bunks. Which bunk you slept in was about the only choice, unless you were last and all the bunks except one were taken.

Youth hostels served meals at the same price for everyone with no choice and no embellishment. One breakfast, one evening meal and one packed lunch with no choice. Everyone ate at communal tables. Everyone shared the same space, with no room for conspicuous consumption.

Simplicity begins to sound dull to a consumer's ear. Choice today is an article of faith, a fundamental of liberty in our free market democracy. But at a time of enormous difference and huge gaps between one class and another the lack of choice was freedom. Many people treasured exactly that sense of all being in it together.

Just as youth hostels were part of the discovery of parts of rural Britain and the landscape, they were part of a rediscovery of social landscapes through fellowship. In 1930s Britain chances to meet people from other parts of Britain and other social backgrounds were few. Gender, home, work and the city trapped most people. Simplicity brought people together. Through it they discovered people from different backgrounds, different places and different cultures. They shared with others of different social classes and of the opposite sex. Youth hostels broke barriers and drew people together.

Youth hostels were a radical departure. Everyone paid the same price, a shilling a night whatever your age. Though different regions and hostels offered different concessions for age a lower price for young people only arrived nationally in 1943. Everyone stayed in the same rooms, washed together without reference to age, class or wealth, separated only by sex.

Self service was fundamental to simplicity. Self service reinforced hearty equality and fellowship, a service not just to the self but to fellow guests and the association. It was an act of loyalty. With no servants in youth hostels, no boot boy and no one to clean up after you, serving fellow members was a sociable process and an education too. Boys and girls learned the rudiments of housekeeping, sweeping and tidying, peeling potatoes. Jack Catchpool thought many young people learned valuable lessons in domestic economy in youth hostels. Perhaps "Mother had done everything for them before..." Self service encouraged a personal exploration of independence, responsibility and self sufficiency particularly amongst young people on the verge of leaving home.

The brand new association demanded little of the first owners of youth hostels. Jack Catchpool wrote on 20 March 1931 to Thomas Thirkill, who proposed a youth hostel at Kirkby Malzeard, near Ripon in West Yorkshire. Catchpool outlined the conditions for opening his youth hostel. Thirkill would keep the one shilling a night each member paid for a night's stay. In return, they would advertise Thirkill's house in the handbook of hostels which would go to every member. Later owners offering youth hostel accommodation shared their income with YHA. Any one taking meals at the youth hostel would pay Thirkill at cost price. Catchpool said he would be glad if simple facilities could be made available for those who preferred to cook their own meals.

Having outlined these terms to Thirkill, Catchpool added they expected him to provide simple beds and blankets. Each member would bring his or her own sheet sleeping bag. When they failed to do so, they would have to hire from Thirkill. Youth hostels in Britain imported the idea of sheet sleeping bags from Germany. Made of two sheets sewn together with a pillow case, light and easy to carry, they kept down costs. They saved their users from the need to buy and carry a heavy camping bag. Catchpool could supply the sheet bags to Thirkill for a small charge.

Catchpool set no standards and indicated nothing about facilities beyond beds, blankets and sheet sleeping bags. Many homes were without indoor sanitation. In rural areas the most usual washing place might be a stream. Many households still used a tin bath in the living room and heated water on a fire. In those circumstances it's no surprise Catchpool expected no other facilities.

Self service, fellowship, one price and everyone sharing: youth hostels were not complicated. They were unadorned, sometimes out of necessity. Early hostels were often basic because funds were limited. Facilities, including beds, in the excitement and headlong rush to open youth hostels, were often inadequate. Sometimes youth hostels opened without them. Bertha Gough described sleeping on mattresses stuffed with straw which rustled all night and at another "slept on beds which had been made out of half-cartwheels with just wire nailed on, with the result that we kept falling in a ball to the middle. It was also in a loft with a current of air blowing straight through holes in the wall, which was decidedly draughty! Still, we were getting hardened to queer hostels and quite enjoyed it."

On the travels which led to his book, *The Road to Wigan Pier*, George Orwell spent two nights in youth hostels in 1936. One hostel was comfortable but he thought the hostel at Rudyard Lake was "a most peculiar place... A great draughty barrack of a house, built in sham-castle style - somebody's Folly - about 1860. All but three or four of the rooms quite empty. Miles of echoing stone passages, no lighting except candles and only smoky oilstoves to cook on. Terribly cold." In the morning, he got out of bed so cold he could not do up any buttons and had to go down and thaw his hands before he could dress.

Some early youth hostels in halls and mansions were grand. But towards the end of a spectrum of meanings, away from plain, simple became austere. In Germany people faced terrible hardships after the first world war. War reparations impoverished the country. The victors occupied their country and saddled them with debt. In those circumstances their youth hostels evolved a pared back style. The first German youth hostel guidebook, in August 1920, exhorted travellers to "Give up cheerfully everything which is not essential."

Britain echoed this austerity. Simple became spartan, a resistance to going cosy, to anything soft. Youth hostels began to base their simplicity on "absence of all kinds of upholstery, physical and mental." Spartan was good for the mind and body. Spartan kept body and soul hard. Exercise and walking toughened it. The physicality and athleticism of youth hostel members should not be underestimated. These were men and women who could walk 21 miles in a day to inspect two potential youth hostels in Wales, and think nothing of it. Others at the end of a hard day's walking in Snowdonia could invite a journalist to climb with them to the top of Tryfan in the dark.

GM Trevelyan settled on the term in the first issue of the *YHA Rucksack* magazine in the autumn of 1932. Youth hostels, he said, started on spartan lines. Trevelyan was an austere figure. He did not indulge himself or his family in the vulgar creature comforts of the middle classes. Life at Wallington Hall, his childhood home had been spartan and his own home at Hallington was hard. David Cannadine recounted, in his biography of Trevelyan, a visitor's description of food that was bad, lukewarm water, no wine and draughty rooms.

Trevelyan's appearance was unostentatious and his mother despaired of him and his dress. When she suggested he buy himself a new suit, he ordered one from his tailor exactly the same as his last. He was untidy, often unkempt. A colleague from the National Trust watched him remove his dentures for a cleaning during a meeting. A bed maker, in a Cambridge college, mistook him for a tramp.

For Trevelyan, youth hostels were not "abodes of luxury." He told *The Times* in 1933 their cheap and spartan fare "has drawn out the right type of young men and women who take their holidays strenuously and joyously, without slacking or rioting, hard walkers or active bicyclists." He epitomised a simplicity that dominated youth hostels, that hardened as a shell against softness. Resistance to softness became a creed for many youth hostel members. Simple became an aspiration for discomfort, became cold water, bare boards, iron beds and thin blankets.

Physical hardship was often seen as enhancing to life. The lack of comfort also created the feelings of fellowship, a feeling bred in young men in the first world war. In the armed services, Olive Coburn wrote, "men had also known a sense of companionship, born of dangers and discomforts shared; and at times they would miss this feeling. After such experiences, civilian life was bound sometimes to seem a little flat. If so, they could find in the YHA a fellowship intimately related to... the comradeship of the Services."

Herbert Gatliff, an early youth hostel fan, had experienced only a short time in the army but he was still, like Trevelyan, an enthusiastic supporter of spartan youth hostels. He invented the motto "we won't go cosy" for his walking group in Surrey, the Southern Pathfinders, in 1932. By it he meant resisting cosiness of the mind as well as of the body.

Gatliff was an assistant secretary at the Treasury. He was an individual in mind and outlook, with a wide ranging love of the outdoors, the countryside and walking. It was not uncommon to find a rucksack and primus stove in his office and a bicycle propped against the wall. Symonds, first chairman of the Merseyside Youth Hostels Group, taught Gatliff at Rugby and gave the boy his love of walking and the outdoors.

After Rugby Gatliff went to Balliol College, Oxford, and then took a commission in the Coldstream Guards in 1917. He relinquished the commission within six months for no clear reason. Ill health may have played a part. Working as a civil servant he settled for a conventional life, marrying in 1923 and living in a modern house in Chipstead in Surrey. But by 1931 he had tired of orthodox life. He joined the Southern Pathfinders walking group. Walking in the Surrey hills brought him to youth hostels where he and the others in the club found the spirit of friendliness that they so much valued.

Gatliff hoped that youth hostels would never "go cosy". "Let us keep always a certain simplicity and hardihood. For the YHA was made for those who, at any rate if they are to taste the full joys of the pilgrim and the country lover, cannot afford to go cosy. We must be sure that we do not become soft or exacting in our demands, else we shall make the hostels too expensive and close them to those for whom above all they are meant, those who have very little money and must think of every penny they spend. But we do not want to turn away those who have more money, so long as they are happy to abide by our simple standards. Rather we welcome them; for it is the privilege of YHA beyond almost any other institution, to bring together just as friends "all sorts and conditions of men" (and women). Bishop and blacksmith shall be equally welcome, provided that they are young in heart and will share the washing up."

Low cost, fellowship and the right kind of people made youth hostels. Those who could afford more than the one shilling a night, could "give what they save quietly to one or other of the many needs of the YHA itself or help save one or other of those beauties of the English countryside for which all true hostellers care." Gatliff followed his own advice. He gave generously and often to youth hostels and to other causes.

Under the influence of Trevelyan, Gatliff and many others, youth hostels adopted spartan as a creed. Gatliff's refusal of cosiness implied a dogged resistance to change. As consumerism grew, as fashions changed, as homes became more comfortable, the term dragged youth hostels into a conservatism far removed from their radical early days. Youth hostels, which had led the way in providing simple accommodation, began to forget who they were aiming to reach. Simplicity became an end in itself.

But that lay in the future. When youth hostels started, they satisfied a hunger for exploration. It is usual to think of this exploration as being entry into the countryside, but youth hostels encouraged an exploration of social landscapes. Through the simple approach of youth hostels people shared space, ate and washed together. Simple accommodation also brought together the sexes in an easy and radical unfamiliarity. Men and women, boys and girls were no longer chaperoned or kept apart. By bringing people together in their simplicity, youth hostels were forerunners and outliers for the post war period.

Simple was also fun. Spartan and the simple had a charm that was part of the adventure and exploration. Young men and women were exploring places dreamed about or read of in the popular books of Morton, Priestley and Trevelyan. For young women especially, youth hostels offered acceptable freedom. Parents allowed their daughters to visit youth hostels in pairs or small groups. They used buses. They walked and cycled. They escaped cities, neighbourhoods and homes.

Youth hostels offered an opportunity for self exploration too, for learning responsibility, independence and self sufficiency. In youth hostels young women discovered their own capabilities and their own self sufficiency. Society denied the fair and gentle sex discomfort and hardship so any amount of either became an adventure. A taste of both for young women and girls signalled independence and freedom.

Two young women, travelling round Yorkshire on their bikes, stayed at the youth hostel in Kirkby Malzeard in July 1949. The rudimentary facilities of Thomas Thirkill's youth hostel were beginning to fail. It closed in 1953. But Margaret and Joan accepted its facilities and failings in good humour. Margaret wrote to her parents in Sheffield. She and Joan were having fun and they were learning along the way. They had learned that Margaret's father had put the brake blocks on her bike the wrong way round. Margaret had fixed that herself. A friendly mechanic in a garage helped when she broke her screwdriver. They learned how not to light a fire with damp wood, how to use Calor gas and how to use an electricity meter. Margaret proudly listed the food she cooked.

People were friendly and helpful. A man and a woman at the Co-op in Masham were cyclists and interested in their travels. "The lady let the bacon slicer 'slip' and we got 4 good rashers, 4 eggs and some Cheshire cheese." They had been to Ripon, Harrogate, Ilkley and Kettlewell before stopping at Thomas Thirkell's youth hostel.

The hostel was "primitive except for an electric fire in our dorm which is small so we are quite cosy. There is a youth and girl here as well, they are trying to get the stove in the Dining Room to go and as they have found an envelope dated 1948 inside they are having to clear out quite a lot of rubbish before lighting it. Today has been fine and fairly warm but there has been a mist all day so we haven't seen much. We are warm at night as there are plenty of extra blankets, we should be very warm tonight as this dorm is getting nicely aired.

"I forgot to say what we are doing with the 4 eggs. One went in the custard with 1/2 pt of milk tonight, 2 have been hard boiled for tomorrow lunch and we are sharing the 4th between us with the bacon for tomorrows breakfast.

"There is a pipe above Joan's bunk which intrigues us, whether it is to let air out and water in we don't know. We have decided not to make some tea as it is much too warm in here and much too cold to go outside to the lean-to shed which is the cookhouse but doesn't lean to on anything except the air. There are numerous pans and frying pans, kettles and we cook by calor gas, very interesting... we have just gone into fits of laughter over the pipe and the cook house and the whole hostel in general.

"The electric fire went out a few minutes ago so I have had to go and investigate the meter, we have to turn a small handle back, insert a penny and turn the handle round again and lo! on comes the fire."

Notes and References

I have relied on Len Clark's biography for much of the background on Gatliff, one of the most intriguing figures behind youth hostels. Like Trevelyan he was closely involved with the National Trust. He set up a trust to run small, simple hostels in the Hebrides, one of those stories I could not shoe-horn into this account of youth hostels. Thanks to Len for permission to quote from the biography he wrote of Gatliff. John Martin pointed me towards Catchpool's letter to Thomas Thirkill and Margaret Southwell's letter card home. I came across Orwell's youth hostel adventures in his *Collected Essays, Journalism and Letters Vo1*. My edition is old, published by Penguin in 1962 and the quote is reproduced by permission of Penguin Books Ltd.

"With a civilisation…" Leonard, *Adventures in Holiday Making*, p36

"There were no privileges…" Catchpool, *Candles in the Darkness*, p146

"Mother had done everything..." Ibid, p146

"slept on beds…" Gough, *A Diary of Seven Years with the YHA*, 19-20 January 1935

"a most peculiar place…" Orwell, George, *The Road to Wigan Pier Diary*, p196

"Give up cheerfully everything which is not essential." Grassl, Heath, *The Magic Triangle*, p40

"has drawn out the right type…" *The Times*, Saturday 21 January 1933

"men had also known…" Coburn, *Youth Hostel Story*, p101

"Let us keep always…" Clark, *An Eccentric Englishman*, p15

"give what they save…" Ibid, p15

"The lady let the bacon slicer…" Margaret Southwell, letter card

-12-

Steps Bridge

I dreamed of running 'my own' youth hostel. Visits to Black Sail reminded me of remote and lonely places where I had lived and wanted to live again. When a couple of youth hostel jobs in the south-west of England came vacant and the region was looking for new wardens, I applied immediately. A gang of us, prospective wardens in our mid 20s, toured the empty properties. We picked them over and smelled the damp, before subjecting ourselves to interviews with a small, friendly and sympathetic committee in Bristol.

They offered me the job at Steps Bridge in Devon. I was already in love with the place. Halfway up a hill, in a woodland clearing, the clump of wooden huts looked over tree tops toward far-away Exeter. The River Teign cruised down from Dartmoor, smooth as glass. At the foot of the hill it snagged for a moment on an untidy weir, plunged into a pool and then shouldered its way under the old stone bridge that gave the place its name. From the youth hostel verandah, in the quiet and gaps in the wind, the constant rush of water was loud.

In the 1920s huts of every description littered that corner of woodland against the river. They included a tea house serving traffic coming up the main road to Dartmoor. Only the hostel and a few ruins remained from that craze for living in the countryside before the second world war.

People living near the hostel told me a local doctor had bought an old army hospital hut and transported it into the woods. Settling it on brick piers and a wooden platform high above the road he took his family there each summer. They camped amongst the trees, having a holiday. The doctor travelled down the hill to visit patients when necessary. His summer house became a youth hostel in 1935, complete with a hand pump for water. The buildings survived requisition and after the war additions and extensions were made; another low hut, two lean to buildings, an extension and an outside toilet. A ram pump replaced the hand pump until mains water arrived.

YHA classed the hostel as 'simple,' the most elemental type of youth hostel. It had three toilets for 24 people, and two misnamed 'washrooms,' for men and women; two plain rooms with bare concrete floors, no baths and no showers. Everyone carried hot water from a tap in the kitchen and washed in plastic basins.

People from round the world visited. Travelling on their own or with a friend or two, they climbed the path to the youth hostel perched on the side of the hill. They loved being 'away from it all' and 'out of the rat race.' They hitchhiked, caught trains or buses, walked, cycled or drove miles to be there.

They loved being so close to nature that, from bed in the morning, they could watch squirrels in the trees and hear bird song. They loved the friendliness of a place so small that, by the end of a night, everyone who stayed knew everyone else. They exchanged stories and made sorties down to the pub. They handed each other advice about places and destinations and made plans made to meet up again at other youth hostels. They moved on to the next youth hostel, up on the moor, or down to Cornwall. Some had stopped on their way to Edinburgh, York or London using their youth hostel handbook as a guide to the world.

They loved the youth hostel's simplicity, its three bedrooms with bunk beds where they slept. Inside the main house, in a common room with three tables, they ate the meals I cooked. If they preferred, they warmed baked-beans, burned toast, grilled bacon and fried eggs to black lace in a self catering kitchen. Each morning, everyone folded blankets, swept floors, cleaned windows and scrubbed out the kitchen before they left.

Goodbyes were sometimes long affairs. It was one of those places that RS Thomas, the Welsh poet, said we find and then spend the rest of our lives looking for. On quiet evenings, guests sat on the long veranda that fronted the building. They leaned back in chairs and studied the distant hills, listening to the river, talking among themselves. Some went into the woods or up the river to the moors. In the woods they found badgers and deer.

I exaggerate. Not everyone loved it. For some the hostel was not so cosy. On Wednesday nights, the youth hostel in Exeter closed so the wardens there could have a night off. With no other youth hostel nearby, people who would rather have stayed in the bigger city hostel struggled up the hill to my hostel perched in the woods. They could hardly believe that anywhere without hot water in a bathroom, let alone without showers, could exist. Outside toilets were beyond belief.

In summer the woods came alive with ants. They streamed through the hostel in long lines. They bit ferociously. At times grass snakes and slow worms found their way inside too. They horrified people who had never seen a snake and knew no difference between the harmless and the deadly. Confident none were poisonous, I swept the intruders out the door with affected nonchalance. In winter, when the hostel closed, deer wandered down through the woods, their footsteps stirring frosty mornings. I could watch them from my bedroom window.

After two seasons at Steps Bridge, when Caroline I had met and we had married, realising the cost of running the place, I was no longer so sure about its idyllic nature. I worried that those who loved its simplicity were a minority. I fretted the hostel could not afford its upkeep with less than 2,000 overnight stays a year. It seemed impossible that it could stand the cost of installing showers and more hot water. The hostel was beginning to slide on its platform. The pillars on which it was built were cracking. I checked them constantly, watching nervously how they leaned.

The hostel needed money and lots of it to keep itself balancing there. At times I worked frantically. I plotted and planned improvements. A working party of volunteers and youth hostel enthusiasts from Exeter beat back woodland that had crept too close to the buildings. They cut down everything that stood nearby including my washing line. We painted bedrooms. Caroline made new curtains to hang at the windows. All that scope for improvement, for running things better, made the work enjoyable. Making somewhere look better brought a sense of achievement. Thorough cleaning and a coat of paint transformed the building.

I could have wondered how it all got like that but I was impatient. I had no time for thinking about the past or understanding what made youth hostels like they were. I wanted to see it all changed. I wanted people to feel more comfortable, more welcome, less constrained by rules. I wanted youth hostels of which we could all be proud.

-13-

Dreams of peace

On a sunny Monday, when the previous day's temperature had hit 29C in London, Lord Allen of Hurtwood officially opened the youth hostel at Holmbury St Mary in Surrey. He set out a role for the new youth hostel movement, to extend international understanding, to take reconciliation from nation to nation. Youth hostels and young people between them would change the world.

Peace and international understanding were abiding causes for Lord Allen and would become so for youth hostels. It was a dream that helped youth hostels shape the future of travel and tourism for young people, especially in the period before and after the second world war.

Youth hostels, at the beginning, were happy to align themselves with radical causes and anti-war beliefs, like those Lord Allen espoused at the opening on July 15, 1935. Lord Allen, with his distinctive looks and auburn hair, was a hero among socialists for his resistance to conscription during the war. He was also a local man and youth hostels were knitted into local communities. He lived at nearby Abinger Common with his wife and family, sharing his wife's enthusiasm for experimental education and her concern for the welfare of children.

Born Clifford Allen, he had been involved with the socialist newspaper, the *Daily Citizen*, before the first world war, forming close connections in the Labour movement. He was anti-war and a determined pacifist. He would have been excused military service, because of poor health, but instead he chose to resist on the grounds of his pacifist work and was then imprisoned for refusing conscription into any non-combatant role in the armed services. After three terms in prison, when his already poor health deteriorated, he was finally released.

Others involved in youth hostels at the beginning had been, like him, opposed to the war. Sir Charles Trevelyan resigned from Asquith's Government in August 1914 because he believed that the war with Germany was not in Britain's interest. TA Leonard was a pacifist who became a Quaker just after the outbreak of war. He was, like Lord Allen, an active supporter of the Independent Labour Party. George Lansbury, another pacifist and socialist, moved the beginning of youth hostels in Scotland.

Jack Catchpool and his brother Corder were also against war. Their pacifist ideals kept them from the fighting but in 1914 they joined the Friends Ambulance Unit on the western front near Dunkirk. They could not fight but they could share the suffering of others while not contributing to the war. Two years later, conscription forced all young men into the war. The two brothers could have taken non-combatant roles as conscientious objectors. But they and many others believed that by working in forestry or in ambulances even as non-combatants they would be part of the war machine. Whatever they did would contribute to war.

They held to their pacifist principles. Called up, they returned to England intending to refuse military service of any kind. Jack faced a tribunal where he made his stand public. Early tribunals were lenient. Jack's, overseen by someone who knew the Catchpool family, exempted him from military service. He was more fortunate than his brother. By the time Corder faced his tribunal, several months later, attitudes had hardened against pacifists. His tribunal exempted him for nothing. The tribunal deemed Corder a deserter. He and others who refused military service were liable to jail and even execution by firing squad. Corder was arrested in January 1917 and spent the next two and a quarter years in prison.

Those involved in youth hostels were not always pacifists. Many served in the military or took non-combatant roles. Barclay Baron, turned down on the grounds of his health, joined the YMCA's work in France. GM Trevelyan, also turned down on the grounds of health, commanded a Red Cross brigade. Quakers like Geoffrey Young and Philip Neville served with the Friends Ambulance Unit under his command in Italy.

Richard Schirrmann fought in the trenches with the German army. During Christmas 1915, in the Vosges in France, he saw German and French troops mingling through disused trenches. They exchanged wine, cognac, French bread and cigarettes for Westphalian black bread, biscuits and ham. That experience inspired him. He dreamed of a new role for youth hostels. If "thoughtful young people of all countries could be provided with suitable meeting places where they could get to know each other" peace and friendliness could be encouraged. "That could and must be the role of our youth hostels, not only in Germany, but throughout the world, building a bridge of peace from nation to nation."

Schirrmann had begun youth hostels in Germany in 1909 but after the war his idea crossed borders. Young people and students aged 19-24 with no adults started youth hostels started in Switzerland in 1924. School children's contributions financed the first hostels in Poland in 1926. Three youth hostels opened in Holland without any organisation. A Dutch association began as a foundation in 1928, without the trappings of democracy or a federation that were so much part of the set up in Germany. Norway, Denmark and France followed in 1930. British youth hostels split into separate associations for Scotland and England and Wales in 1931 and Ireland began its own youth hostels in 1931 including Northern Ireland as an autonomous branch. Belgium also began youth hostels in Flanders in 1931.

Youth hostel regulations developed in different countries. They had various styles of membership card. They recognised different age limits, different aims and objects. They used varying standards of equipment. None of that was a problem until the members of each visited another country and wanted to stay in youth hostels there. They wanted their membership cards recognised. They expected similar regulations and standards and found none.

The benefits of establishing formal links and working together were plain. In December 1931, the secretaries of the Dutch, English and

Scottish associations met Schirrmann and Münker from the German association in Hildenbach, near Wunsiedel in north eastern Bavaria, close to the Czech border. They talked about convening a conference of youth hostel organisers, like themselves. A meeting might create better and more formal links.

They delegated Dr HLFJ Deelen, the Dutch Secretary, to continue working with neighbouring countries. Deelen, a stiff formal man with a penchant for fashionable dress and plus fours, visited the Flemish, Danish and Norwegian associations. They welcomed his proposals. If he organised a conference they would attend. In August 1932 Deelen invited them all to Amsterdam.

The Dutch offered hospitality for the meeting and arranged for the visitors to see their youth hostels. Jack Catchpool went with Mary Lander from the office in Welwyn Garden City. Terry Trench, from *An Óige*, attended despite the misgivings of colleagues back in Ireland. Scotland was missing. Representatives from Switzerland, Czechoslovakia, Poland, Norway, Denmark, France, and Belgium were there along with the Dutch organisers. Schirrmann and Wilhelm Münker represented Germany.

They met in October. They held their meetings in German. Schirrmann presided and Trench recalled him coming up with the phrase *solvitur ambulando*, it is solved in walking. Trench recalled the phrase "would have made an excellent motto for the international organisation, but it was never taken up."

Deelen stressed the importance of education and Münker emphasised young people. He was clear that youth hostels must cater for and give priority to young people. Young people should pay less. On October 20th, 1932, they created the *Internationale Arbeitsgemeinschaft für Jugendherbergen* (IAJH). Poland, hosting a later meeting, translated the title as the International Union of the Youth Hostels Associations. When the federation created an international guest membership in 1935 it became the International Federation of Youth Hostels.

Their meetings were good natured and optimistic. They elected Schirrmann as their president and chairman with Deelen as secretary. They agreed principles and laid foundations that would see a boom in youth travel in future years.

Youth hostels would be primarily for young people, to help young people travel freely. Youth hostels had to be open to all the young people of a country. There could be no discrimination. Young people would pay lower fees, for membership and for accommodation. Youth hostels would give them priority over other guests when they allocated beds. They would accommodate boys and girls in separate dormitories, one to a bed, in simple and homely accommodation. Müncker insisted that nothing was too good for young people. They were not inferior. They deserved nothing less than the best.

Membership cards would have a uniform style and size but they couldn't agree to recognise each others membership cards. Germany with 2,000 youth hostels, many more than any of the others, would not agree reciprocal memberships until they achieved a more equal balance of hostels across Europe. They feared members from beyond Germany might swamp their hostels.

They agreed they would only recognise one youth hostel association from any one country. Exceptions were made for Belgium, with its two different language groups, and for Czechoslovakia, with its German minority.

In true international style, none of the conference's conclusions bound anyone to anything. For Catchpool that was fortunate. His association had already rejected and would never give priority in booking or the allocation of beds to young people.

They agreed to meet the next year in Germany. By then the Nazis had taken power in Germany. They had dissolved the youth hostel organisation in Germany that treated all boys and girls equally without discrimination. The Nazis incorporated youth hostels into their own youth movement, the Hitler Youth. Girls had their own movement, *Bund Deutscher Mädel* (League of German Girls). Münker resigned. Schirrmann, impressed with the idealism of the new movement, agreed to stay on as honorary president, a decision he would later bitterly repent and regret. Johannes Rodatz, a young Nazi who knew nothing of youth hostels, took over.

Nazi officials in party uniform attended the conference in Bad Godesberg. Hitler Youth, also in uniform, made a guard of honour. In contrast with the Scouts, the Guides and the Boys Brigade, youth hostels had always been non-militaristic. Members had no uniforms. They dressed informally, often in shorts, and respected no hierarchy. There was no military drill and no athletics except walking and cycling. The appearance of Hitler Youth and uniforms at the international conference was a shock, if not an insult, against youth hostel traditions.

The conference drew up a constitution and agreed contributions to a secretariat in Amsterdam. But those there refused to commit to a formal federation. Against the principle of recognising no more than one association from each country, German youth organisations in Latvia, Rumania, and Denmark applied to join the federation.

Two teachers from America, touring Europe with a group of Scouts, turned up at the meeting. Isabel and Monroe Smith had met Richard Schirrmann and after the conference, returning home, they started youth hostels in the USA in March 1934. Youth hostels began in Canada around the same time, when two young teachers opened a youth hostel in a tent. In July 1934 the Smiths were back in Europe with the first of their members, travelling through Germany, Austria, Czechoslovakia, Holland and Switzerland. Returning home, they opened their first youth hostel in December 1934 at Northfield, Massachusetts, in a chateau which was as close as they could find to the youth hostel at Altena in Germany.

The Smiths missed the third international conference, held in October 1934 in England. The conference aimed to pool ideas and to achieve greater freedom of travel as the threat of a second world war grew ever greater. Despite events in Germany Richard Schirrmann attended. Lord Snell, chair of London County Council, welcomed delegates from Belgium, Czechoslovakia, Danzig, France, Germany, Holland, the Irish Free State, Luxembourg, Northern Ireland, Poland, Scotland and Switzerland. They met in rooms in London's grand County Hall at Westminster Bridge.

The Times of London reported the meeting and the BBC broadcast Lord Snell's speech. Richard Schirrmann, GM Trevelyan and Barclay Baron also spoke before delegates went off to tea at the prime minister's home in Downing Street. Ramsay Macdonald, prime minister at the time, was in parliament. They tried to decipher scribblings left on blotting paper in the cabinet room and took tea with Macdonald's daughter, Ishbel. Her mother had died more than 20 years before and she had taken over many of the duties of a prime minister's wife.

From Euston they travelled north by train to the little village of Cromford in Derbyshire. Willersley Castle, a Methodist hotel and conference centre, where they would meet for the next three days, was a short walk from the village's station. With an agenda 60 pages long, their work included admitting Danzig, Luxembourg and Rumania to membership of the federation. After two long sessions on Thursday, they set aside Friday for visiting youth hostels.

They went by bus to youth hostels at Chester and Maeshafn. They stopped at the youth hostel in Llangollen for lunch before continuing to Shrewsbury for tea. During the long journey, in mist and rain, they amused themselves by singing. A concert of folk music and a film about youth hostels in England and Wales, *Youth Hails Adventure*, entertained them that night. The story of a young man's adventures using youth hostels on holiday the film, screened in village halls and clubhouses, publicised the new youth hostels and their organisation.

After another conference session on Saturday morning, they were off to nearby Hartington Hall. Schirrmann planted a copper beech tree as a symbol of the friendship of the youth of all nations. They visited the youth hostel at Derwent Hall and joined an informal dinner party of English members at Overton Hall youth hostel. Afterwards they held an international social evening. They played traditional games and taught each other their own countries' dances.

Some of the hostels they saw amused Schirrmann. He had not expected to find youth hostels in grand mansions and Derbyshire was gaining a reputation as a county with many grand youth hostels. Though they had great hostels in Germany, Schirrmann declared they had not got the atmosphere of these wonderful halls. On Sunday, following a final session, delegates climbed Black Rocks, a weathered outcrop of gritstone with panoramic views of the Derwent Valley.

Catchpool and Baron could reflect afterwards on a conference that had passed well. The delegates might have reflected on the smooth, well planned arrangements. Tensions from Germany had not emerged into their meetings. The next year's conference in Cracow, Poland, passed equally well but the meeting in 1936 in Copenhagen was stormy.

Again, the Nazis wanted German speaking associations from neighbouring countries admitted to the federation. Worse, their youth hostels now went against one of the federation's key principles. They discriminated against Jewish people, trade unionists and others. They excluded 'German non-aryans and German emigres.' Laws banned Jewish and trade union members from office in youth hostels as in the rest of Germany. The Nazis dismissed youth hostel wardens and the chair of a youth hostel committee in North East Prussia took his own life rather than wear a yellow star as the law demanded all Jewish people must. The Nazis changed the name of the official youth hostel magazine, *Die Jugendherberge* (The Youth Hostel) to *Jugend und Heimat* (Youth and Native Land).

Reassuring house parents in youth hostels were gone. House parents now wore uniforms. They were often party officials and the walls of hostels displayed pictures of Hitler. Individuals and small groups stopped wandering between youth hostels. Large uniformed groups of Hitler Youth, marching in step, singing political songs, replaced them.

The Dutch sought assurance that youth hostels in Germany would continue welcoming their members irrespective of politics or religion. The federation tried for a compromise. They stated foreign guests had a duty to respect the traditions of the country they were visiting. Disagreements caused long wrangles. The Nazi delegates walked out, putting pressure on Schirrmann to resign too. Schirrmann despaired that their failures would break up the federation and make international youth travel impossible. As the conference closed Isabel Smith, there again for the new US youth hostels, handed out roses as a symbol of peace to departing guests.

In July 1937 Schirrmann finally gave in to the inevitable. Under pressure, he resigned as president of the international federation and gave up any role in the German association. He regretted his earlier support for the Nazis. Germany withdrew from the federation. The Nazis claimed the existing framework was frustrating the big expansion of the movement they wished to see. In reality they left because their new German associations, in countries like Latvia and Rumania, were not accepted into the federation. Without Münker and Schirrmann, they sensed they no longer led the youth hostel movement.

Germany returned to the conference in Switzerland in 1938. Many problems seemed to have been resolved. They recognised each others' memberships, overcoming objections particularly from Germany which had held up discussions since the first international meeting. They discussed peaceful topics like 'Youth hostels and the Use of Leisure' and 'Youth Hostel Construction.' But when they came to elect officers for that year harmony collapsed. The Nazis tried once again to take control and to reassert their leadership of the movement. The meeting fell into wrangling, manoeuvring and vote trading. Finally, against the wishes of the Nazis and their bloc, the conference elected Catchpool, secretary of the England and Wales association, as their new president.

The decision was momentous, full of consequence and implication for the future. Catchpool may have been a compromise candidate but, a year from war, their choice was fortunate. They kept the key person of the movement out of mainland Europe after the Nazis occupied Europe. When war did begin Catchpool maintained the federation. He kept in touch with associations out of Europe in the USA and Canada. New Zealand had its own youth hostels from 1932 and Australians set up youth hostels in 1939. When war finally ended Catchpool was in place to resurrect the movement as part of the wider reconstruction of Europe.

Catchpool's many personal qualities served the international federation well. He had drive, energy and enthusiasm. He was a committed internationalist with a gift for reconciling others and bringing them together. He believed the aims "of our associations though variously worded and expressed in a dozen different languages, are essentially one in spirit." He became the great driving force for youth hostels during the war and especially in the post-war period, striving "to bring together the peoples of the world, so that... they may appreciate each other's view point and outlook, and realise that we are a world brotherhood."

Catchpool was well travelled. He had an international outlook. Having gained exemption from military service in the first world war, the Friends War Victims Relief Committee had invited him to join their work. In 1916 he travelled to Russia from where horrifying reports of conditions amongst refugees were coming. The Russian armies, retreating in front of the German armies, burned and destroyed everything behind them as they left, sending "some three million peasant families fleeing into the heart of Russia, one of the greatest migrations then known to history".

In Moscow Catchpool found English speaking helpers. Trainloads of old people, women and children fleeing the fighting arrived every day in Moscow. They had worn out their boots walking. Clothing moulted from their skins. Catchpool and his helpers set up soup kitchens and aid stations for the refugees.

Wherever he went Catchpool made connections and made the best he could from terrible conditions. He was indomitable, never giving up or losing his cheer. He met the family of Leo Tolstoy, studied Russian, went to the opera at the Bolshoi Theatre, met the composer Stanislavsky and saw Anna Pavlova dance Swan Lake. Moving from Moscow, living in villages, he worked for a time in Armenia. He recovered from typhoid fever. When the Russian revolution brought peace, the Turkish army invaded Armenia and forced Catchpool along with the relief unit back to Moscow.

In the aftermath of the revolution his hunger for reconciliation came to the fore. He organised the rescue of children. At home in England they assumed he was dead. As war between the Bolsheviks and White Russians flared he tried to reconcile the opposing armies, to end escalating atrocities against hostages on both sides. Trotsky supported him. He crossed between the warring armies and began arranging a first transfer of hostages. But his bold plan failed. The White Russians captured and threatened him with shooting before they expelled him across Siberia to Vladivostok from where he could finally travel home.

Reaching Tokyo as war ended he sent a telegram home. For the first time in his trials and adventures he was able to tell his family that he was safe. With time on his hands, before a ship back to England, he went to Korea and Manchuria, visiting the Great Wall of China and Peking. He glimpsed hideous slums, underfed children, tuberculosis and grinding poverty. The terrible conditions in China convinced him that a time of reckoning was bound to come there as it had in Russia.

On his way home by ship he went ashore at Suez. He travelled overland to Jerusalem and passed documents, given to him in Armenia, to the Archimandrite of the Armenian church. He found time to visit Armenia once more, investigating the needs of refugees there, before he continued his journey home. He had picked up American ways of speech during the four years he had been away. Boy, he muttered as his train pulled in, "I sure am glad to see Victoria Station."

Even before his appointment as president of the international federation he had thrown himself into helping colleagues in Europe. Touring France in his Baby Austin with his French counterpart in 1935, he had seen the need for youth hostels there. His faith in the power of volunteers was immense. Through the youth hostel magazine, back in England, he invited volunteers to join him in France, to set up a youth hostel on the edge of the forest at Fontainebleau. He arranged another volunteer camp in Denmark.

His plans were sometimes vague but they always were practical. Believing that young people achieved reconciliation by coming together in work he took volunteers to the Irish Free State. He aimed they should "show our regret for the tragic misunderstandings between Ireland and England in days gone by." Over six weeks, 100 volunteers created a youth hostel at Bunnaton, Donegal, from five coast guard cottages destroyed in the Irish war of independence. The volunteers included Ruth Catchpool and family. Catchpool organised a final camp in Norway before war began. They opened a new youth hostel at Mjolfjell in June 1939 including cutting a road from the station.

The federation cancelled its next international conference, planned for Scotland in August 1939. A rally for young people went ahead at the youth hostel at Ardgarten on Saturday 26 August. The Scottish organisers had hoped for delegates from 18 countries but for the event only those from France, Belgium, Holland, USA, Canada, Luxembourg, Norway, Finland and Denmark were there. *The Scotsman* newspaper reported that about 1,500 attended. The majority were Scottish, though large parties were present from England, Ireland and Wales.

Duties as an army reservist stopped Leo Meilink, secretary-treasurer of the international federation, from leaving Holland. He wrote instead that experience taught him that where young people met in youth hostels, they showed that mankind could live in peace and friendship. The next week his hopes were dashed. War began. The dreams of men like Meilink, Schirrmann and Lord Allen, that youth hostels could be a bridge for peace between nations, had been an illusion. They had not prevented another war.

When the Nazis took over youth hostels in Germany they made others, particularly in Britain, wary of mixing youth hostels and politics. They had learned to fear large groups and any kind of officialdom, an attitude which rose to prominence after the war as youth hostels struggled to rid themselves of the stain of the Nazis. For a long time, without any truth, many people associated youth hostels with Nazis. The Nazis poisoned the well of ideals that created youth hostels. Ideas from the *Wandervögel*, of the benefits of fresh air and countryside, of health and exercise suffered through links with the Nazis. In Britain, a sense of idealism slipped from youth hostels as people became wary of notions like fresh air, health and beauty. Nature became the realm of nature studies and countryside the preserve of planning laws and conservation.

But those who dreamed of international peace through youth hostels achieved much. At a time when European and international travel was almost illusory, working together in the international federation Schirrmann, Catchpool and others laid the ground for a post war boom in travel by young people. Their far sighted agreements on reciprocal memberships, on common standards and on small practical steps like providing agreements and vouchers for bookings across borders survived war. As the war ended people turned their eyes to travel to other countries. The resurrection of youth hostels would set their dreams free once again.

Notes and references

Graham Heath and Anton Grassl provided the main account of the development of the International Federation of Youth Hostels in their book *The Magic Triangle*. The story of Graham Heath's life is a gap in the story of youth hostels. His accounts are invaluable but I have found little of his life in records. I relied on Catchpool's autobiography for the story of Catch's life as well as detail from the development of the international movement. The biography of Isabel Smith was another invaluable source. In 1940 John Biesanz wrote about the Nazis and their influence on youth hostels which provided useful detail and a near contemporary account of the changes the Nazis brought about in youth hostels in Germany.

"thoughtful young people…" Heath, *Richard Schirrman*, p28
"would have made an excellent motto…" Trench, *Fifty Years Young*, p48
"of our associations though variously worded…" Catchpool, *Candles in the Darkness*, p91
"to bring together the peoples…" Ibid p91
"some three million…" Ibid, p26
"I sure am glad to see Victoria Station." Ibid, p111
"show our regret…" Ibid, p152

-14-

Colchester

Caroline and I married in that second summer at Steps Bridge. We met when Caroline worked in the youth hostel at Hawkshead in the Lake District. We liked the people, the routine and the variety of work in a youth hostel and wanted to carry on, after we married.

But we couldn't carry on at Steps Bridge. The job was for a single person. Single people ran small youth hostels, open only for the summer season, and married couples ran bigger hostels. For a couple of months, through the winter of 1980, Caroline and I travelled about attending interviews, getting more and more despondent as interview followed interview with no job until, finally, we found work in Colchester in Essex.

Colchester and its hostel was perfect for us. The town was open, friendly and welcoming. Its youth hostel, at the bottom of a hill, overlooked an old bridge across the River Colne. Built of soft red brick, set in its own small garden, East Bay House had been a youth hostel since 1949.

The ports of Harwich and Felixstowe were nearby. Cyclists poured over the North Sea every summer. They came on ferries from Bremerhaven, from the Hook of Holland, from Esbjerg and Zeebrugge. They streamed towards Colchester riding old fashioned bikes, the kind we called 'sit up and beg' with wide flat handlebars. They were wonderful times when young people were discovering travel, testing their wings, before heading further and further afield.

Ferries, hitchhiking, trains, buses and the bicycle were the only ways to travel in those days before budget airlines. Few could afford a car. Youth hostels worked like a system of travel, feeding users along determined routes. From Colchester they went by train to London, heading for Devon or Cornwall. Adventurous cyclists crossed the Thames to a youth hostel at Kemsing, in Kent. Others took an easier route on their bikes to Castle Hedingham, to Saffron Walden, to Cambridge and the Norfolk coast. Often their routes looped back to Colchester, days or weeks later, for a last leg back to Harwich and a ferry home.

The region, influenced by the previous warden, had spent money on the youth hostel. Roger was a dynamic ex-salesman. With his wife, Kitty, he was intent on shaking up hostels. Leaving the hostel at Colchester with new carpets, new showers, new washrooms, new beds and new bedding, they had gone up the road to the bigger and busier hostel at Cambridge, where I had worked a couple of years before.

The hostel at Colchester, in a Queen Anne style house, held 67 people when it was full. Caroline and I lived in an upstairs flat, with three bedrooms, a bathroom, a lounge and kitchen. Big windows flooded high ceilinged rooms with light.

We were happy. The job was fun. A babel of languages echoed up and down stairs. The excitement of people on a first or last night in a strange, foreign town filled the rooms. Work was always a kind of travel with people of all backgrounds, from all kinds of places, arriving to stay each night.

The surrounding countryside, tucked into the Suffolk border, was rural and pretty. Our daughters were born and the summers were always long and hot. We cycled out to the nearby villages in the Stour valley where the great English landscape painter, John Constable, lived and worked. We went down to the sea at Mersea Island or along the coast to Walton-on-Naze, Frinton or Clacton-on-Sea.

Through the autumn fewer and fewer people arrived until we shut down the hostel for a couple of months. Winters were long and cold and often snowy. The hostel was empty. The house, in its garden, sank into silence, in deep muffling layers of snow. We painted, tidied and cleaned. The building recovered and we breathed more easily for a while until spring began.

By then the emptiness bored us. We were sick of the smell of paint. We looked forward to the crowds and busy days and friendly strangers. Early crowds emerged into the weak sun of Easter, finding their way to us as the season once again got underway.

-15-

A good war

Youth hostels had a good war. Less than ten years old when hostilities began war could have destroyed them. They depended on people to stay in them and to run them. As more and more people left their homes, friends, and work to fight in the war, youth hostels without people to stay in them or to run them might have gone under.

Against the odds they kept youth hostels open. Volunteers took their fate in their own hands. They begged, borrowed and sometimes stole what they needed. With men away fighting, as in other walks of life in Britain, women played more than an equal part. They walked and cycled for miles, giving up free time, just so that they and others would have somewhere to stay for a night, away from the bombing, away from stress and constant uncertainty. Ironically, having opposed war, youth hostels prospered, with help, support and funding from government.

The executive committee decided to carry on. Catchpool was still secretary and Trevelyan the president, but Barclay Baron had gone from being chairman. He now chaired the Youth Hostels Trust, the body that held all the association's youth hostels and properties.

John Cadbury took up the chairmanship from John Major who had only been chairman for a couple of years after Barclay Baron. Cadbury came from the Birmingham regional group of youth hostels. He was a successful businessman and had been a member of the National Executive Committee since 1933. Like Major and Cadbury subsequent chairmen came out of the membership, from people familiar with the workings of the organisation at a regional and national level. The association chose familiar, known and trusted men.

"War makes the need for our service greater, not less" Trevelyan wrote in 1939. "For boys and girls engaged in arduous war work, occasional escape into the quiet countryside is necessary both to maintain the quality of their work now and to enable them to grow up into the right kind of men and women in the future."

War heightened the need for youth hostels, for getting outdoors, for rest and recreation. Youth hostels could help win the war. "Holidays to reinvigorate war workers of all occupations and of both sexes are essential to the effort of the country in the fight for its own life and for the world's freedom. The YHA supplies the means for the best kind of such holidays."

In the time known as the phoney war, when Germany did not attack, Catchpool settled to a new way of working. The executive committee would only meet three times a year. A War Emergency Committee handled the executive's routine business. *The Rucksack* carried news of youth hostels still open in autumn 1939 and the national handbook, listing all youth hostels, continued, though it dropped in size to save paper in 1943. Membership figures plummeted, reaching a low point of 50,000 in 1940.

The authorities requisitioned a third of all youth hostels immediately. Requisitioning happened quickly with sudden closures. Soldiers, mothers and children, schoolchildren, schoolteachers, the aged and infirm, and people made homeless as a result of air raids used requisitioned youth hostels. Others accommodated soldiers on leave, a Friends Ambulance Unit training camp and Czech refugees or became emergency meeting rooms and feeding stations.

Schools from large cities took over youth hostels. Moved, because of the threat of bombing, children took up residence. The youth hostel at Ilam, in Derbyshire, housed children from nearby Derby. 80 schoolchildren from Manchester went to Ravenstor, also in Derbyshire, until the Ministry of Health took over the youth hostel, in June 1940, for a special school from London. Sir Charles Trevelyan managed to keep the youth hostel at Wallington open. Troops occupied the tiny youth hostel, a former cheese factory, in the Dorset village of Litton Cheney not far from the sea. Judging by graffiti on the walls there would seem to have been "very few units of the British Army (not to mention Americans) who were not there at some time during the War!"

Families bombed from their homes in Coventry took refuge in Warwick's youth hostel. A bomb scored a direct hit on the roof of the youth hostel at Swanage and bombs damaged The Folk House, home of the Gloucester and Somerset region, in Bristol. The coastline of southern England and East Anglia expected an invasion and youth hostels close to the sea and the beaches, in restricted areas, closed for the duration of the war. The youth hostel at Scarborough in North Yorkshire continued through the first months of the war. In October 1940 it was still operating but only to members resident in the restricted area along the coast. By 1941 it was open again.

Monroe and Isabel Smith invited the Catchpool family to join them in the US. Jack and Ruth Catchpool faced a difficult choice. Authorities were evacuating children from the cities and Ruth was pregnant. In that uncertain period, at the beginning of war, they were unsure what facilities for a pregnant woman might continue. Ruth took three of their four children to America. May, their eldest at 17, could not leave because the authorities planned conscription.

Jack and Ruth had been apart through the long years before they married when he was in Russia during the first world war. They settled for a second separation, not knowing when Ruth might be able to return. Their fifth child, Carol, was born in America on Christmas Day 1940. With her other children at school, Ruth ran the youth hostel at Northfield, 70 miles from Boston, for the next four years.

The regional group in London moved their office from Toynbee Hall in the East End to a hostel in the countryside away from the threat of bombs. The national office at Trevelyan House turned into an emergency hospital. Catchpool moved the association's office into his empty family home but Meadow Cottage wasn't empty for long. A Jewish family of refugees from Vienna joined Catchpool. He ran the youth hostel organisation from his home with the help of a couple of conscientious objectors until he found a new office.

By 1939 attitudes to conscientious objectors had changed. The authorities treated them with more humanity than they had done in 1916. They no longer classified objectors as deserters and locked them in prison for their beliefs. Panels again reviewed the applications of conscientious objectors but a lawyer or county court judge chaired each panel. They included a trade unionist and a woman, if the conscientious objector was a woman. An appeal system was in place. Tribunals gave conscientious objectors non-combatant roles. Objectors worked in agriculture or forestry, in hospitals and social service. They worked in youth hostels and with Catchpool in his office. Some conscientious objectors took up the dangers of bomb disposal.

Catchpool continued to work as tirelessly as ever on behalf of youth hostels and found time for other causes too. He arranged talks and lectures for American servicemen stationed in England once the US joined the war. He managed to stay in touch with colleagues in the US, Canada and New Zealand.

Catchpool always believed that youth hostels were doing the work of government. Youth hostels contributed as much to young people's learning as schools and in more practical ways. Youth hostels deserved backing by government, especially by the Board of Education. Youth hostels were doing the work of the board. Young people learned in youth hostels, about the countryside, about others, and about themselves. They took part in healthy and informal outdoor exercise in ways that they could continue out of school at weekends and when they grew up and left school. Youth hostels, with their open easy comradeship, educated them in the ways of independence and responsibility and turned them into better citizens more quickly than any school. So, in Catchpool's equation, the board should be helping youth hostels.

In the years leading up to 1939, when it was becoming clear to many that another war was coming, interest in physical training had been growing. The nation was going to need fit and healthy adults. Britain couldn't afford to repeat the experience of earlier wars when she lacked healthy people to fight on her behalf.

When the board set up a new department to promote national fitness in 1938, Catchpool saw his chance to win government support. Youth hostels were playing their part in building the nation's health and educating young people. The new National Fitness Council, with 20 area committees, had funds to appoint and train leaders and capital grants to improve facilities. The council's voluntary ethos and regional structure exactly suited youth hostels. Catchpool and his colleagues in the regions applied with careful plans for improving existing youth hostels or establishing new ones. The council responded with nearly £8,500 for 14 youth hostels.

War put an end to the scheme. It dissolved in October 1939. It had never been popular. Liaising with existing statutory bodies was tricky. Absorbing existing committees into the work of the council caused resentment. Many thought a voluntary ethos for national fitness training was a waste of time, effort and resource. Compulsory training grew more appealing as the threat of war grew. Local Education Authorities (LEAs) resented the new committees. The new work lacked any relation to the existing good work of schools and the LEAs resented the host of new amateur officials the system created.

In the tangle of war beginning, details of the exact funds paid by the council to youth hostels were lost. Funding was made and recorded for youth hostels in Wales, at Snowdon Ranger, Bala and Llangollen. Other funds may or may not have been paid and Catchpool's figure of £8,500 (£500,000 today) may have been optimistic. But the council's funding was an important first step towards central government support for youth hostels.

Having gained the Board of Education's backing and then lost it, Catchpool turned to persuading government to recognise youth hostels and the role they were playing in winning the war. With government backing he could get requisitioned youth hostels returned to use. He could argue the case for others not to be taken. He could get supplies for youth hostels as essential services and in return youth hostels could help war-weary workers to rest. Children could holiday away from the terrors of air raids and bombing, and servicemen and women could take short breaks between periods of active service.

He persuaded two government departments. The Board of Education and Ministry of Labour threw their support behind youth hostels. The board wanted young people, after they left school and particularly those engaged in wartime industries, to take part in outdoor exercise and relaxation. Officials agreed that youth hostels, offering healthy and inexpensive holidays and a change of surroundings, made a real contribution to the country's morale and strength.

The board replaced support from the National Fitness Council with a direct grant for the salary and expenses of a liaison officer. Mary Lander, who had been with Catchpool since 1932 and who had joined him at the first meeting of the international federation in Amsterdam, took up the post. Her job was to help the regional groups, bringing back youth hostels from requisitioning and promoting youth hostels to a public that knew little of the opportunities they offered. She would continue as liaison officer until 1946, supported throughout by the Ministry of Education which replaced the old board.

The Ministry of Labour also stepped in and recognised the contribution of holidays in the countryside for reinvigorating war-workers of all occupations and both sexes. The Minister for Labour wanted to make all possible provision for the needs of young industrial workers and hoped youth hostels could make more accommodation available.

With two departments backing them, volunteers worked hard at promoting youth hostels in factories and in the armed services. They gave talks, standing up in canteens at meal breaks to tell others about youth hostels. They showed *Hostelling Holidays*, a film extracted from an earlier film, *The Magic Shilling*, to factory workers during their lunch breaks. Mary Lander organised and carried out much of the work. She was also busy assisting regions that were short of people and at times she acted as a deputy or relief warden for youth hostels.

Men and women from the armed services used youth hostels during their leave as youth hostels extended special introductory memberships to them. Air Raid Precautions wardens supervised the black out, kept order in air raid shelters, administered first aid and helped assess bomb damage. During heavy bombing in the winter of 1940 they used youth hostels within easy reach of large towns for rest before the next onslaught.

From the summer of 1941 the two government departments began releasing youth hostels from requisitioning. Once released they were not supposed to be requisitioned again, except in case of most urgent necessity. Elterwater and High Cross Castle, in the Lake District, Wilderhope Manor in Shropshire, Marlborough in Wiltshire and two in Cornwall were among those returning to use. Release from requisitioning could be uncertain. Troops occupied the youth hostel at Crickhowell, in Powys on the edge of the Brecon Beacons. Released in May 1940, the Sub-

Area Quartering Commandant, Cardiff, requisitioned it again the next month. Telling members and others which youth hostels were available became a constant task.

More people were using youth hostels. The London region reported overcrowding and unexpected requisitioning created disappointments for those wanting to stay. The region was trying to find new youth hostels in all parts of the region but "country properties were at a premium and rents and purchase prices [had] risen steeply." The region looked to the future with optimism even in 1941 when it purchased Tun House, in Whitwell, Herts, for a new youth hostel, with assistance from the Ministry of Education.

Membership numbers began to rise, from the low of 50,000 in 1940 to 78,382. The 180 hostels which were open were busier than ever. For anyone wanting to get away for a weekend or to take a holiday, there were very few other places left to go. "Hotels, pubs with a few rooms to let, the CTC's beloved bed-and-breakfast places, all had disappeared, filled with all the people and businesses that had to move house in wartime."

Even if the government released youth hostels from requisitioning, finding people to run them was often a battle. Vera Watson dealt with bookings for the youth hostel at Houghton Mill near Cambridge. A National Trust property on the edge of a placid pond, old machinery and the mill workings littered its interior. Watson cycled the 15 miles to the mill where she acted as warden at weekends, before cycling back to Cambridge in time for work on Monday morning. Her dedication made the hostel one of the most popular in the region. With petrol rationed, cycling was her only choice.

New youth hostels continued to open. The London Region took the lease of an old pub in Leatherhead, Surrey. Volunteers reconstructed and adapted the Old Rising Sun and made it into a well used and popular youth hostel. New youth hostels opened at Castleton and Edale, in the Peak District's Hope Valley, to replace Derwent Hall. That youth hostel finally closed when the River Derwent was dammed and flooded to create Lady Bower reservoir.

The path to opening a new youth hostel could be long and protracted. The Lakeland regional group bought Esthwaite Lodge, outside the village of Hawkshead, in 1942. But the women's land army was already using the house and it took two years for the Regency mansion, built by a Liverpool shipping magnate and then the house of the novelist Francis Brett Young, to fully open as a youth hostel.

On other occasions, volunteers working long hard hours prevailed. Noel Vincent was one of those volunteers. He joined YHA in 1937. When war broke out he found himself in a reserved occupation. As a 'boffin' in a small back room he had a job he couldn't leave, even if he had wanted. His wife was warden at the new youth hostel in Leatherhead. On a Sunday afternoon, cycling up a muddy lane towards Ranmore Common, Vincent and his wife came across an apple tree, with apples, in an abandoned garden. They climbed through head-high nettles, in shorts, and found not only a fruitful tree but an abandoned cottage. "It really was a mess – roof full of holes, bushes growing in the fallen plaster inside, glassless and occasionally frameless windows, wide cracks in the walls."

The cottage was part of the Polesden Lacey Estate. William McEwan, one of the most successful brewers of his generation, had bought the estate in 1906. He was a shrewd, hard headed, hard working businessman. Offered a title, he turned it down because he would rather be first in his own order than last in someone else's. On his death in 1913 his daughter, Margaret Greville, inherited his fortune. She remodelled the original Regency house at Polesden Lacey with the architects of the Ritz Hotel and became a famous hostess. King George VI honeymooned there.

During the blitz Mrs Greville lived in hotels in London and, after a long period of disablement, died on 15 September 1942 at the Dorchester. She left Polesden Lacey to the National Trust. The trust agreed to lease the derelict cottage as a youth hostel and threw in another nearby, where a warden could live, for one pound a year for each building.

Vincent took charge of work to create a youth hostel from the ruined cottage. He lived at Leatherhead and could be out at the cottage, called Tanners Hatch, every weekend. He found enough volunteers to run a working party every week-end for two and a half years. He also left a detailed record of the creation of the youth hostel, *The Tanners Hatch Story*.

"…Sometimes the response was embarrassing and we had to find worth-while jobs and tools for forty enthusiastic volunteers." Two professional building tradesmen, George the plasterer and Tom the carpenter, also appeared. Both were fine workmen and excellent teachers with a great capacity for suffering fools gladly, Vincent remembered.

Volunteers stayed on Saturday nights at the youth hostel in

Leatherhead. After breakfast they cycled or walked up the long muddy track to Tanners Hatch, loaded with tools, food and materials. "We worked all day with lunch supplied on the job (the only freebie we got), then cycled or walked and trained home in the evening. If we needed heavy supplies – sand, gravel, cement, bricks, etc – a group who could get there early on Saturday afternoon would take a three-ton lorry, hired with driver, load it at the local builder's yard and try to see how near they could get to Tanners before it bogged down and could go no more. Sometimes we actually got there, but too often the mud won and Sunday's gang spent their day ferrying a ton or two of sand in rucksacks and wheelbarrows from wherever we had to unload."

Both buildings had almost to be rebuilt. Vincent bought heavy building materials except timber without much difficulty. Britain imported timber at a great cost in shipping and lives lost. Civilians needed permission to buy it. The team at Tanners worked out their needs with care and great parsimony, and requested their license. An official summoned Vincent to put his case. "The official who heard me out seemed to be so stunned by the fact that we were going to do all this with no paid labour at all that he gave us a license at once. Later on we wished desperately that we had asked for more but we hadn't got the nerve to go back."

The wood was of poor quality. "There was no picking and choosing of nice bits without cracks and knots, or even of any particular sort of timber. It was all just wood. To fill that modest order we got larch, spruce, hemlock, Parana pine, Columbian pine, Quebec spruce, and something that in my battered working notebook is called 'Reb. spruce'. And some of it looked and felt as if they had only just scraped the leaves off. But in it had to go, camouflaged with a hopeful lick of creosote, and out the ruins of the old roof rose the skeleton of the new."

The work went on. They laid concrete floors to replace the old timber ones, "scraping rotting wood off the outside of massive timbers to find out how much sound wood was left (and this was often a surprisingly large amount on an apparently hopeless beam) and then splicing in bits from a beam that really was hopeless to mend the worst holes, cutting away all the loose brick and flint work that bordered the great cracks in the walls so that we could rebuild from a sound(?) base, and then building in with brick and flint right up to roof level again."

The team carried water from Polesden Farm using an old timber yoke, probably once used by milkmaids to carry two buckets. "Some unlucky chap or girl would spend Sunday as a water-maid, staggering half a mile uphill with two galvanised buckets, each with twenty pounds of water in, to feed teams of concrete mixers and plasterers and bricklayers…"

Vincent recognised the importance of food in bringing volunteers. "Special rations were issued to registered catering establishments, which could then serve meals without asking their customers for ration coupons, so that every sensible person took every opportunity to eat out and save coupons for meals at home. The rations to catering establishments were of exactly the same quantity per meal for a Youth Hostel or, say, the Savoy Hotel, though I believe that unsuccessful attempts were made to convince the Minister that Hostellers were likely to be a lot hungrier than customers of The Savoy."

Help came from other sources as the work went on. The International Voluntary Service for Peace (now the IVS) sent volunteers who bivouacked in the ruins. A lecturer at the Architectural Association brought young architects to learn about handling materials the hard way. A group came from the London School of Building. But youth hostel members were the backbone of the work-force. Two-thirds of them were girls. They dug and laid drains. They mixed and poured concrete. They cemented bricks and set flints. They tiled roofs, carpentered and plumbed. They needed another youth hostel and saw building their own as the best way to get one.

During the war groups like Vincent's took hold within youth hostels and increased in number. The first local groups started before the war. Some existed in 1935 following the example of an extremely successful group in Croydon. By 1941 the London Region had 36 local groups, each with 80-100 members. Their main aim was propaganda or public relations, promotion and publicity in today's terms. The groups became increasingly important within the grass roots of the youth hostel organisation. They administered youth hostels. They arranged visitors to support wardens and maintained contact between hostels and members. They organised working parties and carried out necessary improvements.

Those staying in youth hostels also changed. Grumbles about anti-social behaviour, rowdyism and noise in dormitories increased. The change dismayed some including the owner of Holt Mill youth hostel near

Kidderminster. "'Old' Gardiner the owner/warden/farmer got fed up with wartime Members who put dirty dishes in the dustbin rather than wash up!' The Birmingham Region lost Holt Mill as a youth hostel when Gardiner left in 1942.

Throughout the war people prepared for peace. Lack of change after the first world war had left a generation feeling let down. Dreams of the countryside had inspired soldiers mired in the trenches. Facing a bombed and blasted landscape they had fought for a better future. Many had expected homes and land for soldiers returning from war.

They would not be disappointed a second time. Planning started for a national health service, a new education act and increased social security. Work began for the creation of national parks and greater protection of the countryside. A greater love of the countryside was integral to the aims of youth hostels. From the beginning youth hostel members had supported increased protection for landscapes.

The association was a founding member of the Standing Committee on National Parks in 1936. Others on the standing committee included the Council for the Preservation of Rural England, the Council for the Protection of Rural Wales, and the Rambler's Association. The committee lobbied for greater protection of the countryside. John Dower, Sir Charles Trevelyan's son-in-law and brother of Yorkshire region's chairman, drafted proposals for national parks ahead of the end of the war.

When war ended in Europe in May 1945 the youth hostel at Tanners Hatch still wasn't finished. It would finally open for Easter 1946, after two and a half years of steady work. The first paying customers included one from France.

Youth hostels were in better shape than anyone might have expected. By the war's end, 234 youth hostels were open in England and Wales, only 63 less than were open in 1939. More people than ever had joined the association, 153,751 in 1945, and almost double the number who had joined in 1939 which had been a record. Of these more than two thirds (67%) were under 21 years of age.

In contrast the situation in Europe was a disaster. Out of 1,130 hostels in the three Allied occupied zones of Germany, 630 still existed. Allied forces requisitioned most of these. In Belgium, eight youth hostels had been destroyed and seven badly damaged. The rest were without equipment which had been requisitioned or stolen. In Holland only nine hostels out of 69 hostels survived. Only 19 of Finland's 45 youth hostels from before the war remained and in France only 50 youth hostels were usable. Catchpool went to France, Belgium and Holland remaking his contacts. International working parties began the practical work of reestablishing youth hostels in Europe.

Each summer in the immediate post war years, volunteers spent their holidays repairing and decorating damaged buildings. In 1946, 400 volunteers from the association were working on seven projects, from Norway to Italy, alongside volunteers from the host countries and the US. They rebuilt the youth hostel at Arnhem, damaged by British paratroopers in the battle that had failed to capture the bridge in 1944. A dozen projects were up and running in 1946, with Catchpool working on getting programmes up in Germany.

Belief in the role of youth hostels in contributing to peace remained. In Wales a small youth hostel opened as evidence that the international spirit of youth hostels continued despite the war. A public appeal brought funds to buy the youth hostel at Blaencaron and, during August 1952, an international work party of 10 Germans and 10 Britons almost rebuilt the premises in a fortnight. The British War Relief Society, an umbrella organisation dealing with the supply of non-military aid from the US, gave £7,000, raised by American Trade Unions, towards new youth hostels at Betwys-y-Coed, Gwynedd, in Wales; Southwell in Nottinghamshire; Cambridge and York.

The war marked another turning point for youth hostels. The London region decided, in 1943, that wherever possible they would establish and manage their own hostels. In nine years 22 hostels, in buildings the region did not control, had closed. Only six of those closed for reasons connected with the war. The region decided direct control would be more effective. The group could ensure youth hostels were in places where they wanted them, rather than where someone else offered one. The region determined to bring an end to instability by purchasing freeholds when they had funds.

In 1945, the region planned to spend several thousand pounds of its own resources and had committed to £10,000 in bank loans. But they did not have the funds to complete their plans. Having borrowed money, they still needed £8,000 to furnish and complete the new hostels. Despite ambition signs for the future financing of youth hostels were not good.

Local groups established themselves at the grass roots of the organisation. A new generation arrived in youth hostels, sometimes to the dismay of their peers, pushing the old pioneering spirit of youth hostels into the past.

Government support became increasingly important. It had helped keep many youth hostels out of requisitioning or returned them to use more quickly than otherwise might have been the case. Government support had helped with supplies, equipment and funds to keep youth hostels open.

The newly created Ministry of Education funded new youth hostels, made payments for equipment and gave grants to assist in administration. It funded, among many others, youth hostels at Wooler and Rock Hall, Northumberland; Chester, Cheshire; Grantham, Lincolnshire; Swanage, Dorset; and Colchester, Essex. The ministry had paid for a liaison officer to support the work of youth hostels, a tradition that would continue after the war. The Carnegie trust had also continued its support.

The state arrived as a player in social service. The 1944 Education completely overhauled education, bringing in free secondary education for students up to the age of 18. The act required LEAs to provide 'adequate facilities for recreation and social and physical training.' It ushered in a style of education which included social and physical training. LEAs used the act's requirements to build their own outdoor education centres. The first centre, White Hall, opened in the Peak District in 1951. They directly rivalled youth hostels.

Youth hostels also benefited from the act. Schools used youth hostels in the post war years in greater and greater numbers. Teachers took children walking using youth hostels as well as camping, to fulfil their role in the social and physical training of young people.

War made clear the role of youth hostels. Authorities gave their work official sanction, a seal of approval that came with financial backing. They recognised how much youth hostels could contribute to changing people. They acknowledged youth hostels' central role in the nation's life and their contribution to the health and welfare of an entire people.

Notes and references

I relied on Noel Vincent's account of the making of Tanners Hatch youth hostel for the heart of this chapter along with records of the London region and Catchpool's autobiography.

"War makes the need for our service greater…" *YHA Annual Report 1939*
"Holidays to reinvigorate war workers…" *YHA Annual Report 1940*
"very few units of the British Army…" Tighe, account of Litton Cheney youth hostel
"country properties were at a premium…" *London, Regional Annual Reports 1931-1965*, 1941
"Hotels, pubs with a few rooms…" Vincent, *The Tanners Hatch Story*
"…Sometimes the response was embarrassing…" This and following quotes from Vincent, *The Tanners Hatch Story*
"'Old' Gardiner the owner warden…" Smith, *Caveat Nostalgia*, p44

-16-

Routine

Youth hostels ran on routine with times and timings for everything. Times to open doors, to turn on ovens, to set tables and greet arrivals and early risers.

Times followed more times, more chores and more routines. Mornings were breathless just keeping up. Ten minutes to bake the croissants. Five minutes to grill the bacon, less for frying an egg. Fill the milk jugs. Boil water. Make tea. Set out jam, marmalade, butter and sugar. Lay out the loaves of sliced white bread ready for toasting. Open the safe in the office, spill bags of coin into the till, check the morning numbers and set out membership cards for the members leaving that day who would collect them later.

Routine flowed but sometimes didn't. A naked guest, clutching a towel, couldn't get her shower to work. Another wanted a pint of milk, a slice of bread or a match to light a stove. One would like to chat, to seek directions or get advice. Apologies for the interruption preceded the question. "I know you are busy but..." More questions followed and, before you knew, the interruption had left you breathless and late.

Soon there would be bins to empty, rooms to sweep, showers and toilets to scrub and dirty laundry to collect. Meals had to be prepared. Letters to answer, forms to fill, money to count and memos to read.

Just at the busiest time of year, when school groups filled every room and the dining room burst with children, the garden sprang into growth. Then the lawn grew ankle deep, demanding the mower for which there was no petrol. When that had been fetched from the nearby filling station it then refused to start. There was always more work than could be done.

Our afternoons were free and even that spare time could disappear. A food delivery could arrive with items missing or we ran out of fruit and had to go shopping. A noisy, enthusiastic group might arrive early. Then it was easier to open the hostel and to let them in, even though we should have been closed. Nothing was gained by keeping the door locked, except unhappiness, dissatisfaction and disgruntlement.

At 5pm we opened again. While people checked in, routine ran. Supper cooked and served by 7pm. Soup on the cooker, pie in the oven, sweet in the fridge and everything ready. The next days' packed lunches made and piles of pots and baking trays to wash.

Things went wrong. In all that rush and hurry notes strayed, bookings went awry and orders were forgotten. A shower flooded, a toilet broke or the fire alarm sounded. I ran, up the stairs, checking rooms, looking for a fire while everyone assembled on the front lawn. There never was a fire more serious than burned toast.

When all the chores were done, the money counted, the numbers entered on the necessary forms and the following day prepared, a little time remained. A shred for a cup of coffee. A chunk for a chat with guests. Time to savour silence and moonlight from the front door. Time for a final walk to lock all the doors and close the windows. A time when all the timings ran out and came to an end when, routine exhausted, the day could finally be said to be done. And then the bell rang for a late arrival or the fire alarm sounded once again.

Celebrations

Youth hostels celebrated coming of age in 1950. Prime Minister Clement Atlee wished in a letter that youth hostels were even older, even "more venerable, for in my young days the countryside was almost unknown to the majority of boys and girls who lived in our cities and towns." *The Times* celebrated too, remarking how the youth hostels movement had grown into a remarkable force in British life. The National Council for Social Services published *Youth Hostel Story*, the first history of youth hostels, by Oliver Coburn. The year's celebration coincided with Jack Catchpool's 60th birthday in August and his retirement after 20 years as YHA's national secretary.

Youth hostels had survived two decades. They had endured a world war. They had begun in 1930 with no money, no buildings and no members. 210,000 members now had 303 youth hostels where they could spend the night in almost every part of England and Wales. Private owners still operated hostels, like Mr and Mrs King who ran the youth hostel at Llanfair Talhairarn in Denbighshire for three years in the 1950s.

But regional groups, whenever they could, bought the buildings they wanted. A member could spend the night in a converted hotel in Ambleside in the Lake District. The Lakeland regional group purchased the Queens Hotel in 1947 after art students, evacuated there during the war, had left behind a mess no one else was willing to clear up. Members could stay in a pair of cottages in the Northamptonshire village of Badby, bought by the Warwickshire and Northamptonshire Regional Group in 1945.

A grass roots organisation was in place. Members and their regional groups recognised no single leader. They emphasised their democratic ways. Members made decisions. They elected a council for each regional group. Members elected an executive and other committees which ran the regions, employed wardens to run youth hostels and, in the bigger more prosperous regions, employed administrators, staff and regional secretaries. 19 regional groups ran the youth hostels. They based themselves in big cities like London, Birmingham and Manchester, on smaller cities like Cambridge and Oxford or on wider geographical areas like the Gloucester, Somerset and Exmoor regional group.

Sub-regional or local groups, in towns and cities, were the heart of many regions. Larger cities, like London and Manchester, might have two or three local groups. They increased in strength and number through the war years when young people in towns and cities banded together. They brought new members to stay in youth hostels and they were the backbone of working parties. They helped clean, decorate, run and even built new youth hostels, repeating the adventure of Tanners Hatch. They worked on wider schemes too. Members of the Wimbledon Local Group surveyed all the footpaths in the Leatherhead area.

None of the original executive from 1930 remained. Five of them continued as vice presidents. They attended meetings, had their say and kept a watchful eye on youth hostels. They maintained a continuity. GM Trevelyan resigned as president in 1950. He was preparing for his retirement and resigned as Master of Trinity College, Cambridge, the following year. When representatives of all the regional groups met they elected PJ Clarke in Trevelyan's place. YHA began to look to its own people for its presidents and vice presidents. Clarke came from the Merseyside regional group and had been YHA's national chairman since 1945.

Youth hostels had become an institution, an established part of British social life. The Ministry of Education continued its support for youth hostels. The department gave £19,522 to youth hostel projects in 1950.

As part of a coalition of outdoors organisations like the CPRE and the Ramblers YHA had achieved a long fought for goal when parliament had passed the National Parks Act in 1949. National parks protected large chunks of countryside from insensitive or inappropriate development. The Peak District became the first national park in 1951. Less than 20 years earlier men had gone to jail for walking on the Derbyshire hills. On Kinder, where the Duke of Devonshire had kept people out so he and his friends could enjoy shooting birds for a few months each year, men and women would walk, run and climb.

The International Youth Hostel Federation (IYHF), with Jack Catchpool as president, also had much to celebrate. The federation had cancelled their last conference at Loch Lomond before the war. With suitable symbolism it met there in 1946. Observers from Australia, Canada, Egypt, Greece, India, Italy, Pakistan, Palestine and South Africa attended.

Richard Schirrmann, the German founder, and his colleague Wilhelm Münker attended the 1946 conference. Monroe Smith, founder of the American Youth Hostels Association, arranged their flight to Scotland. Hostility met the two Germans. Many at the conference were not willing to forgive or forget the war. They agreed with the Czechoslovakians "no help should be given to those countries responsible for the war, before considering the just claims of their victims."

Catchpool ignored the federation's wishes. He arranged an international work camp in Germany the next year. Bombing had destroyed the youth hostel in Hamburg. To replace it, in what had once been "a range of barracks, then a POW camp for men from the east, then a collecting place for small Hamburg waifs and strays," young people from Germany and Britain built a temporary hostel. Many more camps followed in the next three years. Young Germans travelled to England too, taking part in various projects. At Tintagel in Cornwall they cleared rolls of barbed wire from wartime coastal defences around the youth hostel.

Catchpool saw such camps contributing to reconciliation and that gave him enough reason to go against the wishes of others in the federation. "In these international work camps, when young people come together in a common purpose and a spirit of good-will, the superficial differences disappear and the individuals are revealed as being strikingly alike, with the same capacity for fun, work, friendship, generosity, kindliness and love."

The IYHF continued its tradition of pre-war rallies bringing young people from member countries together in a rally at the same time as their conference. At the 1948 conference in the Wicklow Hills in Ireland, "the flags of many nations fluttered from a row of tall flagstaffs, against a background of bracken and purple heather." Youth hostellers toiled up the steep road on foot or pushing their bicycles. *An Óige* accommodated and fed 800 and 500 more camped in their own tents and fed themselves from Primus stoves and fires.

They entertained each other. "One after another representatives of each nation mounted the platform. Singing-dances by a Norwegian group in picturesque national costume, solo songs by a sweet-voiced Flemish girl, lively Morris Dances by an English team in cap and bells, sad French folk-songs sung in delicate harmony by a team from Tunisia, lively modern folk-music from the USA, a Dutch team led by a versatile hostel warden singing to the guitar, kilted Scots hostellers performing an intricate sword dance… The audience sat enthralled whilst the cool of night set in, pulling blankets around them as protection against the chill mountain breeze. Finally a huge bonfire was lit and the evening ended in a babel of talk and song around a blazing fire."

The rally reminded the IYHF of the reasons for its meeting. The presence of so many young people prevented conference from becoming solemn and self important with nothing but papers and agendas. The rally surrounded the conference with celebration and young people from many different backgrounds and countries. Despite the war and despite the efforts of the Nazis to change youth hostels, the federation reaffirmed the purpose of youth hostels in bringing people together.

YHA in England and Wales hosted the conference and rally in 1950 coinciding with their own anniversary celebrations. 2,000 young people from 20 countries travelled to the Bridgewater Memorial Field near Ashridge, Hertfordshire, on Saturday 19 and Sunday 20 August. *The Rucksack* described the setting for the rally as typically English, on a meadow circled by oak and beech trees.

Catchpool had a big job preparing for the rally. A team of 200 volunteers drawn from local groups helped him. They hired tents, fixed a large platform for the national dances and brought a water supply to the rally field. They arranged toilet facilities and provided a hospital tent, post office and bank. They flood lit the camp grounds and helped put together a mass of documents for the conference. Catchpool was in his element. He thrived on bringing together young volunteers from all walks of life in a shared effort with a common goal.

Accommodation and meals for the weekend cost 20/- and day visitors paid 2/6. Weather for the weekend alternated between bright spells and showers. The showers were not enough to dampen spirits. The first visitors arrived on Friday evening and continued through the night. A group from Tunisia lost its leader and their money with him. An American party got the dates wrong and had to leave before the rally began.

Community singing began the event on Saturday evening. Dancers and singers in national costumes from more than a dozen countries took part. A BBC recording van captured their voices and song and the evening finished with fireworks. The rector from the nearby church at Ivinghoe led a united service on Sunday and the programme continued with a puppet show and discussion groups.

The IYHF conference began on Monday morning. King George VI, the prime minister and the Archbishop of Canterbury sent messages of congratulation. GM Trevelyan welcomed 80 delegates from 25 different countries to the Great Hall of Ashridge House. He read a message from the first United Nations Secretary General, Trygve Lie. Sir John Maud, Permanent Secretary of the Ministry of Education, opened the main business of conference.

They reviewed statistics. They discussed co-operation with government departments. On the continent youth hostels were often extensions of government. In Britain the education department was extending itself into the social well being of young people, moving closer to the work of youth hostels. But the conference recommended that youth hostels should continue without direct government involvement. The experience of youth hostels in Germany under the Nazis was a deterrent.

They debated long and hard over banning hitchhikers from youth hostels. Many associations saw hitchhiking as another form of motorised travel like using a private car or motor bike. They opposed it as they opposed travel by car or motor bike. The argument ended without conclusion in a resolution supporting lower fares for public transport. Finally, five years after the end of war, the federation readmitted German youth hostels to their midst.

Jack Catchpool retired. He had been president of the federation since 1938. The conference elected lively, dynamic Leo Meilink to replace him. Meilink had been secretary of the Dutch association and had played a leading role in the international federation before the war.

When the meeting closed everyone went by coach to London. They joined 5,000 young people for YHA's official birthday celebrations at the Albert Hall on Saturday 26 August. Tickets for this event were again 2/6. 12 teams danced national dances. Singers entertained them and they all sang together. Lord Baden-Powell and John D Rockefeller, president of the United States youth hostels, gave speeches. Barclay Baron, YHA's first chairman, spoke and then it was Catchpool's turn. *The Times* reported his speech in full. He delighted at how youth hostels had provided opportunities for young people to gain knowledge of the beauty and history of their country. From youth hostels they gained the capability of looking after themselves and a tolerance that came from mixing with others from different backgrounds.

He anticipated a future with more hostels on long distance paths and in national parks and with more school children using youth hostels to continue learning in beautiful surroundings. He would not drop the subject of government support for youth hostels. He looked across the North Sea to the Netherlands, Denmark and Germany. Local authorities provided youth hostels in those countries and handed them over to the associations who ran them. He saw it as a way of providing more youth hostels. He envied those countries for the pride they took in their youth hostels. Catchpool recalled that when visiting a Danish town, "your guide, showing you round, will point to the lovely church, take you a little further, and show you that wonderful old bridge or the river, then turn to you and say; 'There is our Youth Hostel, up on the hill.'" He longed for that sense of responsibility towards young people in Britain and was glad to see so many MPs in his audience. He urged them to think on the problems of young people.

Ceremonies done, they went to supper in two reserved restaurants in Hyde Park. A group of young people, chosen for the honour because they, like youth hostels, turned 21 that year, planted a tree 'of international friendship' beside the Serpentine. A dance with 'amplified music' was held in the flood-lit Cockpit, where the Rolling Stones would give their free concert in 1969. Illuminated boats with a large YHA sign processed on the Serpentine. 400 torch bearers weaved in and out of the trees, their lights reflected in the water. According to Catchpool, *The Times* reported what was "probably the gayest scene ever enacted in Hyde Park". As dusk fell in 1950 they sang Auld Lang Syne.

Barclay Baron wrote to Catchpool afterwards. "We felt we had seldom seen anything so beautiful and moving as the scene when the torches came into the arena, with the August full-moon over the Serpentine behind, and those thousands of eager faces on the grass slopes lit up by moonlight. You must have been very proud of your 21-year-old (for the YHA is very much your child) ... I hope you are not dead with exhaustion. Do take a little time off to rest soon."

The Times had observed on 12 August that any celebration of the factors making youth hostels one of the most important developments for young people had to include the character of Jack Catchpool. He had brought youth hostels from infancy to adulthood. Catchpool was an unorthodox man. He was patient and dogged. He had a playful witty nature according to *The Times*, without pretensions and with a very practical mind.

As president of the IYHF, he had "turned a blind eye to Constitutions and disregarded Standing Orders." But at every conference over which he presided there was "an unmistakeable atmosphere of friendship and trust." He had "brought to youth hostel workers... a spirit of kindness, understanding and good humour." "He had links with many leading Liberal and Labour politicians... [and] influential figures in public life (notably with the First Secretary to the Cabinet)." His contacts ensured wide ranging support for youth hostels and smoothed their way to growth.

He found committee and paper work uncongenial. He was happier promoting new projects. Regional groups sometimes viewed him with suspicion. At times he pushed centralisation and a public service ethos too much for their tastes. But throughout his time the youth hostel organisation prospered and grew, even in war. His charm drew support and funds from others. Colleagues like Mary Lander and John Simpson, the association's accountant, stood behind him. They carried out the backroom work and held it all together for him while he was away, busy raising money or finding projects.

Catchpool believed in the power of voluntary work. He had been a volunteer in Britain and abroad. The role of president in the IYHF was honorary. His influence on YHA, as an organisation built on voluntary effort, was long lasting. In helping to build youth hostels, he showed the same characteristics as he did during his war time travels. "He was doing what to many people often seemed impossible, crazy, or absurdly idealistic. But if Jack got an idea it had to be put into action; when he had a vision of something which would make life more tolerable and would increase understanding, especially among young people, then others must be made to do it."

Once he got an idea and was convinced it was worth fighting for, he would fight, but he was also a great reconciler, a born mediator and democrat. He was broad and open minded, wanting to bring other people with him and never trying to exclude anyone. Leo Meilink, secretary of the international federation for much of the same time as Catchpool, observed to him "You have always been broad, never narrow; you have always tried to bring other people into our family, and you have never tried to keep people out." His aptitude for reconciliation was important to his work in England and Wales. He held together the developing regions and their differences. He brought together strong minded people from regional groups in the same way he united nationalities.

Even when he no longer held any official role in youth hostels he involved himself in their work. On his retirement, he vowed to give such help as he could, in the remaining years of his life, to those overseas associations that might welcome him in their midst. In 1951 he went to India. He persuaded Prime Minister Nehru to help arrange exchanges of students between India and Pakistan. He discovered disused government bungalows and organised work parties to convert them to youth hostels. Volunteers taking part included the US ambassador's wife, embassy car drivers and Indian MPs.

His enthusiasm for youth hostels sent him to Afghanistan, Iraq, Syria, Jordan, Lebanon, Cyprus and Greece. He planned an overland chain of youth hostels, from Europe to India, that never came to fruition. He met groups of hostel enthusiasts in South Africa, Rhodesia and Kenya. When the British and French attacks on Suez in 1955 damaged an Egyptian youth hostel he organised a volunteer work party of young people from England to help restore the hostel. He remained as keen as ever on practical reconciliation and he continued to intervene even when his interventions were not invited.

Catchpool and Trevelyan departed. The executive committee after a long search appointed Dick Knapp as Catchpool's replacement. Knapp brought knowledge of rural affairs and a long standing involvement in youth hostels. He had been working in a county agricultural service. His first experience of youth hostels had been in Germany in the early 30s and he had been the first honorary secretary of the Wiltshire regional group. As with the president and vice presidents, YHA began looking to its own people for its appointments.

The Times, in an article from 1953, noted the different social classes using youth hostels, making it difficult to define a typical youth hostel user. The writer observed that it would not be unusual to find a university professor sitting next to a steel worker from Glasgow or Sheffield. Though many members might be teachers or students, men and women from all kinds of backgrounds made the life of youth hostels.

Youth hostels continued to give young women opportunities to travel. *The Times* noted an emphasis in hostels on young people and particularly on young women who travelled together in twos and threes.

Success brought difficulties. The annual report of 1949 noted with surprise that, for the first time since 1940, membership numbers and overnight stays at youth hostels had dropped slightly. The previous year, controversially, fees had been increased. When membership numbers stalled an expected increase in income disappeared.

Youth hostels were not immune to outside forces. A run on sterling followed the freeing up of financial markets. With sterling over valued, the government could not avoid devaluation and youth hostel costs increased.

Arthur Dower, elected chairman when PJ Clarke became president, had been sounding warnings about YHA's finances since 1946 when he informed council "hostel running has risen very greatly in cost and there are six war years' arrears of maintenance which will absorb many thousands of pounds. The cost of opening new hostels is two or three times the pre-war cost, since, as everyone knows, property is at a premium."

Dower came from a family with impeccable credentials in the countryside movement. His brother, John, wrote the report that led to the founding of national parks. Arthur had been brought up to regard walking as the natural state of man and the Lake District as next to paradise. He was also a keen boat sailor with a fleet of small boats on Ullswater. He rock climbed, scrambled and walked in most of the mountains of Western Europe and discovered youth hostels during a bicycle tour in Norway. He joined the West Riding regional group in 1933 and was its chairman from 1935 to the outbreak of war.

The dozen or so hostels that, for one reason or another, closed their doors each year concerned him. Replacements for those alone could take all the free money available. Property values continued to rise, making the goal of owning youth hostels even more difficult to achieve. Without more youth hostels, demand in popular areas would continue to outstrip supply.

Dower concluded that, with limited resources, development would be slow and some hostels would be too busy at peak times. At the height of summer, in places like the Lake District, Wales and the Peak District, there weren't enough beds for everyone who wanted to stay. This was the beginning of the long standing problem of 'peak loading,' when demand exceeded supply and too many people tried to stay in popular youth hostels. People had to book months in advance to get into those youth hostels in the short British summer.

Dower reached a simple conclusion. If they wanted less crowded hostels "we must have more hostels, and this means more money." The simple solution of more hostels would become an obsession in the coming years. The regional structure of youth hostels made the problem worse. The Lake District, Wales and the Peak District suffered from excess demand in the summer. Profit from those regions went to national funds that other regions could call upon to finance hostel developments. But the regions were autonomous. They ran their own finances and buying a youth hostel at Saffron Walden in Essex would not overcome the shortage of beds and youth hostels in the Lake District, the Peak District or Wales. Neither would opening new youth hostels at Bawtry on the Great North Road, at Lyonshall near Kington in Herefordshire or at Gosport in Hampshire where new youth hostels opened in 1950. Opening more hostels was not in itself enough.

That year YHA agreed a national framework for the wages of wardens running youth hostels. Negotiations had been protracted and added a significant burden to the limited resources of youth hostels. The annual report of that year predicted that the agreement would cost the association some thousands of pounds each year. The North Midlands regional group resorted to employing part-time wardens at lesser used hostels to save money.

A different generation was taking up travel with a taste for European destinations. British youth hostel members were the principal international visitors to youth hostels on the continent. They accounted for 25% of the international guests in some countries and almost 50% in French youth hostels in 1950. English replaced German as the international language of youth hostels.

Before the war many of those going to Europe had been students. Now a less privileged group of office staff, nurses and skilled manual workers was travelling there. Many of them knew no foreign languages. YHA set up a small foreign travel office in London, at 5 Tavistock Square, to help them make arrangements. Graham Heath, who had been assistant national secretary to Jack Catchpool during the war, took up post at the office. As International Information Officer he answered enquiries in person or by post. He arranged itineraries to cover chains of youth hostels in the most interesting parts of the Netherlands, Switzerland and France.

Passenger air travel began to shape youth hostels and the way that people who stayed in them travelled. Heath's office in London arranged popular air charters for flights to Amsterdam, Basel, Copenhagen, Munich and Oslo. Flights made it possible for young Americans to travel quickly to Europe. Monroe Smith, who with his wife, Isabel, had started youth hostels in the USA in 1934, resigned from the US association. He started a company, Youth Argosy, flying young Americans to Europe in 1949.

Youth hostels had reached a pinnacle. They had survived a depression at the outset and a world war. They had arrived in the post war world in strength. Membership numbers hit a high point in 1948 and for the rest of the 1950s remained close to that high with around 1,000,000 overnight stays recorded each year. The number of youth hostels peaked in 1950 when the annual handbook listed 303. It never listed as many again and, like figures so often are, the figure may be unreliable. Some that were supposed to open didn't and others, not listed, opened after the handbook went to press.

The figures for the number of youth hostels open, often quoted as a record, flatter. The years immediately after the war were not a record measured by the numbers staying in youth hostels. Youth hostels still had to face the difficulties Arthur Dower had identified. Costs were rising including wages.

Changes in youth hostels unsettled some. In 1946 a demobbed soldier had expected changes in youth hostels since the war but "we were really amazed at what we saw... the days of the real enthusiastic cyclist and rambler are over. In their place we appear to have large numbers of juveniles who turn up in parties of six or more and have not, judging by their style of dress, done any real walking or cycling. Instead they seem to have caught the train or bus to the nearest station and are merely using hostels as a cheap means of board and lodging..." The sight of a girl wearing silk stockings, suede shoes and a light summer frock accosted his eye. He had never seen anything like her before in any hostel.

The demobbed soldier may have been right. The days of the real enthusiastic walker might have been over. Increasingly older members began to discover that youth hostels had ushered a new world into existence. They might have thought that youth hostels were for really keen walkers and cyclists. Young people and juveniles catching trains and buses had very different ideas of the purposes youth hostels might serve including attending dances and meeting members of the opposite sex.

Notes and references

Grassl and Heath's history of the international federation of youth hostels was a valuable source for this chapter along with Catchpool's autobiography again.

"more venerable..." *The Rucksack*, July-August 1950
"no help should be given..." Grassl and Heath, *The Magic Triangle*, p90
"a range of barracks..." Catchpool, *Candles in the Darkness*, p169
"In these international work camps..." Ibid, p167
"the flags of many nations..." Grassl and Heath, *The Magic Triangle*, p109
"One after another representatives..." Ibid, p109
"your guide, showing you..."" Catchpool, *Candles in the Darkness*, p176
"probably the gayest scene..." Ibid, p177
"We felt we had seldom seen..." Ibid, p177
"turned a blind eye..." Grassl and Heath, *The Magic Triangle*, p110
"an unmistakeable atmosphere..." Ibid, p110

"brought to youth hostel workers..." Ibid, p110

"He had links..." Ibid p.75

"He was doing what to many people..." Harris, *Friends Quarterly*, July 1971

"You have always been..." Catchpool, *Candles in the Darkness*, p175

"hostel running has risen..." *National Minutes 1949-1950*, National Council 1949

"we were really amazed..." *The Rucksack*, Autumn 1946, p20

-18-

Family life

I was a privileged father. I spent more time with my daughters when they were growing up than most fathers could. I shared their growing up. I was nearby when they woke and at their bedtime. I took them to playgroups, fetched them from school. They could share a kiss at bedtime or eat breakfast while we were working. I was there to forget them more often than I should have.

Youth hostels were fine places to bring up children. Our daughters grew up in a big gracious home. Their bedroom was large. They had plenty of space and a big garden outside the kitchen door where they and their friends could play. Caroline and I were never far away. They played in the dining room when no guests were there. They came along when we cleaned rooms. One or another sat on a tall stool beside me at reception while I signed in guests. They learned how to set tables with cutlery, crockery and condiments. They took part in everything. They did their homework in the hostel office and watched television in the dining room. When Caroline went shopping for hostel food Anna went too on the back of Caroline's tricycle, clutching her favourite toy elephant.

Anna rode her little bicycle round the kitchen while we prepared meals. She played in an up turned laundry basket. An enormous, catering size cardboard box that once held cornflakes, empty and on its side, became a play house for her. Fiona grew up with the shelves of a sweet shop just out of reach and knew that, if she was careful, the reward of a sweet was always there.

If we chose our times with care, the youth hostel was perfect for parties and games. The girls and their friends could have the hostel to themselves and mothers could collect their children before anyone arrived for the night. A big rambling house cannot be beaten for hide and seek. In winter when the hostel was quiet the two of them made dens from bunkbeds, mattresses and blankets in empty bedrooms. In summer they took part in games with school children. They listened to a brass band from Germany rehearse on the lawn in front of the hostel.

They never went without company. When their father was busy, out of sorts or in a huff, they could find a member of staff wiling to talk and play. For those assistants who loved children, two little girls were a welcome distraction. Assistants became friends, came to school concerts and applauded their success.

I like to think our daughters have a sociability, friendliness and an interest in the world that comes from growing up in a house full of staff and strangers. Families and their children staying for a night became friends. They filled our daughters' lives with transient friendships. Cards or small gifts from distant towns in Britain, France or Germany arrived in the post.

Growing up in a hostel brought benefits. Fuel, heat and light came with the job. We never went cold. Food was plentiful. The girls helped themselves to fruit juice from the fridge. Eggs sat in trays in the pantry, milk came in five litre packs and cornflakes in six kg boxes. Everything was large. Even the vacuum cleaners were big.

But life in a hostel could be isolated and strange. Their friends did not understand how they came to live in such a large house, how so many people stayed at once in their home. Their teachers puzzled over the people who shared their house, who cleaned rooms and worked in the kitchen with their mother. We had no front door of our own. We lacked privacy in that rambling home. On their way to school in the morning they struggled through boisterous crowds of older children to get down the stairs.

The kitchen below their bedroom was noisy and hot. On long summer evenings in overheated beds they roasted, tired, fractious and sweating. Loud groups woke them late at night and they woke in the mornings to the rush of feet down corridors and stairs, to the roar of hairdryers, to the rush of water in showers and toilets and the scent of shampoo and deodorant.

Pay was low. We depended on the government's family allowance for shoes for the children. We began to want more privacy. The union demanded better pay and accommodation for staff that was apart from the hostel. Accommodation with its own front door, insulated from noise began to seem like paradise. We dreamed of no more noise, no more disturbance and a home with its own front door. Since youth hostels had first employed staff, accommodation was included as part of the job. Rooms, free fuel, heat, light and food kept down cash pay and made staff cheaper to employ. In a big house with plenty of space, arrangements like that must have made sense.

In the 1980s life began changing as Margaret Thatcher's revolution bit down. Colchester was entering boom times as people bought and sold their council houses, as privatisation swept its way through Britain.

The girls grew older. They wanted space, freedom and a family life unshared with others and without noisy interruptions. We worried when they disappeared in the hostel or its garden. We watched older wardens approach retirement with no home once they finished work. Everyone relied on a council house. They put their names on housing lists as retirement approached. But council housing was being sold.

When business in the hostel was slack, when a roof repair loomed, we worried that if the hostel closed we would lose not just our jobs and wages but our home and the roof above our heads.

-19-

The motor car rules

Ursula Bailes had come across hitch-hikers before. They came from Canada, Australia or New Zealand and from the other countries of the British Commonwealth. Having come so far from their homes they had to see the whole of the British Isles in a week or two with little money. They did it by staying in youth hostels and hitch-hiking, getting lifts from place to place, in cars or trucks.

But in Avignon in France in 1953 Bailes came across a different kind of hitch-hiker. They covered the ground with "a night at Avignon, a day on the beach at Nice, and on to the Italian frontier." They travelled in "beautiful cars… or sometimes a lorry, or even the back of motor-bike." One "with a week's growth of beard in a fringe from ear to ear… looked a first rate brigand." A young English-woman appeared in the common room wearing long ear rings and nibbling grapes. She might have emerged straight from an upper class English drawing room. A petite blonde was "clad in very little besides brief linen shorts and a red hankie round her head..."

Bailes supposed it was an 'adventure'. By her tone she did not approve of their dress, their habits or their appearance in youth hostels. She preferred to go as far as her purse allowed. Then she explored the region under her own steam "in the best tradition of British youth hosteling". Under your own steam meant walking or cycling. Canoeing was acceptable but horse riding was frowned on as being not quite travel under your own steam. Horses required stables, food and equipment and took youth hostels too close to the inns they were never meant to be.

Hitching was not acceptable. Hitch-hikers travelled some of their time under someone else's steam and they didn't pay for that steam. Others also abused the purpose of youth hostels. Suitcase hostellers, people who carried suitcases and toured from hostel to hostel, were as bad. They travelled as quickly as they could from one hostel to another. YHA's democratic principles stressed independence and self help. Some thought that youth hostels should only offer self catering because self sufficiency was part of the true spirit of youth hostels.

Members ran youth hostels. They elected regional councils to run regional groups. Regional councils in turn sent representatives to a national council held each year in April. National council elected national officers and with regional councils elected the members of national committees. Through this representative democracy, members determined rules and policies and set prices for youth hostels.

Members maintained and sometimes built youth hostels. They cleaned them after a night's stay. Youth hostels were as good as the members made them. And those with the true spirit worked for youth hostels and loved the countryside. They were keen, as the object stated, to learn about and understand the countryside better. They visited it whenever they could. Those like hitch-hikers, without the true spirit, were a threat. They used and abused youth hostels, thoughtlessly. Some members feared youth hostels without the spirit would become cheap hotels, nothing but a chain of cheap doss-houses. Boarding houses could be dirty, overcrowded places.

Members looked to the rules to preserve the right spirit in youth hostels. When youth hostels began that hadn't been the purpose of rules. At the beginning when youth hostels were a radically new style of accommodation, they needed rules to reassure and console. Invited to become president, GM Trevelyan had doubted the wisdom of mixing sexes in youth hostels. Bringing young men and women together, unchaperoned, to sleep in the same building had seemed in 1930 a dangerous and immoral thing to do. Jack Catchpool had responded to Trevelyan's concern with his usual clarity and practicality. Young men and women would tramp together whether Trevelyan wanted them to or not. If suitable accommodation wasn't available, they would sleep in haystacks.

Youth hostels were not universally welcomed when they began. Landowners, estate managers and game keepers saw the countryside as their exclusive domain. Wordsworth had thought countryside recreation was a privilege, for those with an eye to perceive and a heart to enjoy natural beauty. Philosopher and writer CEM Joad feared townspeople invading the countryside. He described "hordes of hikers cackling insanely in the woods, or singing raucous songs as they walk arm in arm at midnight down the quiet village street. There are people, wherever there is water, upon sea shores or upon river banks, lying in every attitude of undressed and inelegant squalor, grilling themselves, for all the world as if they were steaks, in the sun. There are tents in meadows and girls in pyjamas dancing beside them to the strains of the gramophone, while stinking disorderly dumps of tins, bags, and cartons bear witness to the tide of invasion for weeks after it has ebbed; there are fat girls in shorts, youths in gaudy ties and plus-fours, and a roadhouse round every corner and a café on top of every hill…"

Walkers could be unwelcome invaders of the countryside. "On cool summer evenings all-night hikes by parties of fifty or more strong shattered the peace of early Sunday mornings in the Peak District, for instance. These night walkers, who hibernated by day, insisted on singing at the top of their voices as they made casual progress along metalled roads and well-marked tracks, dropping litter in all directions… Country folk were rightly annoyed and disturbed: dogs barked incessantly and constables on bicycles were summoned to deal with the noisy weekend interlopers from the sleeping cities of the Midlands and North. Parts of the Lake District and Derbyshire were by no means pleasant places on summer weekends…"

Catchpool had seen the dangers. "The new Association had its enemies and even well wishers were sceptical. Sabbatarians thought young people should be in church on Sundays, not encouraged to spend weekends in the country. Farmers were horrified at the idea of ignorant townsmen invading their fields, leaving gates open, disturbing stock. Hotel keepers feared we would take their clients and wiseacres predicted grave scandals if boys and girls were to sleep in the same hostels."

Catchpool and Tevelyan reassured critics youth hostels would be properly regulated. Regulations appeared for the first time in the 1934 handbook; quiet in the dormitories after 10pm, sleeping accommodation separate for boys and girls. Rules stipulated meal times. Members had to report at once to the warden on arrival at a hostel. On departure they were expected to shake and fold blankets and sweep and tidy rooms. Youth hostels closed their doors from 10am to 5pm.. The rules guided conduct such as cleaning cooking utensils, reporting breakages and not using naked lights in dormitories. Rules allowed no dogs and limited when meals could be cooked.

Rules banned intoxicating liquors. German youth hostels stressed abstinence but complete abstinence never became a part of the spirit of youth hostels in England. People smoked in British youth hostels, avidly at times. Youth hostels sold cigarettes until a policy change banned that in 1962. Smoking in dining rooms during meals wasn't stopped until 1967. A complete ban on smoking in youth hostel common rooms waited until legislation demanded it. But alcohol was banned from the outset.

Rules had various uses. They fostered a new morality of social mixing. They mediated between people of different backgrounds and cultures, from different countries. They established a common code of behaviour and expectation when people staying in youth hostels didn't know each other and came from different social classes and different countries. Youth hostels promoted all faiths. Policy required they display the times of local services for all churches and faiths on notice boards. Many also displayed a metal sign at the front gate or by the front door, stating "this youth hostel is one of many, both in this country and abroad, where young people, regardless of race or creed, may spend the night."

Rules were a way of imposing policy on the 19 regional groups responsible for running youth hostels in the 1950s. They told a large and far flung organisation how to run its youth hostels creating consistent standards and approaches. By 1958 YHA National Chairman, Arthur Dower, considered "reasonable, flexible rules evenly administered integral to the smooth running of youth hostels."

Wardens guaranteed good conduct within youth hostels and rules gave them authority. They could fine or eject from youth hostels members who broke the rules. They could do so on the spot with complete immediate authority. They could keep members' cards and thus prevent future stays in youth hostels. A system of appeals within the regional groups tempered these powers but didn't prevent many wardens from becoming petty tyrants with their own made-up rules, called house rules.

Rules were not always popular. Some members looked at them with suspicion. One retorted he had no desire to go round "telling other people to shake their blankets and turn off the lights at 10.30 prompt." As early as 1948 some spoke against the moral fervour of rules. Opponents said they had no wish to join in the democracy of youth hostels. They had no reason to go out of their way to organise common-room evenings or to get involved in running the organisation.

For others rules were integral to what made a Youth Hostel. "A Youth Hostel is not a cheap hotel," Leo Meilink, president of the International Federation of Youth Hostels, pointed out in 1952. In his view a youth hostel represented "an ideal of world fellowship." Rules promoted and protected that fellowship. Others agreed with Meilink. Rules were "the elementary decencies... a true consideration for the rights of others... because the whole of the hostel scheme is bound up with the word 'community'."

The rule against touring by motor car summed up concerns about the appropriate use of youth hostels. The first meetings to set up youth hostels rejected the idea of restricting youth hostels to walkers and cyclists and insisted youth hostels would be open to anyone. Restricting youth hostels to those who walked or cycled waited until 1934 when it became a broad intention. The handbook of that year stated, as a fourth regulation, youth hostels were "intended for members when walking or cycling and are not open to motorists or motor-cyclists (unless they are using the hostel for the purpose of walking or cycling. In any case motor-cars and motor-cycles must not be garaged at a hostel.)"

The intention went through changes. By 1936 it had become rule six and the wording was more specific; "hostels are intended for the use of members when walking or cycling and not when motoring or motor-cycling. Motor-cars and motor-cycles must not be garaged or parked at a hostel."

Early members opposed the car for many reasons. In his radio address on behalf of youth hostels in 1931 GM Trevelyan was clear that a car had limited value. Not everyone could afford a private car. The car had "to stick to the road, and the roads are every year becoming more like the towns, owing to our failure to control building and advertising along the roadside." Trevelyan believed the internal combustion engine ruined most of what was good in English civilisation as England headed to become one great, unplanned suburb.

Trevelyan set a tone for youth hostels. The one true way to appreciate the countryside was by walking. "To be at one with nature you must leave the roads, and tramp across the fields and moors, and by hedgerows and lanes and bypaths..." For Trevelyan, motoring and "charabancing" stood in relation to walking and cycling as watching football did to playing football. It was "a poor substitute though better than nothing."

Walking was not an idle dream or a lackadaisical pursuit for Trevelyan. He considered solitary walking across country to be one of the three best things in life. He could walk 60 miles in a day. On their honeymoon, travelling by train to Cornwall, he abandoned his wife with their luggage saying he could not face a whole day without a little walk. He walked 40 miles before he joined his wife at their destination.

He walked to get out in the countryside, in fresh air, to lift his spirits and because walking was healthy. He boasted that he had two doctors; his right leg and his left leg. He walked for company, for hardship, for the simplicity of it and perhaps because walking kept bouts of depression away. He walked from Cambridge to Marble Arch, a distance of about 55 miles, with his friend Geoffrey Winthrop Young in twelve and three quarter hours.

Cars were destroying the countryside. Ribbon development was eating its way out of towns. Petrol filling stations were so ugly competitions were held to design attractive and fitting types of building. Roadside signs proliferated in another sign of the disruption motor cars brought. In 1950 one farmer continued to see car users as destructive. "By far the greater amount of week-end damage to crops is done by picnicking motorists. Walkers, either singly or in herds, usually go from place to place harmlessly enough, but motorists, having parked their cars (sometimes having driven through a gate on to a field in the process) and eaten their meal, look around for something else to do in the vicinity of their car." Youth hostel members were not like that. The farmer praised them and singled out their approach. They had "an admirable country code... I must say I have never had the slightest problem from people such as these."

Cars at youth hostels offended justice and fairness. Car owners could arrive quickly at youth hostels and get beds before slower walkers arrived. If motorists filled a youth hostel, a walker arriving late might find herself with nowhere to sleep. The motorist could move on to a nearby less busy youth hostel or at a push could sleep in the car. A walker would have to sleep under a bush, in a ditch or find somewhere more expensive to stay.

Motorists as a minority with a luxury hobby had been just about tolerable to walkers and cyclists. But as manufacturers started to make small, lightweight and cheaper vehicles for a wider market the number of vehicles rose. Driving licences issued to London addresses rose from 100,000 in 1920 to 261,000 in 1930 and after the war car ownership rose further.

The rule against motorists was vague. It did not and could not ban members from owning cars. It banned members from touring by car and travelling from one youth hostel to another. Owners could use their cars to get to an area but they could not travel from hostel to hostel using them. They had to garage their cars whilst they toured under their own steam. Enforcing the rule was difficult. Car users hid their cars and walked the remaining distance to the youth hostel. Over zealous wardens searched the hedgerows for hidden cars and neighbours complained about thoughtlessly parked cars blocking lanes and villages.

The national council of 1954 tried to make a ban on cars part of the constitution but failed. A motion at the same meeting, to allow motorists to stay at hostels, was also defeated.

Abhorrence of cars as an article of faith had a hypocritical strain about it. Plenty of people owned cars and needed cars to get to youth hostels. Work parties used them for shifting tools and equipment. Cars were essential for keeping youth hostels supplied with food, fuel and equipment. The Merseyside pioneers hunted by car for properties in Wales to open as youth hostels. Jack Catchpool travelled widely in his baby Austin. He travelled around France in search of youth hostels with a French colleague.

The rule twisted YHA in contradictions. In 1957 national council recognised that youth hostels were open to hitch-hikers and that hostels shouldn't actively discourage hitch-hiking. Later that year, a warden withdrew membership from some members because they were hitch-hiking. The following year's national council contradicted itself, supported his action and decided regional groups should keep the cards of anyone using motorised transport.

Regional groups struggling to finance themselves looked for ways of getting more people to stay in their hostels. But national council threw out a proposal that would have allowed members using motorised transport to stay at hostels when they would not normally be full. The members of national council voted by 72 to 19 against the motion. Even if hostels were empty national council would rather not have motorists staying in them.

In 1956 Dower acknowledged conflicting opinions about youth hostels. At that year's annual council meeting, he set out his thoughts about the YHA he wanted. It was one where voluntary work and enthusiasm were central, paying good wages with good conditions and a just approach to all employees, with well maintained buildings and grounds.

Dower maintained the association should be an organisation of good countrymen who knew the countryside and its lore well. It should be a good neighbour for others working in the countryside and for young people. At national council the following year he added that youth hostels were simple countryside accommodation at reasonable costs for those travelling under their own steam and with adventure as the call.

Len Clark followed Dower as national chairman in 1959. He had worked his way up through the London Region, having stayed at his first youth hostel at Holmbury St Mary before the war. After that first visit he had started a local group in London. Clark came from a modest background. Before the war he worked as a clerk in the London County Council and his father had been a shop assistant. Throughout the war, as a conscientious objector in a non-combatant role in the army, he continued staying in youth hostels whenever he could. He started a local group in Hereford where he was based for a time. Involved in developing youth hostels in Wales and then back in London, from 1951-59 he served as national treasurer for YHA.

In his first address as chairman in 1960, he rejected two views of YHA. It was not a religious sect. Neither would it become a public service, within or outside the education system. He believed YHA was a great club with a small group of enthusiasts at its centre. These enthusiasts were people for whom the association had come to mean much in their lives. The much larger number of other members were less involved and might only use youth hostels once a year for a holiday. For Clark the club sprang "from a love of the countryside, comradeship, tolerance and adventure."

When a member proposed a ballot of all members about the rule prohibiting cars national council refused. An organisation, proud of its democracy, refused to give all members a say on the matter and insisted on the right of elected representatives to make decisions.

In November 1959 Jack Catchpool entered the debate from his retirement. He saw rules holding youth hostels back. He sensed exclusivity staining an organisation that had prided itself on an ethos of public service. YHA was becoming a select club for a chosen few. He wrote in *The Rucksack*, "Committees hold different opinions. One group feels that YHA is so good and precious that they want to keep it for themselves and the select few whom they regard as worthy of what YHA has to offer. But there are others who believe YHA is so good that they want to share it with all... If the YHA is left in the hands of the first group, there is, I believe, no long future for our Association – and the YHA will fade away. But the YHA is meant for all as stated in the objects of our Association... We are weighed down with too many regulations... let us away with many of our restrictions."

His article caused an outcry. Youth Hostels provide "something intangible – an atmosphere that makes all genuine hostels more than a building." If motorists were admitted something that had grown with YHA would be lost. It would take the heart out of the whole movement. Others supported Catchpool, who responded to the outcry he had prompted "many young people are bitter against the thoughtlessness and bigotry that excludes them from our hostels."

Argument and division continued until national council met at Ambleside in April 1962. The meeting that year ran out of time to discuss a motion altering the wording of the rule on car use. The motion aimed to replace the complex and misunderstood rule with a simpler and more easily administered one. The matter was left to the national executive committee for their decision. The national executive found the subject "not easy" and after long discussion the majority favoured removing the rule. They proposed placing an explanation of YHA's attitude to the use of cars elsewhere in the annual handbook and not amongst the rules.

When news of their decision leaked out, an uproar surfaced in *The Rucksack*. Removing rule one would bring about the complete disintegration of YHA. Writers defended 'our present way of life'. Motorists "are a race apart from genuine hostellers and do not hold the countryside in the same respect as the latter." "To abolish Rule One completely is to destroy the original aims of the movement at one fell swoop, a blow from which the Association would never recover." "To know 'this amazing England' a man must travel it slowly and keep his intimate touch with its age and loveliness."

A movement rose to call an extraordinary national council meeting to rescind the decision. A petition to summon an extraordinary meeting needed 50 supporters and before the end of August 48 had already signed it. With every prospect of two more at least, Clark decided to save the expense of a special meeting. He put the withdrawal of rule one on hold until the following year's national council which defeated the proposal.

National council remained steadfastly against admitting motorists throughout the 60s. Motions proposing experimental change were lost by large majorities. The rule remained in place until members forced change by their sheer numbers. Members arriving at youth hostels by car parked them nearby, blocking surrounding roads and disrupting villages and small towns. Stratford-on-Avon reported particular problems. National council carried a 1968 motion by 69 votes to 30 to allow car parking at youth hostels where there was no alternative. Council had finally accepted the parking of cars at youth hostels because they had no other choice. Motor car use overwhelmed the principle against them.

Walter Martin, who had followed Len Clark as chairman, by 1969 detected "the whiff of progress was growing strong in the Association's nostrils and the delegates were showing maturity with YHA on the verge of a great leap forward." The 1973 handbook simply stated that youth hostels would no longer exclude anyone by reason of their mode of transport, exactly as Jack Catchpool had wanted more than ten years before. The decision was too late for him. He had died in 1971.

By the 1950s youth hostels had faced down the suspicions and fears of farmers and landowners. They had gained the trust of parents, of teachers and priests. That they had achieved respectability so quickly had been astonishing, exceeding the hopes of men like Catchpool and Barclay Baron. Youth hostels became respectable more quickly than he had dared hope, Catchpool later observed.

Rules had played their part in creating a modest, respectable atmosphere for youth hostels. But those rules gave youth hostels a moral tone. They encouraged a prissy, authoritarian environment increasingly out of sorts with the rest of society. Youth hostels had been at the forefront of liberating young people in the 1930s, freely mixing the sexes and encouraging travel and freedom. By the 1950s YHA enthusiasts at the heart of what was now a club no longer cared. They were very satisfied with things as they were. They pushed youth hostels against the lives of young people and their fashions with which they had once been so closely linked.

Rules gave authority to wardens. They allowed petty interpretations. They allowed wardens to exclude those they thought unsuitable to be members. Perhaps more damagingly, the rules gave wardens the potential to become severe, arbitrary figures of authority, the most disliked aspect of youth hostels.

Youth hostels had defied their radical origins. They had passed from being radical and offering an outstandingly different style of accommodation. They had become safe, conservative and backward looking. They had turned their backs on being the education movement Catchpool had foreseen in 1930. They had established a reputation for being old fashioned and conservative, for being all about rules. They had shown how slowly they could change. For more than ten years they had resisted change. They had dug their heels in at every turn until eventually they could no longer resist and they were forced to surrender to change.

Banning cars and rules created a sense of exclusion, as Jack Catchpool had feared. Youth hostels came to look like and to act as clubs which only welcomed the right kind of person. The rules became a test of membership. Those who would not accept them, who insisted upon their use of the car, failed the test and excluded themselves. The debate about cars is what many people remember most about youth hostels, their defining reputation.

Of far greater consequence for the image of youth hostels, reluctance to accept cars set youth hostels against youth. The debate about cars hid other problems for youth hostels as a generation familiar with national service grew up and moved on. Young people came into youth hostels unfamiliar with rules and regulations and the sharing of barrack life. Rules to them were a moral clampdown and a restriction. Spartan conditions were less and less familiar, less and less redolent of a carefree happy time. "As well as enjoying what the economic experts describe as more 'spending power,' the present day youngsters are accustomed to a higher standard of living provided by both their parents and by the education authorities. A hostel which compared favourably with the local school in the 1930s will seem poverty-stricken to the youngster attending schools built in the 1950s."

Young people took to using scooters and motor bikes. Ursula Bailes, when she met hitch-hikers at Arles and Avignon, was seeing a new generation of travellers. The youth hostels where she stayed were busy with young Germans traveling by scooter. She went as far as trying to hitch a lift herself, but she was impatient. After a three hour wait she gave up, went back and drank coffee before catching a coach.

The world was opening more quickly than Bailes expected. Whether she wanted it or not, what she considered the best tradition of youth hostels, of travelling under your own steam, was loosening its grip. Those who opposed the car in 1960 were not ahead of their times.

People were hurrying more and more, travelling further and faster than ever before. Youth hostels were opening the world for the young people Bailes had seen, for the unshaven young man who looked like a brigand, for the young woman with long ear rings, nibbling grapes, and for the petite blonde clad in very little besides brief linen shorts. They were the coming generation and youth hostels would open the world for them, just as they had for the previous generation. Youth hostels were opening the world for young people whether Ursula Bailes wanted them to or not.

Notes and references

Many sources contributed to this chapter. Len Clark pointed me towards the central events of the debate about cars. I have more sympathy with those who opposed the car than this chapter might show. I don't own a car. I agree with Trevelyan that the car has ruined much of what was beautiful in English life. But those who opposed the car in 1960 were not leading a debate about the use of the car in society and the damage it was causing to us all. They were an orthodoxy, against change.

"a night at Avignon..." *The Rucksack*, Nov-Dec 1953, p12

"hordes of hikers..." Williams-Ellis, B*ritain and the Beast*, p72

"On cool summer evenings..." Cox, *The Hike Book*, p14

"The new Association..." Catchpool, *Candles in the Darkness*, p138

"reasonable, flexible rules..." *National Minutes 1958*, National Council

"telling other people ..." *London Regional News Vol 3*, June 1948, p2

"A Youth Hostel is not..." Grassl and Heath, *The Magic Triangle*, p138

"stick to the road..." *Address by Prof. G.M.Trevelyan*, 21 January, 1931

"To be at one with nature..." ibid

"By far the greater..." *The Youth Hosteller*, Nov–Dec 1950

"Committees hold different opinions..." *The Youth Hosteller*, Nov-Dec 1960

"the whiff of progress..." *YHA National Minutes 1969*, National Council

"As well as enjoying..." *YHA Annual Report 1958*

.

-20-

Make do and mend

Only the seasons varied. In winter we dawdled, deep-cleaned and decorated. The hours were slow and we relaxed. We had time to stop and stare, time to tackle jobs long delayed, time to dream and plan, time for friends and family time.

Summer holidays were unusual for us. Only those who worked at hostels with lots of staff managed holidays during the summer which everyone called 'the season'. The rest of us took our breaks when we could and never in the summer. Some youth hostels closed for the wardens' holiday. Others drafted volunteers, friends or relations to care for the hostel while they took a break. Seasonal staff took pay instead of a holiday when work finished at the end of summer.

Autumn brought a change of pace but first we took stock. We counted every knife, every fork and spoon, every blanket, every pillow, every table and chair, every bit of equipment the hostel held. We completed a requisition, to bring the number of each item back to where it had been at the start of the year. When I wanted a bucket, so I could clean windows without using a saucepan to carry water, the chairman of the committee responsible for buying equipment told me I couldn't have one. The hostel had never had a bucket. If my predecessor had managed without one for 20 years, I should too.

The approach was called make do and mend. It was a hang over from the second world war when shortages had caused such problems. People had learned to do without and to mend whatever broke. In youth hostels it survived long after the war ended, almost a religion even in the 1970s.

Pride had encrusted it, leading to a self sufficiency that was endemic. Volunteers and wardens did everything in many regions. Professional builders or maintenance couldn't be afforded. One warden was reputed to have used old bicycle tires for nosing on the stairs of his hostel. Jobs were left undone for want of money. At Keld in North Yorkshire I saw a handbasin laid on the floor. The pipes, which had fed the taps above it, had been carefully sealed. New taps were wanted but no one could afford to buy them.

When beds sagged so much that they no longer supported sleeping bodies, boards replaced missing springs and bodies now slept on mattresses that once might have been four inches thick but were no longer and through which hard board pressed against bone.

Youth hostels didn't need signs, a joke went. If you looked for the most rundown building, in the most overgrown garden, usually in the most inconvenient location, on top of a hill or as far as possible from the railway station, that's where you would find a youth hostel.

Youth hostels were everywhere in tumble down buildings, in old mills, in old manor houses and old vicarages. Some were neglected beyond belief, with overgrown gardens and paint peeling from windows and doors. Some were new and well maintained and some regions were prosperous, with plenty of money. But more needed attention, needed cleaning and decorating. Some liked it, like a pair of shapeless slippers worn too long. Others did not. The number of those content with make do and mend slipped and declined.

Habit and routine are narcotics. Tradition blinds. But they could not disguise the fact. Youth hostels were becoming horribly out of date. The world was changing. People were becoming used to paying for what they wanted. They were becoming used to comfort. More and more people owned their own cars. They had the freedom to come and go. They spent summer holidays in Spain. At home they had indoor toilets and plumbing. Fitted kitchens and carpeted floors were becoming common and those without aspired. By the end of the 1970s they aspired to the new and shiny, to shop on Sundays and to do away with limits and restriction. A future without hot showers seemed less and less likely.

People were less and less keen to cram into crowded bedrooms with strangers, to share washrooms. When someone was paying to stay for the night, for a bed in a room with ten others, explaining she must be back 10.30 was becoming increasingly impossible. That there were only two showers for 30 or more young women at Colchester was becoming incomprehensible.

There were only two options. There only ever are. You accept the hand that fate has dealt, or you don't. Some accepted and others didn't. Those who accepted stayed. Those who didn't didn't.

As wardens and staff we accepted that youth hostels were like that, full of rules, old fashioned and out of date, or we pushed for change. A generation of wardens was arriving, less content with discomfort, less deferential and less tolerant of make do and mend. We were brash, unsympathetic and impatient. A gentle spirit of kindliness, epitomised by the best of the older wardens, was going.

We ignored the rules. We stayed open late. We let non-members stay. We gave couples and families rooms for themselves. We broke the rules, hoped no one noticed and prayed for better days. Sometimes it seemed the days were only getting worse.

Worst was when a young mother, who had been upstairs to check the rooms and bathrooms, looked me in the eye and told me that she could see our standards were not the same as hers.

Best was when we found our way to make people happy. Best was when the days were smooth, when the routine ended, when the list of jobs to do had all been ticked. Best was when the sun shone when we settled back with cups of coffee in the back garden, under the apple tree, and reflected on a job that could be the best in the world. Best was when people enjoying travel had surrounded us, people who had enjoyed every moment of their time under the roof of our youth hostel and who had left as friends.

PART 3

A MODERN SPIRIT

Democracy

Youth hostel president GM Trevelyan saw youth hostels in the best tradition of self government. Standing down as president in 1950, he declared that youth hostels and their spirit represented the best British tradition of debate and co-operation. The democracy of youth hostels had brought about phenomenal growth and had opened more places for young people to travel than anyone might have dreamed. Ten years later the system Trevelyan admired so much was struggling.

John Parfitt, an upstart member from London, showed those responsible for running youth hostels a different picture of their democracy. They were no longer the 'grass roots' by the early 60s. A tiny minority, only 1.5% of all members, involved themselves in committees and councils administering youth hostels. More, but still only 7% of all members, took part in running youth hostels, in work parties or as hostel visitors.

Throughout the 50s youth hostels had been stagnating. Numbers joining and staying in youth hostels had peaked in 1950. A record of around 300 youth hostels were open that year, a high point not reached again. Regions had watched the numbers coming to stay remain about the same with only London and the Lakeland group seeing increases. Too many members joined for a year, made their journey, stayed for a night or longer in a youth hostel and returned home. Once their holiday was over they let their membership lapse and never came back to hostels.

To reverse the slow decline, Parfitt encouraged his colleagues to break with the past. His was a strong voice. He stood against the traditionalists. He was in favour of hard headed business tactics. He challenged youth hostels to face the present and modernise. He had studied at the London School of Economics and taken an early interest in politics with the Labour party. For a time he was the youngest borough councillor in the country. But his interest in politics waned. His political views changed and he left politics. He took a greater and greater interest in youth hostels.

Youth hostels were political in a non party way. Parfitt made his way through the complexities of the organisation. He voted in committees. He took part in debate. He wrote an explanation of how YHA worked. For the novice, he set out how a small, lively democracy operated through local elected officials and a maze of committees, sub-committees and councils, making decisions in rooms where the air could be as thick as the argument. In one region after a meeting it was "necessary to sweep up the ash and the dogends before leaving." Starting as a volunteer in the London Regional Group, Parfitt rose quickly, making a name for himself as a bright and forthright young man. He joined the national executive committee in 1959, was its vice chairman in 1963 and six years later was elected as its chairman. He remained in that office for 12 years.

He came from a professional background. He was one of the new breed of social scientists with marketing skills and expertise. His work with surveys and consumer panels had a profound and long lasting influence on youth hostels. After university he began his career in the market research division of the giant Anglo Dutch soap and food company, Unilever. He started an 'ad hoc' research division in another market research company, Attwood Statistics, before becoming managing director of Mass Observation. Under his guidance the research organisation became a successful company once again.

He combined his passion for market research with his love of youth hostels. When passions exploded over the rule banning motorists from youth hostels, he persuaded the executive to commission a survey of youth hostel members. A survey would give them much greater understanding of members and their views. Through a survey, they would hear what members thought. A survey would reveal what members really believed. It would help the executive understand current problems like the rule banning motor vehicles at youth hostels.

The executive agreed. A questionnaire went by post to a selected sample of 2,492 members on 27 September 1962. Two reminders followed. The response rate was high. 92% of those who received the questionnaire returned it.

The survey showed that people were generally satisfied with youth hostels. Even those who had not renewed their membership were satisfied. They generally liked youth hostels and wanted them to carry on the same. Though they owned cars, few wanted the rule against cars abolished. They did want some change. They wanted youth hostels open later at night, instead of closing at 10pm. They wanted showers, hot water, better toilets and improved drying facilities. But they were not prepared to pay more. Hot water and better toilets were becoming standard in everyone's homes. Members expected the same in youth hostels.

Satisfaction among members was not surprising. Stepping into the debate about cars in 1959 Jack Catchpool had warned that this was so. They were "a walled-in-membership". A survey or referendum would not reveal the views of those who had never been members. Asking members about changing rules was, in his view, like asking a society of drunks to vote for shorter drinking hours. The answer, Catchpool observed, was a foregone conclusion.

The survey only went to members or those who had recently been members. It had shown that the majority of members thought school parties using youth hostels were a good thing. But they wanted a limit on the size of parties. No one asked the children or young people who used youth hostels as part of groups for their views, an irony for an organisation started by a school teacher for groups of school children in Germany. 15% of those who stayed at youth hostels in 1962 came from school and youth groups.

Neither did anyone seek the views of those from other countries arriving at youth hostels in increasing numbers. People from Germany, Australia, the Netherlands and more than 30 other nations stayed in youth hostels that year. They accounted for 22% of overnight stays. Surveys only went to members and never reached all of those who were staying in youth hostels.

Parfitt did want to understand why so many members joined for a year and then let their membership lapse. Between 1958 and 1961, 445,000 people had been members of YHA. Only 75,000 of them were still members in 1962. Parfitt concluded that the vast majority of members enjoyed youth hostels. They appreciated youth hostels but, in modern terms, youth hostels had become commodities. Most people came to youth hostels, enjoyed them and moved on. They had no particular reason why they did not stay again. They had used a youth hostel, or two or three, and then they moved on to other things. Most were not loyal or committed in any way to youth hostels.

The finding ran against everything that youth hostels stood for. Herbert Gatliff had vowed in 1934 "We do not want the YHA to be run by some people for others; we want it to be a true democracy run by all its members for all its members. We want its committees to consist largely of members who are themselves constantly using hostels – so long as in the hostels they are hostellers and not committee members. Above all we want every committee to have a large proportion of young members."

Members were happy. They came and went. They left a small group of enthusiasts running youth hostels. The democratic approach of men like Gatliff had run out of steam. YHA was no longer run by all its members for all its members. Volunteers reported falling attendances at regional AGMs. In 1946 the burden of administration had "grown too great for voluntary effort, and with the introduction of paid officers the cost has risen appreciably." One correspondent warned "unless the YHA member is prepared to play his part, the YHA will have to rely more and more on paid staff." By 1961 the situation was more threatening. There was an "increasing difficulty in finding members, willing to serve on committees or tackle other responsible jobs."

Members' ideals no longer provided youth hostels with everything they needed. Volunteers often did not have the necessary sound business acumen required. They kept failing youth hostels open too long. They subsidised uneconomic hostels that members had largely given up visiting. Sentimentality submerged the financial facts of life too often.

Running a youth hostel could show a small surplus. That soon disappeared through depreciation and increased maintenance costs. Little was left to repay money borrowed from the bank. Regions had problems maintaining the youth hostels they already had. As early as 1949, regions were unable to afford all the hostels they had. At Keld in North Yorkshire, the hostel had deteriorated to such an extent that at the end of September 1949 the regional group decided to close it until spring. The group hoped that by then essential repairs would be carried out. Keld had to wait until 1951 for repairs before it could reopen.

The cost of acquiring new hostels was also rising. The days of cheap and empty property had ended. A house or other building was reckoned to cost three times its pre-war price. Too many hostels were running at a loss. Too many regions were not popular enough to warrant the youth hostels they already had. The financial weakness of some regions was "a cumulative evil, few newer hostels and existing hostels in bad repair, fewer visitors and less funds for administration." Poorer regions drained money from successful ones.

As early as 1947 the people in charge of finances at a national level knew they had problems. They considered centralising the funds of all the regions so that they had enough money for all youth hostels. But the regional treasurers dismissed their idea. Regional treasurers, not surprisingly, thought centralisation would be a step too far. A loss of control would frustrate the regional groups and, despite financial difficulties, they feared the need for a decision from the centre might also hold up any new schemes. Regional groups still thought new youth hostels were more important than the ones they had. They still had their eye on new schemes and expansion.

In 1964 after two years of study, a report to national council proposed major changes to the regions. The distribution of youth hostels throughout England and Wales was far from ideal. It had not adjusted to changes in the ways members used youth hostels. Facilities had not kept pace with modern trends, as shown by the survey results on members' attitudes to showers and hot water. Rather than retaining an attractive and pleasant simplicity some youth hostels had become just dowdy. The report called for "the most fundamental changes in YHA's structure since the Association was founded".

National council debated the report on 11 and 12 April 1964, in Durham, agreeing most it. But change concentrated on the structures of the organisation, not its finances. The original 19 groups had become 18 in 1960 when the East Anglia and Cambridge regional groups amalgamated. Now 18 regional groups became ten provinces. The new 'provinces' would have a two year period for transition, while they agreed minor variations between themselves.

Some of the old regional groups amalgamated to form the new 'provinces'. The name never lasted. They called themselves regions instead. Some, like London, split to create new regions. And some continued with little change. Many of the same people took up roles in the new regions with similar committees, sub-committees and councils. Walter Martin continued as chairman of the executive. Half of the members of the executive in 1964 were still members three years later.

Merseyside continued to run youth hostels in North Wales region but without Tom Fairclough, their long-standing secretary. He had been the driving force in establishing the group, after his trip to Germany in 1929. He retired in 1965, after more than 35 years. The region would miss his patience and his ability to smooth out difficulties. Other regions would miss his willing advice based on his long and wide experience. His old friend Connie Alexander scoffed at the idea of his retirement. She had been to Germany with him on that first trip. She wrote in the pages of the youth hostel magazine he was simply handing over to a younger man, to carry on his life's work. His retirement came a year after the death of Barclay Baron, the first national chairman.

The report proposed national executive should have greater powers. But as with the attempt to centralise finances at the end of the 40s, regional groups refused to give way. They wanted to wait until experience showed that giving power to a central authority was necessary and practical. They postponed. It took until 1984 before they finally agreed. By then two regional groups were nearly bankrupt. National council was willing to continue with financial inequalities between the new provinces. Whilst geographically the new provinces were roughly equal and a rough equality of hostels was intended, they could not be financial equals. Members flocked to youth hostels in areas like the Lake District but fewer went to regions like East Anglia.

National council also agreed that every youth hostel should pay its normal running expenses. Each hostel should pay for maintaining the building and its equipment. But the decision was only an ideal. National council allowed some youth hostels should continue running at a loss because of their special responsibilities "to encourage a greater knowledge... of the countryside." They allowed similar excuses, for running uneconomic hostels, for years to come.

Youth hostels did improve financially. In 1962, more than half of all youth hostels had been losing money. More profitable youth hostels had covered the £24,000 those hostels lost. By 1967 the regions reduced the number making a loss. But their aim, for all youth hostels to finance themselves, remained out of reach. 117 youth hostels between them still lost £17,000 that year. Those losses again reduced the money available for improving youth hostels. Profitable youth hostels propped up uneconomic ones.

Youth hostels needed more than restructuring. The days when ex-service men, used to "years of huggermugger communal living in tents and huts with all and sundry thrown together," flocked to youth hostels were over. Members had shown in Parfitt's survey that they wanted hot water. They wanted better showers and toilets. They wanted youth hostels open later at night.

One correspondent wrote to the youth hostel magazine, now called *The Youth Hosteller*. He complained "there is nothing worse... than to find after a hard day's walking, hard and lumpy mattresses, ice cold water, nothing but oil with which to power [an] electric razor and then to be humiliated by being told that he cannot be trusted out after 10pm. The lack of facilities and outdated rule may be deterring people from joining or renewing."

Members who loved the spartan life, cold water and hard beds dismissed the complaint. "After a hard day's walking [who] wants to be out after 10pm," one retorted. Another added "It is only those who possess an inferiority complex or a big head who feel humiliated at having to be in by 10pm and the weak-skinned who cannot stand cold water on a proper razor." Writers to the magazine advised the original correspondent to resign his membership. He should stay at the Savoy or Claridges. At those hotels he could stay out all night, if he chose. A barber would shave him in the morning though it would cost more.

Others joined the debate. In 1964 Labour won at the polls. New prime minister, Harold Wilson, appointed Denis Howell, an MP from Birmingham, to his cabinet. Howell was a fortunate minister. During his time as the minister of sport in the Department of Education England won football's world cup. In 1976 he was appointed as minister for drought. Rain fell. The drought ended.

Howell was a friend of youth hostels. If he had money, he said, and had to give it to one organisation more than another, he would give it to youth hostels. Nothing gave him more pleasure "when driving around the countryside than to see so many of our young people, rucksack on shoulder, getting away from it all and into the countryside, and to know that when they reach a youth hostel they will find there a very real spirit of fellowship." He was also a minister who made decisions on funding to bodies like YHA.

In March 1966, in Keele, he told the members of national council that they were too modest. He was well aware that over 270 youth hostels recorded more than 1.5 million overnight stays. But "as good as those figures are, they are nothing like good enough." The minister, saw a new generation coming from the rising post-war birth rate. He called for youth hostels to prepare themselves. An increasing population of young people would have greater needs for leisure. National council immediately told their executive to consider the points Howell had raised and to come back the next year with a report on action taken.

In a political game of chairs, the executive passed the problem to John Parfitt. He led a special committee to plan for the future of youth hostels. The committee's report, completed in 1968, took a devastating view of the present. Reorganising had not been enough. Youth hostels themselves were ill prepared to meet the needs of a generation of baby-boomers.

The report stated that a large number of hostels were "scruffy and... ill equipped." Complacency, a lack of care and poor management meant many youth hostels never looked really clean. "A complete stranger entering some of our hostels might well be forgiven for believing that we are an organisation devoid of imagination and energy." "Common rooms often look as if they have been equipped exclusively by attending jumble sales in the last ten minutes before closing."

Youth hostels needed adequate lighting so people could read and see what they were doing without straining their eyes. Youth hostels needed fixed curtains in all rooms. Paint used wisely and decoratively would give hostels a clean, bright and attractive air. Hostels should be equipped for users who were welcome. They should stop giving an impression of catering for refugees in a crisis. Public rooms were bleak and unwelcoming. Hostels treated members as if they were unused to and could not be trusted with anything better.

The report tackled the myth that members joined youth hostels in pursuit of an abstract ideal of simplicity. Members did not join to help those of limited means enjoy the countryside. They joined because youth hostels had something to offer which they needed. They left when they no longer had that need. They stopped staying at youth hostels when youth hostels did not offer what they required.

"YHA is not a religion and cannot, therefore, expect its 'adherents' to make big sacrifices in its name. Shabby hostels, cold dormitories, undried clothes, off-hand wardens, unreasonable rules rudely asserted on glaring notices, etc; are not crosses to be borne... They are disadvantages at best to be tolerated, at worst to be avoided by trying some other leisure time activity." Discomfort in a hostel was not fun. Neither was it an end in itself. Discomfort was not simplicity.

Parfitt and the others who prepared the report recognised that a new generation was arriving in youth hostels. Young people born since the war had no collective memory of poverty. They had no respect for the causes of poverty. They considered the atmosphere of the 1930s in hostels was drab and not related to any concept of simple accommodation. The standard of facilities they expected had risen as living standards climbed. Young people were not used to a lack of restraint. They had money to make wider choices. Believing that facilities beyond those of the average hostel encouraged softness, attracted the wrong type of member or conflicted with the aim of youth hostels was false.

Voluntary democracy, whether restructured or not, created many of the problems. "A crowd of satisfied customers" running youth hostels were not likely to drive change. Voluntary management ineffectively controlled hostels. It delayed or protracted maintenance. Volunteers were often unable to choose good wardens. They failed to dispose of bad ones. Volunteers often solved problems by talking about them. They rarely bothered to follow through or record who was going to do what. They spent heavily on travel for long discussions on mundane and trivial matters. They made the mistake of never paying for anything they could do themselves "however slowly or badly."

Too few regions seemed to think it was important that 117 hostels were running at a loss. They thought it rather "indecent" to delve too far into hostel results. "Seeking higher profits (or smaller losses) is often thought of as a non-YHA activity, best reserved for commercial undertakings. Yet we are a commercial undertaking, even if we are also a charity and we have a responsibility to the membership to see that that their money is not wasted. If we had shareholders instead of easy-going members most of us would have been thrown out of office long ago for mis-use of the Company's capital! Only our unique position protects us from a take-over bid."

Parfitt and his four colleagues concluded that YHA should "pay for jobs that need doing if we don't have a competent volunteer to do it." Youth hostels needed expansion, a fresh spirit, new blood and strong finance.

Their proposal was simple and radical. YHA would improve facilities at youth hostels, then promote new youth hostels and finally tackle the uneconomic youth hostels, concentrating on a long term policy for the location of youth hostels. They proposed youth hostels with more and better toilets, hot water, baths and showers, laundry, winter heating and drying facilities.

They would abolish the single type of simple accommodation which youth hostels offered. Not all youth hostels would be equipped to a similar degree. They would be graded according to their facilities; simple for the genuine simple hostel, standard to cover the general run of hostel, and superior for the better equipped. A handful of 'special' hostels, never more than three or four, with all the facilities and longer opening times were also planned.

The report disposed of a single price for all youth hostels irrespective of their facilities. Youth hostels with better facilities would charge more. Regions would have an incentive to invest in youth hostels to increase their income. Members would know exactly what facilities each youth hostel offered. A new category of young members replaced the old juvenile membership category. The plan projected cutting 20 rules in the handbook, a mixture of the superfluous and unnecessary, to the reasonable and necessary.

Wardens were central to the success of the proposals. Wardens represented YHA. Geoff Smith, chairman of the South West region in the 1970s, said unequivocally "the warden is the hostel - the hostel is the warden." The plan recommended training, better pay and improved accommodation for staff.

The committee proposed reducing the 30 strong executive committee. Regions would no longer send two representatives to the committee. They would have fewer sub-committee meetings too. Finally they asked regions to look at themselves and to produce their own development plans. The availability of money would determine how quickly the plan was implemented.

National council debated and agreed the plan presented by John Parfitt on 6 and 7 April 1968. They recognised that the Policy Report, as it was called, aimed to improve the financial position of youth hostels. They saw the dangers of delay with so many youth hostels making losses. "Most of the Association's capital is in its hostels and equipment... If by some miracle all our loss-making hostels were sold tomorrow and the capital thus freed was invested in the right locations our financial problems would disappear overnight and many of [the] policy recommendations would be superfluous or easily achieved."

From 1971 youth hostels no longer offered one style of accommodation. Four grades of youth hostel charged four different sets of prices. Three special hostels opened, at Pen y Pass in Snowdonia and at Ambleside and Patterdale in the Lake District. The new youth hostel at Patterdale, purpose built in a Scandinavian style, replaced TA Leonard's old country house, Goldrill House. When Leonard retired from the Holiday Fellowship, friends and supporters had talked about presenting him with a portrait. Leonard had resented what he called an outrage and suggested buying a third of Snowdon and passing it to the National Trust would be better. When funds were raised the owner wouldn't sell land on Snowdon and instead they had bought the house in Patterdale, in 1932, as a gift. Leonard immediately loaned it and then sold it to YHA in 1945.

Two years after national council accepted his policy report John Parfitt stood for and was elected chairman of the national executive. He took the place of Walter Martin, who had been chairman since 1963.

Youth hostels entered a golden era. Regions invested in hostels, and closed others. Denis Howell's prediction came true. From 1968 to 1980, membership numbers soared, from 217,842 to 309,341. Even the pioneering years of the 1930s had not achieved such growth. Overnight stays shot up, by more than a quarter of a million, an increase of 52%.

Only the war years had exceeded that rate of growth. Visitors from overseas almost doubled as did those from school groups.

Youth hostels continued to spread, into Africa, Latin America and Asia. In Japan membership numbers increased at an annual average of 14%. Overnight stays rose by 20% between 1963 and 1970. International travel grew as Americans and Australians discovered youth hostels as a low cost way of travelling. Northern Europeans headed to the Mediterranean for sea and sun in greater numbers. Overcrowding brought problems. Surveys in Germany and the Netherlands showed very similar issues to those Parfitt had uncovered. Having released young people to greater freedom, increasing affluence among young people, a greater desire for increased freedom and more comfort now threatened youth hostels.

Youth hostels had broken with their past. Restructuring broke the link between cities and their hinterland of hostels. No longer would people band together, venturing into the countryside, to open and run youth hostels, as they had done from Liverpool, Manchester, London and other towns and cities. Those days were gone, as the price of property rose, planning laws grew and legal complexities multiplied.

Youth hostels had shifted from the grass roots organisation of the early years and reduced their ties with the old affiliate bodies. The Holiday Fellowship, the Headmasters and Headmistresses Association, the Ramblers, the CTC and many other national organisations had been instrumental in starting youth hostels. Their impetus had forced the first national meeting for youth hostels. As part of the restructuring of democracy they lost all specific representation on the national executive committee. Though they continued to be part of the youth hostels' national council, they turned up in smaller numbers. They took less and less part in youth hostel affairs.

The years of boom rewarded the work of John Parfitt. Rather than relying on the outmoded 'grass roots' way of doing things, with committees, councils and the executive telling themselves what needed fixing, Parfitt used his professional background in market research to explore and assess the thinking of YHA's members. He used the techniques of consumer research, of surveys, panels and focus groups, to develop hostels. He persuaded colleagues to look beyond their own views, to what members thought and wanted, to understand the problems and to fix them.

Under Parfitt's influence, youth hostels began a long march to modernising themselves. Due largely to his initiative, major changes in the structure and policies of youth hostels came about. He equipped the association to better administer youth hostels, to benefit young people and to provide facilities at a level and price they needed and could afford.

Youth hostels opened their doors to a new group of young people who were beginning to flex their freedom in greater and greater numbers. Before the advent of *Rough Guides* or the internet youth hostel handbooks gave them ready made itineraries. Handbooks told them of places where accommodation awaited them. They could travel safely knowing where they could afford to stay.

In May 1971, Which, the consumer organisation, studied youth hostels in the UK. Their report concluded that, apart from camping or renting a caravan, youth hostels were the only available accommodation for young people. A night in a youth hostel for an adult cost from 30p to 60p a night. Bed and breakfast accommodation was difficult to find for less than £1.25 a night and, it seemed, prices were often inflated when young, long-haired walkers tried to stay.

At a youth hostel young or long haired walkers were welcome. They were not "made to feel poor." Young people no longer had to sneak into hotels, feeling that they were unwelcome, paying inflated prices, as JB Priestley had found in 1930. They now had places where they were welcome, places where they could stay in comfort. Youth hostels had changed the world of travel for everyone, and especially for young people. Now they had to face the consequences of that change.

Notes and references

The *YHA National Membership Survey* of March 1963 and *The National Policy Report* were prime documents for this chapter. The membership survey was the first of a series YHA commissioned through John Parfitt on the views of its membership. Parfitt conducted similar surveys at regular intervals and carried out research for the international federation. His surveys were a model for YHA into the 90s. The National Policy report outlined in detail and at length the rationale for the first sweeping changes to youth hostels since they began in 1930. Geoff Smith's recollections of youth hostels in the period of this chapter were invaluable for background.

"necessary to sweep up…" Smith, *Caveat Nostalgia*, p42

"We do not want…" Clark, *Herbert Gatliff, An English Eccentric*, p15

"grown too great…" *The Rucksack*, Midsummer 1946

"unless the YHA member…" *The Youth Hosteller*, Feb 1961

"a cumulative evil…" Coburn, *Youth Hostel Story*, p103

"the most fundamental changes…" *The Youth Hosteller*, May 1964

"huggermugger… in tents…" Smith, *Caveat Nostalgia*, p32

"there is nothing worse…" *The Youth Hosteller*, May 1963

"when driving around the countryside…" *YHA National Minutes* 1966 National Council

"scruffy and… ill equipped…" and following quotes, National Policy Report 1968

"the warden was the youth hostel…" Smith, *Caveat Nostalgia*, p39

"Most of the Association's capital…" YHA National Minutes, *1966*, National Council

"made to feel poor." *Which*, May 1971

22

The Union

I joined the union with my first pay packet. Coming from a country which outlawed trade unions, I believed in them and their power to create a better, more equal world. I was proud to join. It was a sign, like voting, I had come to live in a decent liberal country.

The concerns of others were less romantic. They joined because the union looked after us. It looked after pay and safety. It negotiated more holidays, shorter hours and better accommodation. We paid our dues and had decent pay and, if things went wrong, someone advised and represented us. It was as simple as that. It was also fun. Union members were our friends. We were isolated in our jobs. We worked alone or in couples and treasured the friendliness the union brought.

Meetings were long, full of quorums counted, votes moved and motions proposed. Older women members, often called wardens' wives in an offhandedly demeaning way, knitted in the front row. Members at the back read newspapers, did crossword puzzles and voted when called upon. Babies played among our feet and children played in the corridors. When the weather was good, they appeared at the window to wonder what the adults were doing inside.

We elected officers from among ourselves. We elected delegates who went to national meetings where they decided policies and voted for national officers. Those national officers were legendary figures. They came from among the older wardens. Years of negotiation and argument had bred in them distrust of the regional councils but a rough respect for the the individuals who ran the organisation. They had tales to tell of olden days when they were so poor they struggled to buy shoes for their children, when they worked through summers without a day off and without other staff.

Caroline had worked with Eric and Jean Booth at Hawkshead in the Lake District when Eric was the union's national chairman. He was a pacifist and had worked in forestry during the war. He had met Jean on the back of a tractor and after the war they came to run the lovely Georgian mansion overlooking Esthwaite Water near Hawkshead. They loved the house and their life there but they had learned the hard way they couldn't live on charity and a view from the kitchen window. They understood how much we gained from better pay and better conditions.

I paid my dues and went to meetings, drawn in. Gradually, by speaking up, you're marked down and drawn in. Barclay Baron, YHA's first chairman noticed it, when he said that eight long years as chairman was the price he paid for asking a question.

In the 1980s at Colchester I was secretary of the branch and then chairman. In a small committee we set agendas, ran meetings and relayed the views of our members to national committee meetings. I went to meetings in London or further. I left home early and came home late. As well as negotiating on behalf of members, the union's power worked in other ways. It was a force for professionalism, for higher standards, better facilities and more flexible hours. We were in touch with guests. We knew what guests wanted. We knew how out of date youth hostels were becoming.

We pushed and argued for change. We watched with dismay how the region's finances fell into disarray. Decent skilled people ran the region but voluntary democracy didn't suit a big property owning business nor an employer with hundreds of staff in its pay. Committees in long meetings to which people travelled after work were not a means of making wise decisions. Wardens and staff picked up the results of a lack of finance and sometimes inconsiderate employment practises.

We argued for change. We held meetings in out of the way locations. We met in a camper van in the car park at Stowmarket railway station. We plotted in parks. We endured long meetings. We debated for more or slower change, for less of this or more of that. We opened back channels with powerful national committees. We passed motions expressing our lack of confidence in the region's management.

We forced the pace of change. We pushed and pushed at the edifice of a weak and troubled organisation. They were exciting times, times when we were beginning to make a difference. Youth hostels could only change or else they would go under and after more than 50 years they would fail. It was as simple as that. We stood on a brink.

23

Professionals

Everyone had experienced wardens who were "rude, abrupt and discourteous... petty dictators in their little strongholds," the National Policy Report of 1968, concluded.

After the lack of hot water, showers and toilets, members criticised wardens the most. At their best wardens made youth hostels unique and attractive places to stay. At their worst they were inflexible in interpreting the rules. They drove guests away and left an abiding impression of rule ridden, poor accommodation. That impression became, for many, the undeserved reputation of youth hostels. Wardens made holidays memorable for the best and worst possible reasons.

Wardens were often the ones driving change in youth hostels. Geoff Smith declared "it was largely wardens as a body who led the campaign against the rule [bannning cars] because they were at the sharp end of impossible enforcement and it was their jobs at stake." In the late 1970s their demands for better pay and conditions drove further major change in youth hostels.

When Richard Schirrmann first dreamed of youth hostels, during a storm while his pupils slept, he expected that teachers would run youth hostels. They would do it for no pay. At the end of a day's teaching, the teacher would shift benches and tables to the walls. He would lay out mattresses and turn the school into a youth hostel.

Time and reality changed his idea. He struggled to get other teachers to follow his lead. Instead of using school rooms temporarily, youth hostels opened in adapted buildings. Some were designed and built as youth hostels. Instead of teachers, married couples ran youth hostels. Those early managers in Germany were called house-fathers and house-mothers. The name reminded children, lonely, away from home for the first time, that a youth hostel was a friendly, welcoming place. They made the youth hostel as close to home as a child could want.

Houseparents worked for little pay. They established a tradition that youth hostel staff worked out of dedication, not for money. They worked because of their interest in young people not for any commercial purpose. They kept down the costs of running youth hostels which, otherwise, might not have survived.

In Britain in the 1930s, youth hostels ran in a different way. Children were less expected to use youth hostels, so the need for a married couple, a substitute mother and father, was less. Youth hostels needed to reassure those who opposed the radical new style of accommodation. Young men and women slept in the same hostels and an emphasis on rules, good behaviour and a new morality grew up in British youth hostels. Youth hostels needed someone to supervise the building and enforce rules.

In Britain, houseparents took the name of warden. It's an old word, coming out of the French into Middle English as early 1200, with many layers of meaning. Not all of the meanings are close to the jailer the word might intend today. At the outset in youth hostels the word meant a keeper or one with care of a building. It's a respectable word, associated with colleges and educational settlements. Jack Catchpool was 'sub-warden' at Toynbee Hall. The title, established, endured until the 1990s when, along with many other changes, the term slipped away. Wardens came to be known as 'managers'.

At the outset, the work was largely administrative, light in nature. The job, in an easy going democracy, in line with an ethos of self service, was "not to wait upon members but to administer the hostel and to share out the housework among the members there." But light duties became more demanding. The tasks became more open ended. When more people wanted to stay than could be accommodated, when there were meals to cook and serve, and food to order, when people wanted bookings made or just to talk, when demands from regional and national offices had to be met, when problems arose with the drains or a roof leaked, the warden met all those and more.

An early warden recalled how hard it was to remain patient. "I remember one poor lad who called after a particularly wearing day asking for change for a Postal Order. The interruption found me in the act of preparing a joint for the oven and I confronted him knife in hand. 'No' I roared, and possibly flourished the carving knife. He ran for it and was gone before I realised that this was the most reasonable request I had had that day."

Connie Alexander was the first warden. She set up the first youth hostel in time for Christmas 1930 at Pennant Hall in Wales. She cooked the first meal using a cookery book hastily bought the day before. When Idwal Cottage youth hostel opened in 1931 she became the warden where she remained until 1940 when she married. Wardens formed a community of their own, recognising kindred spirits. Bertha Gough was grateful to have Connie Alexander with her whenever they went on youth hostel trips. She helped with getting privileges from the wardens.

On 5 May 1932, MLJ Cozens and his wife, the first wardens of the youth hostel at Street, signed a contract with SD Dalston of the Gloucester and Somerset Regional Group. The agreement they signed was three pages long. Its simple requirements were closer to that of an employer with a servant. Either side could terminate the appointment on the "usual quarter days by giving three months notice." Tenancies began and ended, servants were hired and rents and other charges became due on quarter days. Their significance has faded since the 1930s, though Lady Day is still the start of the British tax year.

The committee supplied Mr and Mrs Cozens with furniture, one bedroom, one sitting-room and a kitchen with pantry. The accommodation was free of rent, rates or taxes. They could cultivate part of the garden for their own use. They could supply "at reasonable prices such meals and stores as Youth Hostels Association members required." They could also supply teas and other refreshments, under arrangements approved by the regional group.

In return they would keep the hostel clean and in good order. They should see that the rules were kept and report to the committee any difficulties or breach of rules. They were responsible for collecting moneys, when members stayed, and for handing them to the secretary of the committee. They were expected to keep the hedges trimmed, to attend to the flower beds, to keep the garden, roadway and other outside property tidy and in good order. They were not allowed to cut trees or alter the garden and they had to make sure that there would always be a responsible person on the premises when the hostel was open.

The contract mentioned no wages. It's likely they kept the income and profit from meals, stores, teas and other refreshments as wages for themselves. The arrangement sometimes gave wardens a commercial interest in running youth hostels. They emphasised meals and downplayed self catering which set them at odds with members who came to stay.

Many early wardens were not employed, like the Cozens, but owned the youth hostels they ran. Courtney Rowe's parents owned and ran the youth hostel near Kuggar, on the Lizard Peninsular, in Cornwall. It was open from 1934. Shut during the war it reopened and ran until 1952. The Rowes were farmers and the youth hostel took its name from the sandy beaches at Kennack, half a mile away.

The hostel, one of the first in Cornwall, started in a barn divided in two. Women slept on one side and men on the other, on wooden bunks. "Two blankets were provided for each bed and each person had to either bring a sleeping bag or hire one for 6d (2.5p)." The "common room" was in a smaller adjacent building, with a rough wooden table, wooden benches and an oil stove. The bicycle shed was in another farm building. With no electricity, no mains water and no mains drainage, lighting, cooking and heating was by oil-lamps and oil-stoves. Men and women washed in bowls in a shed, carrying water from the nearby well. The toilet, in a small corrugated-iron privy, was a bucket under a seat.

The youth hostel closed in winter when Rowe's parents turned it back into a grain store. Once the grain was gone, the barn could be used again as a hostel for the summer. In 1937, the Rowes built a hostel they could keep open all year round. "Its ground floor was a single large common room, the scene of many jolly evenings; there was a small side-kitchen for those who wanted to do their own cooking." Two upstairs dormitories accommodated sixteen and, in summer, when the barn was emptied of grain, the hostel accommodated about 40 in total.

Each year, the numbers staying increased. Hikers or cyclists, carrying everything on their backs or on their bicycles or tandems, made their way across Goonhilly Downs towards Kuggar. "It was not unknown for unbooked persons to sleep on the hay in a farm building when the hostel was full. The new building had its own water well and flush toilets, though all water had to be pumped by hand as there was still no electricity in the village. Pumping water now became one of the regular jobs of the hostellers. A new wash-room was built for the ladies and the old common room… became the men's wash-room."

"Hostellers checked-in at the farmhouse on arrival, hiring sleeping bags if necessary, and leaving their membership cards which would be stamped with the name of the hostel before they left. Each was given a job-card which stated a task that had to be done during the evening or before departure the next day – brush dormitory, clean common room, wash dishes, carry water, etc; no job done – no membership card back. The maximum period of stay was three nights and travel by car was forbidden."

The routine of stamping slips of paper attached to membership cards for each night stayed began around 1939. Wardens at larger hostels may have wanted to record the number of nights a member had stayed, to stop members staying too long at one hostel. The stamps became enthusiastic collectors' items. Members proudly displayed their collection attached to their membership card. Some grew as thick as books. They were a source of pride for avid members spurring competition, conversation and even special visits to hostels to collect sought after stamps.

As well as stamping cards, wardens made meals. For farmers the income from meals supplemented their low income. "Fresh milk was very popular and was sold and drunk by the pint… My mother offered supper and breakfast at 1/- each (5p) and typically about thirty people would take advantage of this each day. Breakfast was two eggs accompanied by two rashers of bacon or two sausages, with plenty of home-made jam and marmalade and toast, and these meals were served in the thatched farmhouse where each person would collect a laden plate on the way to the dining-room."

Many youth hostels were in remote places, far from towns and pubs.

Robert Gummerson and his wife were, or thought they were, urban to the core, unlike Courtney Rowe and his family. For holidays the Gummersons went to the seaside. The "the slow heart-beat of rural England" was quite unknown to them, until Gummerson went to work, building the Haweswater dam, on the eastern edge of the Lake District, as secretary to the engineer. He and his wife enjoyed their time on the contract, among companionable men who had worked on big contracts around the world. They enjoyed the isolation, nine miles from Kendal, the nearest shopping centre. The 'local' pub was a six mile walk and the nearest bus four miles away. "On the other hand we had a sense of freedom we had never known before, and amidst beautiful surroundings we had leisure to appreciate."

Work ended in 1936. The couple prepared to move to another contract in Ireland, outside Dublin, until a lady from the Youth Hostels Association arrived one day. She told them the association was taking over the building where they had been living. After looking over the house, she asked if they would like to be wardens if the house, Swinklebank, became a youth hostel. They had fallen in love with Longsleddale and they agreed. The house became a hostel and they became its wardens on £1 a week plus somewhere to live, with fuel, lighting and food included.

Various people trained or, as Gummerson described it, groomed them for the job. They found out more from *Instructions to Wardens*, an eight page booklet, issued in 1934. They learned that they had to see everyone off the premises each morning, by 10am. That seemed, to Gummerson, a dubious proceeding and one impossible to execute though they later learned its benefit. They allowed no one in again until 5pm and thus had a time of relative peace and quiet. As soon as a member arrived, Gummerson collected their membership card. He checked that they had a sleeping bag and issued blankets and a pillow. He collected the shilling every member paid for a night's stay and saw that members signed the house-book.

Before a member left, the warden collected blankets and pillow. She or he saw that the member did a full share of the 'orderly work'. The warden entered any charges in the house-book, the ledger in which they kept a record of every member who stayed. Then, if everything had been left in order, the warden returned the membership card.

The warden had the power of "ejection of members and retention of membership cards" but, instructions reminded Gummerson and his wife, "this should only be exercised as a last resort." Although members did the 'orderly work' of washing up and daily cleaning, instructions reminded wardens they remained responsible for the general cleanliness and neat appearance of the hostel.

When the lease for Swinklebank wasn't renewed the Gummersons moved to the youth hostel at Jerusalem Farm, near Colne in Lancashire, in 1940. Local members from Colne, Nelson and Burnley visited the couple. "They were untiring in their efforts to help us settle in." Gummerson and his wife ran a series of youth hostels. From Jerusalem Farm they moved to Kettlewell in the Dales and then the Rookery in Bishopdale. Gummerson became well known for his dog, Punch, a Labrador cross sheep dog. He taught the dog and later her pup, Mij, to play dominoes. Gummerson and his wife moved around youth hostels in Yorkshire to Aysgarth, Stainforth, and then back to Aysgarth. They did the job because of the people, not for the pay. They remained friends with some of the members they met for the rest of their lives. "Our great interest has always been in the people who came to stay with us."

Throughout the 1950s and into the 1960s, Dick Knapp was the youth hostels' national secretary. He had followed Jack Catchpool into the job and was happiest with wardens. He was an enthusiast for training wardens and felt they needed help in doing a difficult job. Wardens could take part in training courses and in exchange visits with wardens from other countries.

Work at youth hostels was often hectic. The work wasn't light and neither did members do most of it, as the climber and writer, Gwen Moffat, discovered. Having found no work for an unqualified woman with a small daughter, she went to the youth hostel at Ro Wen in Wales. It was always difficult to keep a warden at that hostel. She remembered in her biography that no one wanted to live up there. The pay was low and the place was lonely. In her view, only a desperate woman who couldn't get enough of mountains would want to live there.

Each morning, after the hostellers left, she cleaned the house properly. She washed sheet sleeping bags used the night before. She repaired Primus stoves, storm lanterns and Tilley lamps almost daily and emptied all the chemical toilets. She put up notices that members should use the toilets 'only when necessary' because of the rate at which they filled. She shopped in Conwy, carrying all the provisions and equipment for the hostel on her back from the bus stop in the valley up to the hostel. But she had a roof over her head and an occasional day for climbing. She considered herself well off, on pay of £1 a week in summer and ten shillings (50p) in the winter. The main draw back to the job was the lack of privacy as she and her daughter shared the common room and cooking arrangements with everyone else.

Youth hostels were forward thinking and didn't discriminate against women. Other single women like Gwen Moffat and Connie Alexander also ran youth hostels. In the early 1950s Joan Chapman was warden at Black Sail. She did all the cooking and slept in the common room on storage boxes. Once a week she went over to the nearby youth hostel on the Honister Pass for a bath. She recalled if it was raining, she had three baths; one going, one there and one coming back. At the end of the season she moved to the youth hostel at Honister. Everyone thought as a single woman she would be safer there but she didn't agree. She thought any man, having walked all the way to Black Sail, would be too tired to be a nuisance when he got there.

Len Clark, chairman at the time, provided an introduction to a rewritten version of the warden's book of instructions in 1960. "Over a million times a year a YHA member arrives at a hostel and signs the house book. He may be an 'old hand,' spending yet another night in familiar surroundings or he may be new to the game, seeing a hostel and meeting a Warden for the first time... The new warden cannot hope to gain in a week or two the 'know how' that it has taken other Wardens years to acquire. In the meantime, he will not go far wrong if he follows these instructions, uses his common-sense, and remembers that as the hostellers are on holiday, they ought to be enjoying themselves."

In 1934, 25 paragraphs had been enough to tell the warden what to do. In 1960 the instructions covered 60 paragraphs. The warden was responsible for proper order in the hostel. He or she could refuse admission, fine late arrivals or withhold a member's card for "wilful damage, flagrant breach of rules, sexual offences, theft and drunkenness." The warden, in an act of positive discrimination, could not refuse admission to 'girls' arriving after 10pm.

Members carried out household tasks. They swept, dusted, washed dishes, cleaned windows, peeled vegetables and pumped and carried water. They could clean fireplaces, prepare fires, fill coal buckets and burn rubbish but those were jobs better left for men. They could clean bathrooms and wash places but not WCs or urinals. The warden was "ultimately responsible for the cleanliness, order and tidiness of the whole hostel. Wardens must clean the hostel to the extent that it is not done by members." Diligent wardens, like Gwen Moffat, cleaned the youth hostel properly over again each day when members had gone.

As part of the job wardens and their families were given accommodation but that could be cramped and mixed with the rest of the accommodation, leaving wardens and their families little or no privacy. Sometimes wardens had to wait until the members left for their privacy. At Jordans, in the Chilterns, in the 1970s, the wardens dragged a tin bath into the self catering kitchen for their weekly bath. Without curtains they relied on steam for privacy. Accommodation for them was a shed which, before it was bought, had been advertised for sale as "a large wooden dog kennel".

Wardens accumulated grievances, about their treatment, poor pay and accommodation. Rules, like closing and opening times, made their jobs tolerable. But a new generation demanded longer opening times and a more relaxed regime. The regions, keen to implement change, negotiated with wardens for longer hours and for fewer restrictions. Wardens resisted, demanding better pay. Conflicts grew between wardens and the regions that employed them. In early 1978 the National Association of Youth Hostel Wardens (NAYHW), formed in the 1950s, told YHA that they had joined the Transport and General Workers Union (TGWU), one of Britain's biggest.

It was a shrewd move. Wardens saw themselves as professionals and they wanted professional expertise. They wanted the benefits a bigger union offered including research, information and professional advice from full time officials. They assured YHA that they had no sinister motive. They would keep their own funds and would continue to represent themselves.

A year later against the background of a lorry drivers' strike, strikes on the railways, an ambulance drivers' strike and a day of action by public sector unions NAYHW presented a claim for a 37.5% increase in pay. On behalf of 500 staff at 267 youth hostels they demanded salary scales, a five-day week, better holidays, more generous redundancy pay and the abolition of joint appointments. Where wardens were appointed as couples, the appointment of both could be terminated if one partner left. With rising divorce rates the practice was getting outdated.

YHA responded that their demands amounted to a 60% increase in pay. Harry Livingstone, the national secretary, then raised this estimate to 100%. Livingstone had become national secretary after Dick Knapp. He was born in Edinburgh but, having grown up in London, he retained only a trace of a Scottish accent. A barrister, he had always wanted to work overseas and took a post in the Colonial Legal Service in Singapore and then in East Africa. Returning to England, he worked as company secretary and director in a family run stationery and colour printing business. Always a keen rambler, with an appreciation of YHA, he took the post of national secretary in 1968.

Livingstone was adamant that YHA could not afford the increases wardens were demanding and certainly not in one go. Meetings followed, one described in minutes as "not one of the best". NAYHW stated that their claim was not just about cash. They would not accept a part offer without discussing other matters. Their members were pushing them and one branch had recommended strike action. Summer was coming and the delay was playing into the hands of more militant wardens. A strike in the summer would be catastrophic for YHA.

Ron Todd, the TGWU's national officer, advised wardens. Born in Walthamstow, east London, Todd was the youngest son in a family of market traders. Leaving school at 14, he had swept the floors in a local barbers' shop and been a plumber's mate before joining the Royal Marines in 1945. After national service he worked as a gas fitter. He went to the Ford motor car plant at Dagenham, in Essex, remaining there until he became a full time TGWU officer. He was reputedly a man of unusual personal integrity. Critics described him as "too bloody honest."

The wardens, with Todd's support, managed their campaign astutely. They handed statements to guests at hostels, asking for support. They expected that members would be surprised to learn that YHA could be paying a warden, at a small simple hostel, as little as £12 a week. Where wardens provided no meals they had to buy their own food. At an average size hostel, of 7,500 overnight stays, the cash wage of £23.50 rose to £25.45 after four years service. At a larger hostel, of 20,000 overnight stays, a warden might earn £35 a week.

Out of this the warden paid for the food and accommodation of children and dependents. Wardens had a savings scheme but no pension plan. Living in tied accommodation, they had to save for a home when they retired. The job often required ownership of a car. Wardens worked a six-day week, with split shifts, often from 7am to noon, and 5–11pm. Their day off ran from midday to midday, so that many wardens had to prepare and cook food even on their day off or take deliveries. Living on top of the job meant they rarely escaped the demands of work.

On 3 July, the *Guardian* newspaper picked up the threat of a strike. Negotiators for the wardens claimed that they had not leaked the news to the press. Both Munro Taylor, NAYHW chairman, based at the youth hostel in Borth, on the coast of mid-Wales, and Harry Livingstone spoke to the *Guardian* writer.

The *Guardian*'s Alan Dunn investigated wardens' plight again on 18 July. He interviewed Robert "Wally" Owen and his wife Ellen, under a headline that proclaimed "You can't live on fresh air alone." The Owens were dedicated to the youth hostel aims of helping all 'especially young people of limited means, to a greater knowledge, love and care of the countryside.' They loved working with and for young people. Wally, who had never been a union member before, was glad now that he was. With the majority of their colleagues, frustration had bubbled up. Goodwill toward their employers had run thin. Wardens couldn't allow journalists into youth hostel premises so the Owens and their two daughters posed for a photo on a hillside away from the hostel. If negotiations were not satisfactorily concluded youth hostel doors could soon close, Dunn concluded.

YHA members were surprised. Their surprise increased when *Nationwide*, an early evening TV news and current affairs programme, covered the dispute immediately after the main news bulletin. YHA National Office received 50 calls after the programme, many from anxious parents with children on or about to go on holiday.

Members called wardens "the underpaid salt of the earth." Another wrote that he was "very sympathetic and greatly surprised that they earn even less than me. I would rather pay more than have the wardens poorer than I am." One member, earning £4.20 an hour and about to start a 12 hour shift, wrote that he would earn more from one shift than a warden earned in a week.

Some were concerned that members were not being told what was happening. An issue of the magazine, now called *Hostelling News*, had not mentioned the issue. "If the YHA is a democracy it is surely important that these issues should be fully ventilated," a member complained. Another was "shocked to find that I am a member of an organisation that pays wages below the poverty level." "Ridiculously low wages." "YHA have [sic] exploited wardens for too long."

Wardens encouraged members to write to their MPs. They wrote to vice presidents too. Lord Lovell-Davis, an original 'spin doctor' and media adviser to Harold Wilson in the 1960s, received letters and read coverage in the newspapers with concern. He wrote to YHA from the House of Lords on 21 August. Wardens "had slipped seriously behind in the matter of pay and remuneration generally... the job did seem to be becoming progressively less attractive."

YHA finally returned with an offer for the 37.5% increase. Wardens would have four weeks holiday each year. At a youth hostel that was open more than six months without closing for a night, staff would get two additional weeks of holiday. Separate but dependent contracts would replace the joint appointment.

In late August NAYHW's national officers Munro Taylor, Rod Sutton, Dennis Glass and Pam Smith reported to their members that they had concluded an interim settlement with YHA. "Thanks in large measure to the publicity and the tremendous amount of support from the membership" there was now no risk of inconvenience to youth hostel members that year.

The settlement partly met their claim and, as a concession, they had suggested to YHA that settlement should take place over two years. On 6 October 1979 the YHA national executive committee expressed its thanks and sympathy to its negotiators who had "had a fairly tough time of it."

Negotiators had agreed a large increase in pay adding to the costs of running youth hostels. They had to meet a direct increase in costs and associated costs such as tax, insurance and pension contributions. Costs would also increase to provide more staff for the shorter working week and longer holidays, pushing costs further above 37.5%. Livingstone's estimate might have been right.

During negotiations YHA's team had to consult the regions, to check that they had authority to reach agreements. Regions and their finances were autonomous and independent. Two were limited companies. Each operated in different ways accountable to the members in its own geographic area. The Lakes and Peak District Regions and to a lesser extent the South West Region were successful and viable. Other regions were less so. How regions would manage the increased costs arising from the award was unclear.

YHA had been left struggling with the issues, outmanoeuvred and out of touch at times. Volunteers had other work and jobs to do. In a quickly changing situation they could not always be available. At the height of the publicity no senior volunteers had been available to make decisions. On occasions negotiators had to leave meetings before they ended to get home to get to work the next day. The patience of their own employers could be exhausted.

Voluntary management had faced the increasing professionalism of the wardens. The events of that summer reminded them of the need for further change in the democratic and voluntary nature of YHA. As wardens became more professional they needed stronger professional management.

YHA also demanded more of wardens. The push to reduce or remove rules completely, the demand to keep youth hostels open longer each day and for more days each year would push wardens to become managers. They would become responsible for recruiting, training and supervising more staff.

They no longer did the job out of love for the ideals of YHA. Neither did they take the job to live somewhere remote, to have a roof over their heads or to satisfy a love of mountains. The relaxed hours with time off in the winter were gone.

The voluntary nature of YHA was caught between a professional workforce and demanding customers. Employment and health and safety legislation expanded. Responsibility for running a multi million pound business affected the voluntary leaders of YHA severely. They too increasingly had to become professional. The days when YHA volunteers and wardens were idealists who contributed their time with little or no pay were coming to an end.

Notes and references

John Martin, YHA Honorary Archivist, pointed me towards some of the records on which I based this chapter including Robert Gummerson's recollections *The Quick and the Dead*, Courtney Rowe's memoir of Kennack Sands which was discovered in the youth hostel common room at Coverack, Cornwall, Gwen Moffat's autobiography *The Space Below My Feet* and Joan Chapman's recollections. Various editions of *Instructions to Youth Hostel Wardens* were essential reading.

"it was largely wardens..." Smith, *Caveat Nostalgia*, p48
"not to wait upon members..." *Concerning Youth Hostels*, YHA booklet c1950
"I remember one poor lad..." Gummerson, *The Quick and the Dead*
"Two blankets were provided..." Rowe, *Recollections*
"Its ground floor..." Ibid
"It was not unknown..." Ibid
"Fresh milk was very popular..." Ibid
"They were untiring...." Gummerson, *The Quick and the Dead*
"Our great interest..." Ibid
"a large wooden dog kennel" *Hostelling News Magazine*, 1973, No 6.
"the underpaid salt of the earth..." and following quotes, from letters in YHA archive
"had slipped seriously behind..." Lord Lovell-Davis, letter to YHA, 21 August 1979
"Thanks in large measure..." letter from NAYHW officers to members

24

Eastern

When we first went to Colchester in 1981, Eastern Region was on a spending spree. In five years, the region had opened four hostels, at Sheringham, in Norfolk; at Brandon, in the Thetford Forest; in the new town of Milton Keynes and one on the outskirts of Norwich. At Colchester, guests had new showers. New lino covered the floors in corridors and bathrooms. New dormitories with new carpets accommodated more guests than ever.

The region expected to break all records for the numbers of guests accommodated. Instead in the early 1980s a savage recession caught it. Hampered by borrowing, costs soared. Many of its youth hostels were under used and most were empty all winter. East Anglia is a lovely part of England but it's no honey pot for tourists. Visitors, compared with the Lake District or Peak District, are few. Its peaceful spaces and easy landscapes draw contemplative tourists, cyclists, walkers and bird watchers.

We did everything we could to bring more people through the front door. We answered the phone, whenever it rang, whether we were working or not. We stayed open late, against the rules, and kept the hostel open all afternoon in the summer. On rainy days we opened early so that people could shelter inside. The rules sometimes seemed daft and got in the way of people having fun and enjoying themselves. We no longer rang bells to wake everyone. We dropped serving breakfast at a strict time and served instead for an hour each morning. We arranged water-colour painting weekends and spinning classes for guests.

In idle conversation with our manager I mused that it might be fun to run murder mystery weekends. Before I had time to think he advertised the weekends and guests began booking. Panicked, we scrounged a cast off and damaged mannequin from a local department store. Splattered with fake blood of jam and paint the mannequin became Debra, victim of a senseless murder. Friends played suspects. We were travelling musicians. For six weekends guests discovered clues hidden round the town and interviewed us. Each Sunday they solved the crime.

We did what we could to draw more guests, to make more money for the youth hostel, to make it successful. The lovely old building needed so much money to keep it running. An old, curving, wooden bay window, fragile with rot, came apart in my hands. A leaking roof brought down a ceiling. A rotten pantry floorboard collapsed in the midst of serving dinner.

The hostel made a profit but only when we delayed repairs and neglected maintenance. As much as we could we did ourselves. But cleaning and a coat of paint couldn't cover all the faults of a 200 year-old building. Money was getting short and tight. Our efforts to save the hostel, to make it pay its way, began to seem more and more quixotic.

The hostel hung on, never getting enough maintenance, never having the money it needed spent on it, never making enough profit. We achieved record levels of business but still it wasn't enough. Running the hostel was always more work than it was worth. All the time the capital value of the building increased as property prices rose and rose. The prospect of selling it grew more tempting. We moved to another job, at another youth hostel with a more secure future.

Numbers staying at Colchester fell by a third after we left until, finally, in 1996, East Bay House closed its doors. Sold, it became two townhouses. The town, with its claim to be Britain's oldest recorded city, lost its youth hostel. Two families lived where once up to 67 people had been able to stay. The lovely city, its Roman walls, and its old castle became a little more difficult to visit, especially for young people, travelling on a budget. But they were finding it quicker to by-pass Colchester anyway. It was easier, even on a very tight budget, to fly direct from Europe through Luton or Stansted airports to London.

25

The Modernisers

At 9am on a Sunday morning in February, 1983, senior YHA people gathered at the youth hostel in Holland Park. Set back from Kensington High Street, where the open spaces of the park give way to woodland, the youth hostel was a mix of styles, with a Jacobean wing hard against a modern box of concrete and glass. The lines of the buildings set together highlighted the problems facing youth hostels. Like the buildings, old ideas were struggling against sharp edged, brightly lit, modern ways.

Former chairman, John Parfitt, who joined those gathering had warned long before that only a fractional change in leisure tastes would leave youth hostels high and dry. But he had not seen fractional change arriving at the same time as rising costs, rising prices and an economic downturn.

They were meeting because a crisis had engulfed youth hostels. On the back of steady growth, an economic depression had swept down on them. That other organisations and companies faced worse difficulties in recession-hit Britain in the early 1980s was no consolation to Parfitt. In the previous two years numbers staying at youth hostels had tumbled by 14%. For youth hostels, on tight margins, the change was catastrophic. As the numbers staying collapsed, debt rose and two regional groups failed. Youth hostels had made many of the problems themselves and they were high and dry before anyone knew what had happened.

Parfitt and his colleagues gathered to make sense of what was happening, if they could. Members of the executive committee and three well respected wardens were among those at the meeting. David Kingsley, a friend and colleague of YHA vice president, Lord Lovell-Davis, also arrived. In the 1960s Kingsley, Lovell-Davis and Denis Lyons had been the 'three wise men' advising the prime minister, Harold Wilson. They had been the first spin doctors. They had backgrounds in advertising, public relations and business. They had been helping Wilson modernise what he called the 'outdated penny farthing machinery' of the Labour Party.

Youth hostels faced a similar challenge. Parfitt had always believed that youth hostels needed to modernise, make profits and attract a new generation of young people. He was a no nonsense, plain speaking man. "Profit may seem sordid to some people, it just seems like sensible housekeeping to me," he had declared once. He had a remarkable gift for expounding a case, combining "an ice cold logic with a white hot passion" for the things he believed were right.

At Holland Park that Sunday in 1983 he presented to colleagues the results of the latest research from Mass Observation, the research agency of which he was managing director. What they had discovered would prompt youth hostels to undo their foundations and unravel what they had become over more than 50 years.

Parfitt and others at the meeting in February had faced many of these problems once already. In the late 1960s they had reorganised youth hostels into 10 regions. An elected council of members living within each region ran each region's youth hostels. Each year the regional council elected some of their members to attend the youth hostels' annual conference where they debated policy with delegates from other regions. They made decisions and elected a national executive committee to run youth hostel affairs on their behalf until the next council met.

Parfitt and his colleagues had expected that a reorganisation in the1960s would make youth hostels more efficient. With fewer regions and fewer committees running them, youth hostels would become better managed. Youth hostels changed. From 1971 four different grades of hostels offered different standards, facilities and services. Hostels with higher standards and improved facilities charged more. They made more money. The changes incentivised improvement and modernisation.

It worked, for a time. With Parfitt as chairman youth hostels had raced through boom times. Through the 1970s they posted record results almost every year. In 1980 they recorded just under two million overnight stays, with 277 hostels open and 390,000 members, another record. The Queen had marked the occasion with a return visit to the youth hostel at Holland Park which she had officially opened in 1959. For that second visit youth hostels had been in a triumphal mood and Parfitt was there to welcome the Queen.

He was made CBE in the New Year Honours list and stepped down as the youth hostels' chairman. Hedley Alcock, a more emollient figure and a youth hostel member since 1946, followed as chairman. Trained as a scientist, Alcock had worked in industries in Derby, Nottingham and Liverpool, before moving south to work for ICL, the computer company, in Feltham, Surrey. He had been treasurer throughout Parfitt's time as chairman.

Parfitt did not step down quietly. In September 1982 he had raised concerns to an executive meeting at Arnside in Cumbria. He pointed out that YHA had become caught in a cycle, pushing up prices to cover rising costs which deflated demand and caused further price rises.

From 1977 the regions had been on a spree of opening new youth hostels. More than 20 youth hostels had opened, including a new one in London at Hampstead Heath and a brand new, purpose-built hostel at Broad Haven in Pembrokeshire. The last ones were nearing completion just as the crisis hit, as the Conservative government, elected in 1979, raised interest rates and cut spending, driving down demand and increasing unemployment. The economy shrank and unemployment more than doubled. The recession hit young people particularly.

Overnight stays slipped at most youth hostels in 1980 but not as far as they might have done. A big new youth hostel at Hampstead Heath ensured that overnights for the whole year were up. The following year, a new hostel in London could not rescue anyone. In two years, the total numbers staying in youth hostels fell by 13.5%. Membership numbers fell 17% from their peak of 1980. The collapse was even more serious in younger age groups, with the number of members aged 16-21, down 19%. The number of members under 16 was down by more than a quarter.

At the same time as the crisis broke, youth hostels had to finance the previous year's wage award of 32.5%, deal with inflation at 20% and pay for a new computerised membership system. In 1980 expenditure at youth hostels shot up by almost one million, from £2,505,792 to £3,303,680. The following year youth hostels cost a further half million more to run. Official interest rates went to 15% in 1981.

As problems mounted, tensions grew. The executive committee disagreed with youth hostels' supreme body, the national council. After council decided youth hostels should charge for car parking, the executive disregarded that clear direction and abolished charges. Council reminded the executive that it did not have power to overturn decisions made by council. John Parfitt retorted that waiting before taking a decision just to meet a technical rule was pedantic. He didn't normally observe pedantic things in time of crisis.

Complex youth hostel finances added to the strain. Regional groups ran youth hostels and paid money to national funds. Money from those national funds financed big projects and capital investment in the regions. But the regions were autonomous. If a national committee refused funding for a region's project, that region could still go ahead with the project, then run out of money, and then expect national aid. National funds had become the bank of last resort. But from 1980, national funds had been declining.

Cash flow problems multiplied. Regional groups ran out of money just when they needed to pay for increased wages and investment. The regional group based on Merseyside, responsible for youth hostels in North Wales and with its proud history of being Britain's founding youth hostel group, ran into difficulties. It fell behind in paying the levies and payments it owed to national funds. Merseyside's debts to the national organisation had risen from £28,000 to £70,000 in 18 months. It also owed money to banks and high interest rates were crippling it. Poor relations with its paid wardens compounded the problem. The risk that one region and its youth hostels might collapse rose.

Hedley Alcock and the executive set up an advisory group to help Merseyside in 1982. They sent Colin Logan, newly appointed assistant to the national secretary, to Merseyside. Logan, an ex-army officer, had risen to the rank of major, serving in Northern Ireland and Germany and finishing his career in Hong Kong. After leaving the army, he worked in Hong Kong and the Middle East before returning to England and taking up work with YHA.

On Merseyside Logan discovered a deteriorating situation. By July the group's current account was in the red to the tune of £100,000. It had already spent money received in advance bookings to keep youth hostels going. It would need more money for the summer season to pay staff and buy food for guests, who had already paid, when they arrived. Cooperation between wardens and the regional management and volunteers had worsened.

The executive was reluctant to take over the democracy of a regional group but the problem was urgent. It had little choice. The executive assumed the functions and authority of the regional group. It enlarged and reformed the advisory group as the North Wales Management Group and appointed Colin Logan as the principal executive officer for a new North Wales regional group. Logan began the process of winding up the old regional group, which took until April the following year. That the original Merseyside group had incorporated as a limited company created additional difficulties.

Just as the executive was stabilising the situation in North Wales, problems in Eastern Region sprang up. The region covered East Anglia through to the Chilterns and Windsor, with 28 youth hostels in total. The executive sent Logan to investigate. He reported another critical financial state with "considerable debt, a severe shortage of liquid assets and falling usage." Debt from opening a new youth hostel in Norwich saddled the region. It was running an over-spend on building work. By October 1982 the region would need a large tranche of financial support to see it through the winter. Once again the executive decided, reluctantly, to become involved. It introduced Derek Hanson, a member of the executive, as chairman and began winding up the Eastern region.

Dealing with failing regions was painful. Regions were at the heart of the organisation. They had found, opened and run the youth hostels. They supplied a shrinking number of volunteers who undertook work at youth hostels. Even more painfully people, particularly young people, were turning away from youth hostels. Some members explained away the drop in numbers as the baby boom tailing off. Others blamed the recession.

When the economy recovered people would return. They denied their actions were the cause of falling numbers.

Less sure, Parfitt had commissioned a third membership survey to get some answers. On that early Sunday morning in February 1983, when his colleagues met at the youth hostel in Holland Park, he had the results in his hands. He gave them a presentation. He explained the problems and quashed both explanations for the decline. The baby boom had not yet come to an end. Rising birth rates in previous decades should still have been increasing the number of members and overnight stays, not the reverse. Neither had the recession caused the problem.

Instead, triumphalism in the 1970s had hidden complacency. Success had masked problems in youth hostels. The boom in youth hostels had hidden the issue that fewer and fewer new members were joining. Parfitt explained that youth hostels were relying more and more on existing members renewing their membership each year. As a result, members on average were growing older. The average member was now aged 25, whereas in 1961 the average age was 20. The average member was more likely to be married, to have children and be better educated with a standard of education well above the rest of the population. Members were older and more middle class than ever. Since 1961 youth hostels had slipped further and further away from the groups of people and the social classes most likely to have the young people and those 'of limited means' that they existed to help.

Parfitt had further worrying news. All members, those who renewed and those who didn't, irrespective of age, were less keen on youth hostels than they had ever been. They disliked the rules. They disliked the closing times and lights out. They disliked dormitories that were too big, too lacking in privacy and too often dirty, cold and uncomfortable. They disliked noisy, out of control school parties filling youth hostels.

All those at Holland House added their own thoughts and conclusions when Parfitt finished. Those present thought they knew the solutions to all their problems. A centralised booking system would make booking easier. Too much money spent on publicity could be better spent improving youth hostels, getting the product right.

Eric Booth, chairman of the wardens' union, expressed frustration. He pointed out that Parfitt was highlighting issues that were already well known. Committees had been discussing these issues for years with little action, no change and no results. The crisis called for less voluntary management and a less restrictive attitude to paid staff running affairs. In short, the democratic way of running youth hostels was the problem.

A loose federation of democracies with no single leader created youth hostels in the heady days of the 1930s. The loose set-up, almost without structure had served them well. It had been the cause of their rampant success in opening the world of travel to millions of young people. But now it was getting in the way of their survival. Alcock and others left the meeting at Holland Park, determined to change the way youth hostels ran.

The previous December YHA had approached the Countryside Commission for funds to carry out market research. Government had set up the commission in 1949 to supervise and co-ordinate the new national parks. Its role expanded over time to cover the whole of countryside. The commission admired and supported youth hostels as important parts of the countryside. Its support extended to funding new youth hostels. Youth hostels at Gerddi Bluog near Harlech in Wales, Broad Haven in Pembrokeshire and Osmotherley in North Yorkshire had been some of the recent hostels the commission had funded. John Parfitt had recently been appointed to the commission.

Staff at the commission rejected the proposed market research. Having invested in youth hostels, they did not think market research would be enough. The future of YHA concerned them. The financial situation facing one of the most important voluntary organisations in the country worried them. They wanted a management survey as well as the marketing survey and gave funds for both. The executive handed the job to David Kingsley as a consultant. He was "to tell YHA the best way to present itself to the world outside."

Like Parfitt, Kingsley had studied at the London School of Economics. He was an active youth hostel member from 1944-47. He had gone on to be one of the founders of KMP, an advertising agency which broke all the rules in British advertising at the time. They defied the gentlemanly ways of advertising. The agency worked for a fee not a commission. They solicited clients. They pitched for business. In another revolution, staff worked in an open office but that was soon abandoned as everyone could overhear everyone else when they were on their phones.

Advising Harold Wilson, Kingsley had learned that things went wrong when people thought they knew it all, when they weren't in touch with what was going on around them. Instead of listening to those who thought they knew everything about youth hostels, Kingsley, Parfitt and Mass Observation undertook further research among 16-24 year olds. They determined to discover exactly how much youth hostels met the requirements of young people for leisure away from home. Kingsley analysed the results.

He found that the number of young people having a main holiday away from home had fallen during the recession. The boom in youth hostels during the 1970s had hidden how much young people and their tastes were changing. Those who were having a holiday were getting an appetite for guaranteed sun and the chance of sex on package holidays in Spain. They wanted sun and beach holidays. Most had heard of youth hostels and most of their views were the same as those of members. Youth hostels had too many rules and too little freedom. The accommodation at youth hostels wasn't a problem but "they nearly all like to go dancing or drinking or both."

Such changes were potentially a disaster for youth hostels. Older members thought that rules were essential youth hostels. "No youth hostel could run without any rules and it is probable that very few young people would like it even if it were tried," a 1977 report on youth hostels in Germany, France and England and Wales had claimed. If young people wanted sex on holiday, there was little youth hostels could or would do about that.

Kingsley disagreed. The conflict, between what young people wanted to do on holiday and what youth hostels offered, could be overcome. They simply needed to relax the rules about hostel closing at night and times to be in bed. Providing the kind of facilities young people wanted, especially entertainments like space invader games, pool tables and juke boxes would make youth hostels more appealing.

When youth hostels started, they provided the only way out of cramped cities. Anton Grassl, president of the International Youth Hostel Federation admitted, in 1976, when youth hostels first started "young people had so little money that no one apart from teachers, priests and youth leaders took any interest in them." But social conditions in the 1960s and 1970s had changed. Young people could travel cheaply and easily if they wished. They could use cars or scooters. They could hitch-hike or travel by bus, train or coach. They could get into the countryside if they wished.

Youth hostels no longer had a monopoly for accommodating young people. Others, seeing the success of youth hostels, were copying or bettering them. Many forms of cheap accommodation including camping, caravanning, bed and breakfast and cheap hotels were springing up, willing to give young people what they wanted. Parents were endorsing alternatives, like PGL, offering American summer camp experiences, action, excitement and adventure for their children.

Peter Gordon Lawrence started the company, which took its name from his initials, after canoeing on the Danube in 1955. He led similar trips for small groups down the River Wye, camping each night on the bank. The company grew from camping into converted properties, former mansions and farms, like youth hostels. It moved into other parts of the youth hostel's traditional business, accommodating schools and colleges. A clear focus on a defined product fuelled its success.

In the 1980s Lord Forte bought the US Travelodge brand and established it in Britain. He attached them to Little Chefs as Little Lodges before rebranding them as Travelodges. In 1983 the first hotel was still two years from opening at Barton-under-Needwood, on the A38 near Lichfield, Staffordshire. But they and other kinds of competition were coming. Soon youth hostels would lose their claim to be the biggest accommodation network in the country and around the world.

Travel abroad to "the forbidden delights of sun, sea and discos" was easier and getting cheaper. It may have sounded decadent, Kingsley agreed, but he pointed out "sun, sea bathing and sports on the beach" were all recreation. It was no longer a question of what was better. These alternatives were not available when youth hostels first opened.

Parfitt had always feared that youth hostels and their members were getting out of touch. He had never believed in a golden age of youth hostels. He said that his experience of youth hostels from 1944 told him that was a myth. Youth hostels may have been fun he thought. But he held no nostalgia for "the discomforts, the damp blankets, the dictatorial wardens, the elitism of the 'genuine' hosteller."

He had warned that anyone looking at the minutes and records of their meetings might not get a good impression of how the association was minding its businesses. When it mattered, decisions were made too late or too far away from places where decisions were needed. Decisions too often called for knowledge volunteers didn't have. Youth hostels had a large turnover. They had to make a surplus to survive. Profit was not a dirty word. Committees did not have as much scope to change things as they thought they had. They could not change things just because they wanted. Neither could they think they were running a private club. The survey showed how right he had been.

Kingsley returned in November 1983 with his marketing recommendations. Youth hostels had to focus on young people. Awareness of youth hostels among young people was high but perception of a clear image was low and the solution depended on an improved product, a new youth hostel. One kind of youth hostel offering similar facilities at different levels of comfort was no longer enough. He proposed dividing youth hostels into categories for different markets. He saw town and tourist centres, country lovers' centres, activity centres, school party and family centres. YHA could then market and promote these new centres to different groups. A new improved YHA with centres and managers would have an upper age limit for ordinary members.

In December Kingsley made his recommendations for reshaping the structure behind youth hostels. He had detected confused roles and a lack of strong leadership in the association. Priorities were muddled. Youth hostels and their teams lacked supervision and were without clear measures of their success. They were isolated from what was going on in the rest of the organisation. They made unilateral decisions as a result. Voluntary management, in the face of this confusion, trespassed from policy making and evaluation into doing and implementing themselves.

Regions ran youth hostels and carried out national policies in the original constitution. The principle 'small is beautiful,' implicit in the regional system, encouraged local interest and widespread 'grassroots' involvement and drove the phenomenal growth of youth hostels in the 1930s and 1940s. But by 1983, Kingsley could see that the resources and organisation of the regions varied. Regions with high numbers of visitors, like the Lakes or Peaks regions, were successful and able to invest in youth hostels and their staff. Others in less busy regions struggled.

The experience in North Wales and in East Anglia was on everyone's minds. Kingsley pointed out that those regional organisations and their finances had broken down or run out of control. With no other choice, national officers had stepped in to rescue the problem regions.

Kingsley solved the issue by removing regions and volunteers from management. They would advise on policy matters and would act as 'watchdogs' for customers. Regional executives would supervise wardens and youth hostels. Executives would be responsible to the relevant marketing manager above them. They would consult the regional groups, their councils and their officers. Centre managers would have more authority and responsibility. Regional managers would break down the isolation of youth hostels and their teams. Better supervision and accountability would become a reality, not a pretence.

Regional groups, made up of volunteers, would control policy through national council and the national executive committee down to the chief executive who headed the paid staff. Operating youth hostels would be left to the chief executive and his or her team. Kingsley's chief executive also shared a representational role with the chairman. Both would focus on the organisation, separate from marketing. The chairman would no longer be a volunteer. He would work full time with pay. National office, located in the same building in St Albans since 1955, would shift from its costly location. The Midlands would offer better communications to youth hostels in the rest of the country.

Implementing the proposals would give youth hostels new viability in the market. Kingsley considered alternatives. He warned that failure would mean reducing the number of youth hostels. He estimated closing up to 50 if things carried on as they were. In that case, funds gained from sales would support a remaining, smaller network.

A long year was drawing to an end. The executive agreed with the broad principles Kingsley outlined. Management of youth hostels would be professionalised. But they placed a caveat on the role of regional councils. They did not like the concept of divorcing regional councils from running their regions.

When proposals arrived at national council, in 1984, the regions would not agree with all the changes proposed. They recognised the line management concept but they saw the need to keep important roles and functions for voluntary management at regional levels. As Jack Catchpool had observed in 1959, asking members about change was like asking a society of drunks to vote for shortening drinking hours. The regions were not ready to give up the management of youth hostels by local democracy. Regional councils needed a purpose with a defined management role, they declared.

On 6 October 1984 the executive reported they had appointed a chief executive, Andrew Chinneck. He came to youth hostels from Community Industry, an organisation providing training and employment for young people, later amalgamated with the young people's charity, Rathbone. He had been chief executive there for five years. Born in Devon and living with his wife Anne and three children in Puckeridge, Hertfordshire, he listed sailing and fell-walking as his interests. He saw his role harnessing a high standard of management with the commitment and enthusiasm of volunteers. He had learned to value volunteers and expected them to take an increasing role in future affairs.

The regions battled against change for more than a year. John Parfitt warned them the signals of danger had been with YHA a great deal longer than the last few years of falling overnights. They now had a last opportunity to change affairs. Alcock as chairman warned council that they could not go back into the past. The principle of reorganisation was not for negotiation.

A special national council meeting finally amended the youth hostels' constitution and created line management on 9 November 1985. They amalgamated all the financial resources of all the regions into a single resource. From then on YHA was a single business with a single set of accounts. They blurred some of Kingsley's intentions. The regions, reorganised and enlarged, kept a form of management role. YHA's chairman never took a paid role. No upper age limit on membership was imposed.

Chinneck's arrival as chief executive ushered in a new era for youth hostels. The association had begun with no single leader and with only voluntary effort. It had clung to democratic ways of working for more than 50 years. Now a chief executive and a hierarchy of professionals ran youth hostels. Chinneck with his directors, a marketing team, operations managers, youth hostel wardens and their teams began relaxing rules and updating youth hostels.

The regions continued to exercise democratic control. Changes were much slower coming than Kingsley might have expected. The new chief executive envisaged the move of the national office to the Midlands would take five or six years. The move didn't happen until 16 years later. Regional groups slimmed down from the previous ten to four geographic groups and for a few years coincided with the structures of paid management. They sought to exercise control over regional directors and their teams.

Youth hostels had introduced new generations to travel. They had released independence, a spirit of adventure and a hunger for travel but they no longer had the market to themselves. Young people were better off financially than ever before and had greater freedom to please themselves. Others had also discovered how they could cater for people of all ages, travelling on limited budgets. Tastes had changed with rising prosperity and youth hostels had to scramble to catch up.

John Parfitt delivered a final membership survey in 1988. He was also involved in the wider affairs of market research and had been chairman of the Market Research Society. He introduced the first strategic marketing plan for the International Youth Hostels Federation and carried out marketing surveys for them. From 1988 until 1994 the federation elected him as president, the role Richard Schirrmann and Jack Catchpool had once occupied. He died on 22 March 2004, after a heart attack.

During his time, youth hostels changed. He was well connected and used his connections well for the benefit of youth hostels. He was as influential as earlier figures, like Jack Catchpool and Barclay Baron. In many ways his times were more difficult. The association had become an institution with embedded ideas and attitudes developed over years.

Others struggled with similar challenges. Voluntary organisations, political parties and established businesses modernised with difficulty just as YHA did. The process took decades. Change challenged the Labour Party in 1997 as much as it had in the 1960s under Harold Wilson. David Cameron also attempted to modernise the Conservative Party.

Changing a big, far flung organisation was not easy. Intellectual and sharp witted, Parfitt was sometimes seen as abrasive but he was always a committed youth hostel member. He had met his wife through youth hostels and he had a strong belief that youth hostels were splendid and unique. He believed youth hostels should have the reasonable comforts everyone expected in their own homes and that the more people used youth hostels the more youth hostels would pay for themselves. He wanted youth hostels open to all, not kept to a small, select few. They had a great future, he was sure, so long as those in charge were always willing to change and not to hang on to myths of a golden past.

Notes and references

David Kingsley produced three reports, commonly called the Kingsley report. They were the results of a *Market Research Study into the 16-24 year-old holiday market, Marketing Recommendations* and *Organisational Recommendations*. These reports form the backbone of this chapter. Quotes from Kingsley come from these reports. Discovering Kingsley's political background, in newspapers and in obituaries following his death in 2014, was a surprise. His name was well known in YHA, his background less so. I read and used minutes of meetings from late 1970s to mid 1980s. John Parfitt was right; they do not leave a good impression of how YHA was minding its business. But they do show the width and depth of problems it faced and they are a valuable record of how YHA went about changing itself.

"Profit may seem sordid…" *Youth Hosteller*, June 1970
"to tell YHA the best way…" *National Minutes 1983*, 9-10 April
"No youth hostel could run…" *International Survey of Youth Travel and Youth Hostels*, October 1977, p95
"young people had so little…" Grassl and Heath, *The Magic Triangle*, p173.
"the discomforts…" *Hostelling News*, Spring 1982

-26-

Salisbury

B y the end of the 1980s youth hostels were changing fast. In the winter
of 1987-8, YHA spent £1.2 million modernising and updating 24
youth hostels as part of the new marketing plan.

In the midst of change and excitement, Caroline and I moved with the
girls to Salisbury. With a couple of friends we drove all we owned in two
vans around London on the M25 to another youth hostel in another
graceful old house. Wide verandas gave Milford Hill House a relaxed
colonial feel. An old cedar of Lebanon crowned secluded lawns behind a
long, high, red-brick wall. The hostel was a short walk from the cathedral's
soaring spire.

The year before we arrived, the hostel had been modernised. In line
with David Kingsley's recommendations it was one of the new 'city tourist'
centres. It had new showers, a cafeteria and better heating. It was busy for
most of the year. We never closed.

Salisbury is one of the best of England's cathedral towns and an
international crowd, from around the world, came to the town and nearby

Stonehenge. They hitch-hiked. They cycled. They travelled by car, by bus and by train. They stayed a night or two before moving to Bath, Oxford, Edinburgh or Paris or Amsterdam. The network, on which youth hostels had been built, stretched. Distances shrank.

We never knew who might turn up next: a Russian linguist from America; young Israelis on leave at the end of their military service; Brazilians and Argentinians. The world was getting confusing as borders came down and new countries formed. I offended a Slovakian when I sympathised with the plight of her home country. There was no war in Slovakia, she pointedly explained. Perhaps I meant Slovenia?

We had more staff, full time and part time. Fresh from travelling the world, assistants were keen to introduce an entrepreneurial spirit they had learned from youth hostels in Thailand, Australia and New Zealand. Youth hostels there ran bars, tours and entertainment. They had cocktail nights and barbecues and swimming pools. We tried different ways of running hostels. We ran two nearby, smaller youth hostels as well as the hostel at Salisbury.

After six years, I changed course and became regional manager. It meant leaving the hostel but with the girls growing up the move made sense. They needed a home of their own. We moved to a house in a terrace. We had neighbours instead of a youth hostel and the fire alarm never went off in the night. We had no nearby fridge to raid when we were hungry except our own. No pantry and no drying room. No guests with whom to chat. Our front door no longer opened on the world.

I had 20 hostels to manage. I worked from home, from a tiny back room off our bedroom. I had a filing cabinet, a desk, a phone and a fax. I had a mobile phone as big as a brick and then a car phone. I travelled. I travelled a lot. I visited youth hostels. I interviewed and settled new managers. I gave advice, drew up plans, developed budgets and wrote reports. I oversaw building work. I went to site meetings in the shut down, icy hostel at Wilderhope in Shropshire, when we sat around a table and blew on our fingers. Emergencies called me out. Plumbing broke. A youth hostel flooded. One Christmas Eve fire alarms sounded in an empty building. With no manager on site to turn them off, I piled the family into the car and drove to Devon to silence the alarms.

I was away a lot, too much for the family. I travelled to the New Forest and to Dorset. I went to some of the best bits of England, to

Lulworth Cove, Swanage and Weymouth. My patch of hostels went as far as the Mendip Hills in Somerset. A year later I took in the Quantocks before reaching to Exmoor. I adopted the Cotswolds, the Isle of Wight and stretched my way into Shropshire. I travelled in heat waves and got lost in snow. I learned my way around England and Wales.

Everything changed all the time. Reorganisation followed reorganisation. I moved to a new job developing youth hostels for schools and groups throughout the south of England and Wales. We were trying to find a secret ingredient that would make youth hostels thrive and succeed, that would bring enough money to pay the bills and pay for investment.

I went to France, Holland, Denmark, Italy, Spain and Austria to learn lessons, finding how youth hostels in those countries, ran. The Dutch had sold two-thirds of their youth hostels and kept only the biggest. They had no swimming pools but they had football and basketball pitches. Youth hostels in Spain were a part of government, running services for young people. In Denmark, town authorities owned and ran youth hostels under franchise agreements. One ran a restaurant more profitable than her hostel. A couple of enterprising owners ran hotels and youth hostels together, switching rooms and prices to match demand.

Few of us admitted the solution to all our problems stared us in the face. Traditional members would not allow too much change. They clung to the idea of a network of hostels covering the country so that people could walk or cycle from one to the other.

Too many youth hostels cost too much money. More than half were less than half full and empty most of the time. They were not making enough money. If the number of youth hostels could be reduced to those that made a profit, youth hostels would thrive. With fewer youth hostels there would be enough to improve and maintain them every year. As it was the money ran out every year or we made a loss covered only by more youth hostels sold. My calculations always arrived at a network of 80 or 90 youth hostels. They were the ones that paid their way.

We kept going. We kept improving what we had. We sold off a youth hostel here and another there to pay bills. Sales paid for investment in buildings, people and equipment. We closed and sold the youth hostels in Southampton, at Cranborne and Overton, then at Ludlow. We opened a new hostel at Ironbridge. Another youth hostel, at Instow on the North Devon coast, closed to balance the books and raise funds for investment elsewhere. The hostel at Duntisbourne Abbots sold and became an executive's home. I grew weary of telling those who had become friends we planned to close and sell the youth hostel that was their home. There's no way of breaking news like that. The old golf club, at Cleeve Hill, on the Cotswold escarpment, high above the Severn Valley, sold.

Those sold buildings are often in better hands now, better cared for, better maintained. Some have continued as youth hostels under new owners. As big homes have come back into fashion some became family homes. Ostentation in homes is desirable, as bankers, football executives and players look for homes a previous generation could not and would not afford. For many the steady loss of youth hostels has been heartbreaking, like watching an ideal, something loved, destroyed. For others, they brought a much needed dose of reality, as youth hostels raced to catch up with changing tastes and fashion.

The changing countryside

On a trip to the Lake District in September 1952 Alan Turner stopped to eat his lunch beside a tarn, to savour the peace and tranquility that drew him into England's highest hills. The Lake District's 31 youth hostels made the region the most used, after the London region, accounting for 13% of the association's entire business. In 1952 the region had opened a new youth hostel at Etterby House, Carlisle, with grant funding from the Ministry of Education.

As Turner relaxed, the peace beside the tarn shattered as "first one and then many perspiring, mud stained and breathless figures came stumbling and staggering down towards us... Wearing agonised expressions, they had no time to look at the grandeur around, nor yet to exchange a friendly greeting." The "miserable participants" had set off that morning from the Dungeon Ghyll Hotel in Langdale. They had climbed Bowfell, Esk Pike and Scafell Pike, the highest hill in England, before coming down the 'corridor' route to Styhead Tarn. From there they climbed to the summit of Great Gable and their return to Langdale by Rossett Gill.

A MODERN SPIRIT

Harry Chapman, the Lakeland region's secretary, ran the mountain trial to celebrate the 21st anniversary of youth hostels in the Lake District that year. He wanted "to discover to just what extent the long years of work by our group in general and myself in particular had developed the courage and character of this generation." Chapman had spent his early life in Lakeland and then in Preston where after the war he worked in iron foundries and on building sites. He was a keen outdoor enthusiast, tough and wiry, a cyclist, walker and climber. In 1931 he joined YHA, becoming the honorary secretary of Lakeland region in 1937 and its first paid secretary in 1945. At the end of the first mountain trial he was "satisfied, proud, and, at the same time, a humble man" because of the wonderful spirit shown "by all, the runners, the helpers, the onlookers."

Turner was less satisfied than Harry Chapman. Outraged by the way the breathless participants in Chapman's trial had shattered his peaceful lunch break, he complained in a letter to *The Rucksack*. In his view time-trials and races of any sort were incompatible with the aims of youth hostels. He had saved his anger for almost a year before writing to the magazine, calling the event a publicity stunt. Youth hostels had an object of encouraging a greater knowledge, love and care of the countryside. They should not, in his view, encourage members into doing foolhardy things on mountains. They should be persuading them to do exactly the opposite. "Unless squashed at an early stage, no doubt further efforts will be misguidedly made to rouse enthusiasm for this sort of thing…" Perhaps he had heard that Chapman was organising a second trial.

Youth hostels had a starring role in the countryside but as the disagreement between Chapman and Turner shows it was not without controversy, risks or danger. Visitors to the countryside had not always been welcome. Landowners, estate managers and game keepers saw the countryside as their exclusive domain. Wordsworth thought countryside recreation was a privilege, for those with an eye to perceive and a heart to enjoy natural beauty.

One of the ways in which people could use nature without disturbing the perceptions of others was for study. The outdoors had attracted the studious from the late 19th century. Early groups from the CHA studied botany and had field talks on place names, rocks and plants and historical associations. Rambling clubs were often based on naturalist societies, on religious institutions or came from the labour movement and cooperatives. A high proportion of youth hostel members were students, teachers or others connected with learning and education.

When youth hostels began they took up the claim of education. They would ensure 'townies' and young people, born in the city, learned to love and understand the countryside. They would learn not to trample down fields of corn, not to leave gates open and not to leave litter. Youth hostels may also have adopted the aim to reassure landowners and farmers that they were responsible, not like the young communists who trespassed on the Duke of Devonshire's land on Kinder Scout in 1932.

Youth hostels claimed another role in the countryside. Leading figures forged links with other countryside organisations. Gatliff and Clark were closely involved in the National Trust. Tom Stephenson, an editor of *The Rucksack*, was secretary of the Ramblers. Parfitt was part of the Countryside Commission. YHA was a member of the Standing Committee for National Parks. YHA members on national and regional countryside committees argued against roads, hydro electric schemes and dams. They fought for footpaths and rights of way. They cemented a place for youth hostels amongst other outdoor organisations and a voice in countryside affairs.

Baron, Catchpool and the first executive felt that youth hostels offered more than an introduction to the countryside. They "felt that the YHA could become the finest out-of-school educational movement in the country; that it was specially designed for boys and girls living in congested city areas." They would learn not only the beauty of the countryside and exhilaration of open air exercise, but "a sense of responsibility and comradeship in our hostels."

Teachers and educationalists were among those at the very beginning who wanted youth hostels. The National Adult School Union was one of the bodies that called on the NCSS to hold a meeting about youth hostels. School teachers were some of the first supporters of youth hostels. Associations of headteachers and assistant headteachers along with the National Union of Teachers cooperated with the early youth hostels association. A scheme of encouraging school groups to use youth hostels began as early as 1934. School groups were able to stay without membership, so long as the teacher or leader was a member.

Not all youth hostel members welcomed school groups. Groups were sometimes unpopular. They monopolised youth hostels. They took over common rooms, caused scrums at meal times and made too much noise. In 1959 YHA's national council debated the purpose of youth hostels. It declared the "primary object of YHA is to enable young people to go about to many places on their own, under their own steam, and whilst school and other organised parties should be welcomed so far as they can be fitted into the YHA as it is, care must always be taken that they do not prejudice our primary object either by altering the character of hostels or by diverting effort from our main job of running them." No one voted against the motion. No one abstained. But YHA's charitable object was not amended or changed. The national council had a way of debating and passing motions and taking no action to put them into effect.

Further motions at later councils cemented the sentiment. In 1968 YHA recognised "its prime function is to encourage and promote individual hostelling". The 1972 Annual Report reiterated "the Association does not regard itself as an extension of school or the education system. Its purpose is to provide facilities, in the way of meals, accommodation and comfort, allowing the members to obtain the education themselves from the physical surroundings, exertion and companionship of like-minded people."

The motions made little difference. Youth hostels continued to welcome school and youth groups. Since the war they had accepted financial support from the government education department. In 1961 youth hostels went a step further and began providing special facilities for schools. Six hostels offered special field study facilities. Dick Knapp, national secretary at the time, was one of the driving forces behind the development. He took to heart a part of the youth hostels object, to help all especially young people of limited means to a greater knowledge, love and care of the countryside. He believed that young people who did not visit youth hostels were deprived of something valuable.

Boggle Hole and Grinton Lodge in Yorkshire; Bryn Gwynant in Gwynedd; High Close in Cumbria; Leam Hall in Derbyshire and Swanage in Dorset each had simple field study facilities. Groups could use a room to write up their outdoor work, examine specimens and consult a small reference library. The scheme expanded to eight more youth hostels the following year. The annual report of 1965 explained that youth hostels would offer "these additional facilities wherever possible without causing disruption to or distraction from the normal purpose of the hostel." No doubt aware of the opposition to school groups, the report maintained in contorted language that school parties using field study facilities were youth hosteling "with a special purpose, not using accommodation for a different purpose."

From 1962 YHA employed field officers. They brought youth hostels "to the notice of those who are most likely to benefit from them," especially underprivileged young people. Field officers visited schools and spoke to teachers. They raised awareness of youth hostels and what they could do for schools and groups of young people. In 1968, one field officer, Diane Cunningham, began arranging trips to the countryside around London. The trips were, for "underprivileged boys and girls... from broken homes, poor homes and those who never went out of their immediate environment."

Children came from Hackney and Tower Hamlets. Cunningham borrowed walking shoes, rucksacks and macs for the children. A girl turned up for a trip in high heels, carrying a suitcase. They took the train and walked to youth hostels in the Chiltern Hills. "The youngsters had plenty of outlet for their energies and revelled in the sense of freedom and space. It came as something of a shock to some to realise that they had lived a whole week-end without the 'telly' and had not missed it," Cunningham recalled after one trip.

Cunningham set up a permanent group for young people. They took short weekend trips and made longer summer journeys out of London. They walked long distance footpaths, like the Pennine and West Highland Ways. The trips encouraged youngsters to travel on their own when they could. Members used letters and the postal service to keep in touch between trips and, amalgamating 'post' and 'hostel,' they called themselves the Postellers.

Trips to the countryside, out of school, were rewarding for teachers and unforgettable for their pupils and students. School trips to the countryside had been the original youth hostels founder's dream. Richard Schirrmann dreamed of youth hostels as a way of getting young people into the countryside. He believed that children learned best out of the classroom, in the real world. Away from the confines of the classroom, children bonded in new and different ways. They learned new skills and their confidence in themselves increased.

But trips away from the classroom could and did go wrong. Things had gone wrong for Schirrmann in 1909. Accommodation he had expected fell through. A storm caught him and his children and forced them to shelter in a school. That night he dreamed of youth hostels where groups like his could stay for the night. At home after the trip he began the first youth hostel. If things hadn't gone wrong he might never have imagined youth hostels.

Attitudes to outdoor education changed after 1945. A generation that had developed self reliance and strength in war wanted others to have the same, without the need for fighting. They turned to the natural world, to overcoming rain and cold. Teachers and educationalists encouraged young people to test themselves against hills and weather. By overcoming their own physical frailties, young people would develop stamina, independence and confidence. Working in teams, they took responsibility for each other. They would become a new, confident citizenry for the new world of post war Britain.

The countryside became a place of adventure and challenge. Young people learned to take responsibility for themselves and others there. They learned to overcome hardship and emerged, stronger and better adults. Harry Chapman's aim in starting the Lake District Mountain Trial had been born from that belief. Ideas about the countryside became more dynamic and more active. They focused less on using the outdoors as a classroom for study and less on preservation of an environment. Instead countryside contributed to the development of young people and ideas of the countryside as a playground for leisure and recreation.

In January 1951 things went wrong for a group of six young men from the Derby Town YHA Group. They spent the night in bitter cold on the summit of Snowdon, while rescue parties searched for them. The pilot who led one of the three RAF rescue parties said that the group's expedition in such weather, on Snowdon, without an ice axe, was sheer suicide.

The episode created controversy between youth hostels and Geoffrey Winthrop Young. He had been with the Friends Ambulance Unit with GM Trevelyan in Italy during the first world war and the two were close friends. Young was a leading figure in outdoor education. He was a president of the Alpine Club and founded the British Mountaineering Council. He had helped Kurt Hahn, founder of Outward Bound, emigrate from Germany in 1934.

Young wrote to *The Times*. He urged "the great rambler and open-air organisations and the Youth Hostels Association" to do more to ensure young people ventured into the hills equipped and prepared. The alternative was, in his view, to "invite the lighthearted or the empty-headed to face dragons in their lairs with a walking-stick." Youth hostel chairman, Arthur Dower, retorted in *The Times* that youth hostels were already doing much to educate young people. The concerns of Young and others led to the Duke of Edinburgh's Award Scheme in 1956.

Despite such efforts and warnings, worse incidents followed. Three Rover Scouts died during a walking challenge in the Peak District in 1964. Five teenagers from an Edinburgh school and their female instructor died in Scotland's Cairngorms in 1971. Youth hostels were linked to neither of these accidents and they happened in wild places, like the Peak District and in the remote Cairngorms, in poor weather. An accident in 1993 seemed worse because it happened within sight of towns and villages on England's southern coast.

On a sunny summer day, a cheerful group of eight young people and three adults set off to paddle kayaks from Lyme Regis to Charmouth, two miles down the coast, in Dorset. The return trip should have taken no more than two hours but, almost immediately, the group got into difficulty. One of the group and then a teacher capsized. Whilst righting themselves, wind blew them out to sea. They had no emergency flares and no way of calling for help. Four hours later, rescue helicopters winched four of the pupils, a teacher and two instructors, out of the sea. Four others were dead or died later in hospital.

Devon County Council held an inquiry into the deaths. Its report noted that there would always be a degree of risk when young people undertook adventurous activities. Parliament passed the Adventure Activities Licensing regulations in 1996 to minimise those risks. They established a regulator for adventurous activities, ushering in a new era of safety considerations for outdoor education.

In the same year parliament approved the new regulations, a party of 40 children and five adults from Launceston College from Cornwall went for a week in Brittany. They stayed at the youth hostel in Pleine-Fougeres, near Mont St Michel, in a quiet area away from towns. Their plans included visiting St Malo, Bayeux and Mont St Michel, sampling French food and practising the language. The school had been enjoying similar trips to

France for many years.

On the morning of 18 July 1996 one of the girls sharing a first floor room with 13 year-old Caroline Dickinson reached out to wake her and found she was cold. The girl told the others and went to find a teacher in a neighbouring room. The teacher cleared the teenagers from their room and raised the alarm. A doctor and ambulance crew arrived, but they were unable to resuscitate Caroline.

The aftermath of the murder for the parents of Caroline, for the school, for the wider world of education and for youth hostels themselves continued for many years. In December 1999 Sue Dickinson, Caroline's mother, sued the county education authorities for negligence and breach of duty. The judge said he recognised Mrs Dickinson's anguish but said that did not allow him to find the county council liable. In June 2004 a Spanish man was sentenced to 30 years in jail for the murder of Caroline.

In October 2000 two teenage girls drowned whilst river walking in the Yorkshire Dales. The inquest into their deaths praised the teacher's efforts to save the girls but also criticised the teachers and education authorities for their part in the tragedy. Teachers were already under pressure from changes, such as the national curriculum and school inspections. They became more and more reluctant to undertake such trips. They had been protesting against poor pay and the government's imposition of a national curriculum. They refused to cover for colleagues taking pupils on trips out of school. Trips often stopped or teachers turned to specialist, licensed instructors.

Difficulties for youth hostels in the countryside increased another degree in February 2001 when a food inspector discovered foot and mouth disease at an abattoir in Essex. Panic spread. As more and more cases appeared the scale of the outbreak overwhelmed the Ministry of Agriculture.

In the panic Ben Gill, president of the National Farmers Union, called for local authorities to close every footpath. He pleaded for everyone to stay away from the countryside. Prime Minister Tony Blair repeated his hope that people would stay away from the countryside. Other organisations supported the call. Some took their own steps to close footpaths. On 2 March the Ministry of Agriculture called in the army to help.

People stayed away from the countryside. By end of March 109 youth hostels out of 230 were closed. They were either close to or reached over farmland. 15 shut in the Lake District National Park. Youth hostels shed 220 jobs, either by delaying start dates or by leaving vacancies unfilled. Wherever possible staff shifted to youth hostels that were open as cancellations poured in.

By September the disease had cost youth hostels £5 million in lost income. The results for youth hostels were worse than expected. Just as foot and mouth ended, the tragic events of 9/11 brought international travel to a temporary halt. City youth hostels, on which YHA relied during the winter months and that had kept it going when youth hostels in the countryside closed, lost business. Youth hostels ended the year with income £7million lower than the previous year and with a loss of £1.5million. Numbers staying in youth hostels had dropped by more than 300,000, the lowest they had been for more than 20 years.

The UK was finally declared free of foot and mouth disease in January 2002, eleven months after the outbreak began. By then the countryside, the background against which youth hostels had launched their starring role, had become a different place.

The outbreak of foot and mouth disease and the closure of the countryside changed the face of outdoor activity in the UK. People discovered walking, climbing and outdoor locations in Europe or further, the equal of or better than those of the UK, if only because of warmer, drier and more reliable weather. People also learned the economic importance of the countryside. After 2001 they began to exercise that strength. Towns like Betwys Coed, Keswick and Ambleside competed for the title of outdoors capital of Britain, England or Wales, for the visitors they could draw to shops, pubs and outdoor retailers, as well as to take part in outdoor activities. For a time everyone working in the countryside learned to work together.

Accidents in the countryside and foot and mouth disease had shown the countryside to be less welcoming. It was not the bucolic place art, literature and advertising portrayed. Neither was it the vision of delight it may have been in 1930. Mad cow disease had worsened the picture. The countryside was risky and less hospitable to town dwellers than they might have thought. People had fled towns and cities in 1930 for weekends and for holidays. Now those towns and cities seemed more attractive, more welcoming and cleaner and safer than the countryside for a weekend or a longer holiday.

Parents became reluctant to let their children wander the countryside as previous generations had done. Roads are busier, parents more protective of their children. In small families, children are more precious. Notorious murders have scared parents. Children have more indoor entertainment than was available 50 years ago. Children are kept closer to home and are left less free to wander. A generation may have missed and lost the freedom of their parents.

An RSPB report in 2009 showed the gulf between generations. Few children played in wild spaces. Less than 10% played in natural spaces whilst 40% of their parents or grandparents did. Children played in their homes when their parents had played in local streets. 62% of children said they played at home indoors more than any other place. 42% of adults said they had played outdoors in local streets more than in any other place. Three quarters of adults claimed to have had a patch of nature near their homes and over half of them went there once or twice a week. 64% of children reckon they have a patch of nature near their homes but less than a quarter go there once or twice a week.

Research shows that outdoor experiences and contact with nature are good for children's health. They enjoy being outdoors. They develop their emotions and their personal and social skills benefit. Their teachers however are less relaxed about taking them walking in the countryside. They involve activity instructors and buy activity packages by the hour or day. The countryside is part of the UK's consumer life. It is no longer a haven from consumerism or what Trevelyan had described as "the intolerable waste of modern mechanical life." Activity holidays increased by 11% between 2004 and 2009 and in 2009 activity holidays were worth an estimated £4.7 billion.

In the face of such changes, youth hostels themselves have changed. Youth hostels offer summer camps for young people with organised activities and supervision. They offer packages to schools and teachers. The youth hostel at Castleton in Derbyshire offers outdoor learning, history and geography packages. Children can take part in a medieval banquet. They can learn archery using a longbow and archaeological digging skills. The outdoor programme at Castleton helps develop confidence and team work skills through activities like outdoor cooking and GPS tracking.

Following the death of Caroline Dickinson youth hostels put in place stringent but necessary security measures. Locks for bedrooms, late night security and vetting of staff all added costs. The event dealt a blow to the open social mixing of youth hostels and interrupted the free and easy atmosphere youth hostels. Within youth hostels, teachers were reluctant to see their groups mix with other adults. They wanted exclusive use of youth hostels for their groups. To accommodate groups of school children, youth hostels ran with empty beds and turned away adults who wanted to stay at the same time. Youth hostels were no longer the simple accommodation invented by a German schoolteacher for colleagues and their pupils.

Youth hostels still contribute. In 2014, according to YHA's figures, more than half a million young people enjoyed youth hostels with their schools and university groups, with friends and family. YHA awarded grants totalling £278,000 for that year, providing 7,458 trips for young people. 649 young people took part in YHA summer camps.

For Harry Chapman's Lake District Mountain Trial there was no reconciliation with YHA and its members. The event ran again in 1953 and 1954 but YHA organised its last event in 1955. A new committee began organising the event in 1956 and dropped the stipulation that participants should be YHA members. The mountain trial still runs today without official involvement from youth hostels. The race is little changed and although participants no longer wear stout boots, they still run, sweating and breathless through the fells. They test themselves, fulfilling Harry Chapman's original idea, demonstrating every bit of their courage, strength and stamina.

Notes and references.

David Rosen supplied useful background on the Lake District Mountain Trial. I used contemporary newspaper accounts and some key reports for this chapter. The Department for the Environment, Food and Rural Affairs carried out an inquiry into the outbreak of foot and mouth disease. I relied on that report for sections of the chapter relating to the outbreak. I read Natural England's report on childhood and nature and used figures from the report which highlight the difference between generations and their experience of nature.

"first one and then many…" *The Rucksack*, July–Aug 1953
"to discover…" *The Rucksack*, Nov–Dec 1953
"satisfied, proud…" ibid
"Unless squashed…" *The Rucksack*, July–Aug 1953
"felt that the YHA could…" Catchpool, *Candles in the Darkness*, p141
"primary object of YHA…" National Minutes, 1959
"its prime function…" *YHA Annual Report 1968*, p5
"the Association does not…" *YHA Annual Report 1972*
"these additional facilities…" *YHA Annual Report 1965*, p6
"to the notice of those…" *YHA Annual Report 1968*, p6
"underprivileged boys and girls…" Ibid
"The youngsters had…" *YHA Annual Report 1968*, p8
"the great rambler and open-air…" Geoffrey Winthrop Young letter in *The Times*, Tuesday 22 May 1951

-28-

Foot and mouth

When I began work as YHA's Head of Corporate Affairs in December 2000 change was in the air. I expected Roger Clarke, the new chief executive, to bring fresh direction to youth hostels. Clarke was YHA's third chief executive after Colin Logan who had replaced Andrew Chinneck in 1992. Clarke arrived in March 2000 from the Countryside Agency, the former Countryside Commission, where he had been a director. He brought a raft of contacts, an inclusive style and a desire to modernise YHA. We both believed youth hostels could do more to raise their profile in the media and in their local communities.

I started work at YHA's national office in St Albans where 24 years before I had enquired for a job in a youth hostel. The old house was still as I remembered in its garden amidst trees and overgrown shrubs. It made an unsuitable office in a maze of rooms and narrow stairs, in attics, in an odd extension with too many windows and a couple of cabins in the garden. I shared a room under the roof with Mags Rivett. She like me had worked in and managed youth hostels including the one in Plymouth. Facilities were poor. To access email, I linked my laptop to a telephone line by a cable thrown from one window to the next.

When an inspector found foot and mouth disease at an abattoir in Essex, I knew little about the disease. Inspectors also found it in Devon. If I knew little, I soon found out the disease caused panic and terror. Calls went up to close footpaths and for people to stay away from the countryside. On 22 February, the Ramblers' Association advised against taking rural walks. On 23 February, the Royal Society for the Protection of Birds closed nature reserves. The National Trust closed all its parks containing livestock. The British Mountaineering Council called on mountaineers and climbers to respect restrictions and stay out of the countryside.

I went at short notice, substituted for another staff member, to an event in the House of Commons. Alun Michael, the Minister for Rural Affairs, was the headline speaker. As a youth and community worker he had been taking groups of young people on trips to hostels before he became an MP and then minister. I raised our concerns and he reassured me that he and his department understood the issues youth hostels faced.

Roger Clarke called it the worst disaster to hit youth hostels since the war. Under hastily amended powers, local authorities could close all paths within their boundaries, without the need to place closure notices on individual paths. Many supported the widespread closure of footpaths at the time. With the benefit of hindsight, with no straightforward mechanism for reopening them, it was a mistake. When farmers, politicians and groups like the Ramblers asked everyone to stay away from the countryside, members did so.

At first we refused to close youth hostels. We maintained they were open and were staying open. But the pressure became intolerable. Cancellations flooded youth hostels and our small central bookings office. People with bookings demanded refunds even in youth hostels miles from any outbreak. Visitors from Europe and America cancelled visits. Youth hostels emptied.

It was the kind of panicked reaction 24-hour media were beginning to create. A vicious news cycle, when stories ran away from everyone, had begun. Demands were easily amplified. Muddled thinking, good intentions and hysteria overcame logic, leaving little time for reasoned debate. Journalists scrambled for comment. And that was before Facebook,

Twitter and social media offered an instant source of comment.

We conceded defeat. We closed youth hostels in affected areas, where they were close to or accessed through farmland. With the countryside closed and people staying away, almost half the youth hostels shut. Margaret Whaley, Director of Marketing, estimated they would face a net loss of £2m, by the end of April. If the outbreak continued until June, she expected another £3.8m of losses.

YHA cancelled its investment programme. We pulled together a small crisis group. We met once a week. We gathered a picture of what was happening at youth hostels across the country. We published a weekly bulletin, updating the list of closed youth hostels and communicating with staff. We had email communication with some but not with others. We relied on paper. Youth hostels worked together and shared staff.

The public remained confused about which parts of the countryside they could visit. The youth hostel at Grinton Lodge was 20 miles from the nearest outbreak at Settle. In a normal year schools would have filled the hostel but most cancelled. When signs opening footpaths around the hostel went up on 20 July, few walkers went out. Most stuck to arrangements made when the disease first hit in spring.

We moved to campaigning, to rescue what we could from the lost business of that summer. We warned we might have to close and sell hostels to make good our losses. Clarke's view was trenchant and direct. He pointed out that the government had said the countryside was closed. The government's announcement caused everyone to go home. That had been a mistake. The government's offer of rate relief was no help to youth hostels because, as a charity, we paid no rates. Neither could youth hostels get the help available to small businesses, as they were not treated as small businesses.

We mailed members asking them to help. We asked them to support us with donations. We suggested they write to their MP. We avoided template letters and petitions. We advised them to tell MPs their own stories of youth hostels. They could explain how much youth hostels had helped them when they were younger. Members gave £260,000 in support and wrote to their MPs. In turn, 200 MPs requested information and support for youth hostels from the government.

Alun Michael spent a night at the youth hostel in St Briavels in the Forest of Dean. Kim Howells, the Minister for Tourism, and Diana Organ, the local MP, joined him and YHA chairman, Chris Boulton, on a walk in the surrounding countryside, to show that the countryside was open. The efforts of lobbying, letter writing and tireless hard work paid off. Government offered help through business recovery funds. The Wales Tourist Board stepped in with recovery funds too.

Throughout it all we were moving YHA's national office. In August the old Trevelyan House in St Albans shut down but the building in Matlock wasn't ready. People started new jobs in a temporary structure and a marque in the yard. My team scattered itself around the Peak District, in the corners of existing offices. We didn't move into our new places for another month. By then foot and mouth was over.

The crisis had exposed the issues youth hostels faced. We had no centralised booking system and no quick way of gathering information. We struggled to shift resources and to move bookings from closed hostels to those still open. We worked on paper using telephones without central records or databases. Financial information took a month to arrive. The move from St Albans to Matlock upended the archive of youth hostel history in its cupboards and filing cabinets. It arrived in chaos which took years to rearrange. It might have been a metaphor for that time.

A month later, settled in our new location, 9/11 struck. In an open plan office news travels fast, especially when it can be seen on the screen of anyone's computer. On that Tuesday afternoon in September I was on the phone, talking to Kate Law, the publisher of our magazine from Haymarket. She was better informed than I was. She suddenly broke into our conversation to tell me one of the towers was coming down. In minutes the 9/11 attacks were across all our computer screens.

World travel ground to a halt. We had depended on visitors to cities throughout foot and mouth. Now that business and the mainstay of youth hostels through the winter stopped. We faced a second crisis.

The cultural value of cities

Youth hostels had a new logo in 1986. The letters 'YHA' appeared outside and below the established triangle, echoing the international sign for youth hostels. The association no longer styled itself 'the Youth Hostels Association'. It dropped the definite article and called itself YHA, distancing itself from its roots as an association of members.

The duty, or chore, that every member carried out as part of their stay began to slip away. Members swept, tidied and washed up, after buying a meal, less and less especially at larger youth hostels. The move was gradual as the idea of chores lost its place for guests who expected to buy a product or purchase a service. The annual handbook no longer mentioned rules. A section titled 'For everyone's benefit' instead included ten points, which the following year became eight.

New hostels in Cardiff, Kendal, Wantage, Manorbier and Bristol opened and investment went to more than 40 existing youth hostels including Windsor, Brighton, Cambridge, Salisbury, York, and Edale. Investment also went to small youth hostels in mid-Wales and to Lady

Trevelyan's Once Brewed youth hostel in Northumberland.

Simple accommodation emerged in Lancashire's Forest of Bowland. The botanist and television personality, David Bellamy, YHA president since 1983, opened the first of five camping barns there in May 1990. Harking back to the early days of youth hostels, farmers offered redundant buildings as camping barns. Accommodation was basic, often no more than a platform where people slept, a space for cooking, a tap for cold water and a toilet.

Hedley Alcock retired as chairman in 1990 and John Patten replaced him. Soaring interest rates, a drop in the value of property and high exchange rates caused a recession in the early 1990s. Iraq invaded Kuwait in 1990, the first Gulf war followed and international travel fell. Numbers staying in youth hostels dropped by 10% between 1989 and 1992. Visitor numbers from overseas countries fell by 16%.

High interest rates, on borrowings to finance youth hostel investment, caused significant issues for youth hostels. Investment hadn't created the expected income to pay back loans. With bank borrowing already high, YHA turned to selling properties to continue funding improvement and investment. 19 youth hostels with high property values were deliberately chosen for sale to raise funds but, in the recession of 1991-2, property sales slowed and youth hostels didn't sell. Investment stalled.

Andrew Chinneck, after eight years as chief executive, left. He had introduced wide change, including the modernisation and professional marketing of youth hostels. His Product Development and Marketing Plan had not always been popular. To traditionalists it seemed to be moving youth hostels away from their roots and from what made them special. They felt the appeal of youth hostels threatened.

Colin Logan, who had overseen the winding up of Wales and Eastern regions in the early 1980s, succeeded Chinneck as chief executive. Logan had immersed himself in youth hostels and their affairs. He had been an eloquent spokesperson for the introduction of paid management, one of the first regional directors and then the national Operations Director. In a nod to traditionalist members he spoke of his determination to maintain the diversity of youth hostels. He was confident youth hostels would keep their simple and recognisable character.

Management restructured to save costs and increase efficiency in 1990 and again in 1992. Derek Hanson replaced Patten as chairman in 1993.

Marketing centralised. YHA put its faith in operational management, buildings and investment, moving away from Kingsley's vision of a marketing led renaissance for youth hostels.

Youth hostels around the world faced challenge and change, as more people travelled. Australian youth hostels felt the changes more than most, as more and more people travelled there. They backpacked through Asia to Australia and over the Pacific to the US. By 1990, two-thirds of those staying in Australia's official youth hostels came from overseas. In one city alone, in Cairns, Queensland, 46 hostels, most of them independent and unofficial, catered for the new travellers.

Until then the only kind of youth hostel had been an official one. The official ones now struggled to compete with rivals who required no membership and no chores. Independent, profit-orientated, entrepreneurial backpacker hostels offered double rooms, mixed dorms, swimming pools, discos and cheap meals. They allowed or sold alcohol. They sold bus tickets. They packaged trips and tours. Even those with poor fire standards and overcrowded dormitories in run down buildings competed with official youth hostels. People discovered them by word of mouth or found their representatives at bus stops and stations. The advantage a printed guide of youth hostels had once given faded. Official youth hostels in Australia were forced to tackle their old fashioned, austere image.

Competition in England and Wales also grew. Generator, the independent hostel chain, launched their first hostel in London in 1994. Youth hostel buildings in England and Wales proved difficult and expensive to change. Youth hostels paid the price for their rapid expansion during the early years, when the grass roots in the regions had found and snapped up any available property. Many youth hostels were too small to easily convert to modern standards. When converted few of them gave a return on the kind of expenditure they required. Throughout the 1990s more youth hostels shut and were sold than opened. 239 youth hostels were open in 1999. Ten years before the figure had been 258.

Technology created challenges. Youth hostels had their first website in April 1998. The first site was an on-line accommodation guide. Users could search for hostels by name, facilities or geographically, using interactive maps. Hostelworld, an independent website was already offering bookings on line, having launched in 1997. Without the constraints of officialdom, Hostelworld listed any youth hostel, private, official or independent. The site took a booking fee and left the hostel to take its charges from the guest when they arrived. Official youth hostels in England and Wales turned down offers from Hostelworld and kept themselves apart.

Youth hostels were losing the advantage a network and guidebook had given them for more than 65 years. The internet brought into being a new kind of world wide network that would overwhelm local, regional and national ones. Youth hostels had always relied on word of mouth. Their members had always been their best sales tools. Members had always introduced workmates, colleagues, friends and family to youth hostels. The internet offered a new relationship and a new word of mouth.

Roger Clarke arrived as the youth hostels' third chief executive in 2000 when Colin Logan retired. Clarke found an organisation he considered had spent a difficult decade, centralising its regional structure, pursuing efficiency and modernising youth hostels with limited funds, often borrowed. It had lost confidence, he believed, and become inward-looking. Chris Boulton replaced Derek Hanson as chairman.

Since the government had introduced the minimum wage and the working time directive in 1998, costs of running youth hostels had risen. Following the losses of foot and mouth in 2001, seven youth hostels shut and sold. Costs at a brand new, purpose-built youth hostel at Lee Valley in Hertfordshire rocketed. A long-awaited, computerised and centralised booking system was cancelled in 2003 after numerous delays. The swiftly changing internet had overtaken the system and its failure was a setback to plans for on line bookings. Without a centralised booking system youth hostels struggled to offer bookings over the internet or by telephone.

Further bad news for youth hostels arrived when, in 2004, Simon Ashworth conducted surveys to better understand attitudes to youth hostels. Ashworth, a psychology graduate from the University of East London, had set up Gabriel Ashworth Limited, a marketing consultancy and research company, with Clive Gabriel in 1993. He took his research amongst the general public, using robust samples across England and Wales, and did not focus only on members.

When improvement and modernisation began in the 1980s most young people had heard of youth hostels. By 2004 the reverse was true. Ashworth's survey revealed that youth hostels had dropped from view.

Among young people few considered youth hostels when looking for accommodation or saw them as relevant. When asked to consider youth hostels as potential places to stay, the response was replete with negatives and misconceptions about quality, standards, facilities and security. None in his sample claimed to know where a youth hostel was. None claimed to have come across one when searching for accommodation and very few claimed to know someone who had stayed in one.

In 2005 youth hostels waived the membership requirement. After that, anyone could stay in a youth hostel without being a member. The non-member simply paid a £3 supplement. The move ended 75 years of history. Since youth hostels first began, membership had been an essential tenet.

Hard on the heels of that decision, in January 2006, YHA announced it was selling 32 of its least popular youth hostels. YHA planned to invest £18 million. Selling the hostels would raise funds to invest in others. The announcement triggered an outcry. Members accused youth hostels of losing their ethos. They complained the priority of youth hostels had become making money and if a hostel didn't reap a profit it was closed down.

People complained that youth hostels were no longer providing a service to young people. But that year, young people, staying with their schools or other groups, recorded more than half a million overnight stays. In 2005 the Big Lottery Fund had awarded £17 million of national lottery funds for youth hostels to run summer camps. The camps were open to anyone. Places were offered at £100 when a conventional summer camp cost more than twice that. Young people, from households receiving income support, paid £25.

The camps ensured that bringing together 'all sorts and conditions of men and women' continued as a central feature of youth hostels. 32,000 young people took part over three years. On a camp they could go climbing, mountain biking and canoeing. They could take part in drama or learn new skills like bushcraft. Activities challenged their fears and contributed to their personal development.

Lindsey Porter, a member of the youth hostels' executive committee, had set up a programme called 'Give us a break.' The fund helped young people who might not otherwise have afforded a trip to a youth hostel. The financial services group, Provident Financial, funded another. The two

l 15,000 young people so they could take part in school
lassmates that year.

Critics also accused youth hostels of abandoning the countryside in favour of cities. Clarke responded in a letter to *The Guardian* that youth hostels were not retreating from rural areas. YHA remained a major provider of countryside accommodation and many of the 32 youth hostels that had been announced for closure were in towns and cities.

Criticism of youth hostels in cities was not new. One member had written in 1963 "hostels in Central London... are actually luring people away from the countryside... We must close these hostels for they do not support our aims." In that critic's view youth hostels were there "to help everyone to a greater knowledge and love of the countryside. Because of this one assumes that all our youth hostels are in a position to encourage this aim." Youth hostels in cities, in that writer's view, did not.

Youth hostels in cities were not a new development. The first youth hostel in London opened in May 1931 at New Talbot House near the Tower of London. The house was the vicarage of All Hallows by the Tower where Tubby Clayton of Toc H was vicar from 1922. The hostel was for men only and closed in September after recording only 33 overnight stays.

After that beginning the hunt for another site in London began. TA Leonard, champion of basic hostels, spoke in favour of a youth hostel for the city. In 1932 he declared there was a crying need for one. "London has the discredit of being the only capital in Europe that cannot welcome impecunious youth into its midst. Teachers, welfare workers, scouts, all sorts of young folk from the benighted provinces, not to forget Continental youth - all want to see this wonderful London..."

Almost immediately he had his wish. From 1933, for two summers, the Welcome Club Rooms at the Alexandra Palace, Wood Green, were London's next hostel. A large restaurant, on the ground floor, offered youth hostel members meals at special prices. The association next leased the youth hostel at Highgate, on West Hill, from 1935 and bought it in 1944. The brick-built townhouse, originally two cottages, continued as a youth hostel until 1997. A bigger youth hostel at 38 Great Ormond Street opened in July 1936. GOSH, as it became known, stayed open until 1952 when the one at Earl's Court, which remains open today, replaced it. In all, London has had at least 30 temporary, short term or seasonal hostels. 12

have been open for longer periods.

Youth hostels sprang up in other cities and towns. The City Mill in Winchester opened in 1931, one of the group of hostels that opened in time for Easter that year. The mill race poured through the centre of the building. To wash, people swung into the water on a rope, proving that even city hostels could provide adventure and a wild, natural experience.

In 1931 Dover had its first youth hostel in a YMCA hut. A first youth hostel opened in Cambridge in 1934 and, when that closed, GM Trevelyan, who was master at Trinity College, officially opened a second in 1939 in Cherry Hinton Hall. That one closed soon afterwards when war broke out. In March 1945 the British War Relief Society of American gave funds to open a new one in Cambridge. The society provided non-military aid to Britain during the war and supported the opening of another youth hostel in York in May 1945. Youth hostels opened in Norwich in 1937 and Southampton in 1938. Bristol had one from 1949.

Post-war, cities began to be cleaner, more pleasant places. Authorities cleared slums and council housing brought about more pleasant cities. The first Clean Air Act, introduced in 1956, created zones where only smokeless fuels could be burned. Air pollution in cities fell. Events like the smog that settled on London for five days in December 1952, when 4,000 more deaths than usual occurred, ended.

Cities were no longer as George Orwell described them in 1933, when he was writing *The Road To Wigan Pier* and staying in youth hostels. Wigan was no longer "a lunar landscape of slag-heaps." Neither was Sheffield "a world from which vegetation had been banished," where "nothing existed except smoke, shale, mud, ashes and foul water... And the stench! If at rare moments you stop smelling sulphur it is because you have begun smelling gas. Even the shallow river that runs through the town is usually bright yellow with some chemical or other."

Youth hostels joined a wider fashion for regeneration, particularly in old ports and docklands. As Britain lost an empire, cities gave up their old docks for new ports. Bristol abandoned its 'floating harbour' for docks at Avonmouth and Portbury and reshaped the old docks for new purposes. Local MP, William Waldegrave, appealed for funds for a youth hostel in September 1986. Converting an old grain warehouse, on the edge of the harbour, into a youth hostel took almost three years. It opened in July 1989, the first of a series of hostels opening in dockland development schemes.

Another opened in 1991 at Rotherhithe in London, on land reclaimed from the old Surrey Docks. The new building had magnetic keys, 24-hour access, security lockers, lifts, a toilet and sink in each bedroom, a cafeteria, kitchen, currency exchange and a sightseeing booking service. The Queen officially opened it in March 1993. Purpose built hostels, in dockland redevelopment schemes in Manchester and in Liverpool followed. The Duke of Edinburgh opened the youth hostel in Liverpool in August 1998, the first permanent youth hostel in the city.

The growth of low budget airlines eased travel from city to city in Europe and further. Ryanair launched in 1985. Stelios Haji-Ioannou founded Easyjet in 1995, flying from Luton to Glasgow. As youth hostels had changed the world after 1930, budget airlines revolutionised travel from the 1980s. They opened international travel to a new audience. By 2000, youth hostels in London recorded more than 350,000 stays, 17% of the total for all youth hostels.

Cities are now the places to be, for a weekend break or a holiday. Cities are lively and entertaining, with music, museums, art galleries, coffee shops, restaurants and bars. As so many people had crowded into cities at the end of the 19th century, the founders of youth hostels feared we were losing touch with the countryside. But the move of populations to cities continues today. After taking account of changes in area reclassification, the urban population of England and Wales was estimated to be nine per cent larger in 2011 than in 2001.

A new youth hostel opened in Oxford, in May 2001, at the height of the foot and mouth outbreak. Close to the centre of Oxford, on Botley Road beside the railway station, the new hostel replaced an older one on the outskirts of town. With its better location, more privacy, with en-suites and smaller rooms, numbers staying at the new hostel rocketed. The old hostel had accommodated 30,000 overnight stays in its last full year, a record for it. Two years later, the new youth hostel accommodated more than 46,000, 50% more.

YHA recognised the importance of town and city hostels and altered its charitable purpose in 2005 to include the "appreciation of the cultural values of towns and cities". In 2006 the hostel at Hampstead Heath closed. A new one, on Bolsover Street in the West End of London, replaced it. Its facilities were a step further than those at the youth hostel at Rotherhithe.

As well as lifts, key coded security and 24-hour 365 day opening, its reception combined a restaurant and bar where people could catch up, eat, and chat, emphasising the sociability of youth hostels. Most bedrooms had four beds and en-suite toilets and showers.

John Parfitt, David Kingsley and others had always said that modern youth hostels could and would draw young people. The popular new youth hostels in London and Oxford showed they were right. The surprise is that it had taken so long to get the facilities right and to find the money to maintain them. Trustees and the executive had had to convince others that they had more under used youth hostels than anyone could afford. Selling youth hostels provided the funds to modernise others and to create the modern systems new ways of booking and travel required.

But the outcry over selling underused hostels had highlighted another overdue change. Some members, offended by closures, complained that they had not been consulted. They felt an organisation founded on democratic principals had let them down. Three regional councils represented members in England with one council for Wales. The national council had become the annual general meeting. A board of trustees had grown from the national executive committee. The board interviewed experts in the field of charity governance and asked Andrew Purkis to lead a review of governance in 2005.

Purkis had worked as an assistant director at the National Council of Voluntary Organisations that had once been the NCSS, the organisation that summoned delegates to the first meeting that created YHA. He had graduated from Oxford and spent six years as a civil servant in the Northern Ireland Office before joining the NCVO. He had also been a director at the Council for the Preservation of Rural England, another organisation involved in the start of youth hostels. He was a keen walker, giving him impeccable connections with youth hostels as well as links to their history.

Purkis concluded the regional structures were no longer working to involve members. The review estimated less than 1% of YHA members were involving themselves in youth hostel democracy. In the early 1960s low participation in youth hostel democracy had caused a major reorganisation. But that had not changed participation. Few members involved themselves in running the affairs of youth hostels.

YHA denied important users of youth hostels a voice in their affairs.

Overseas guests, schools and groups were unrepresented in the democratic ways of youth hostels. Affiliated organisations had not been on the youth hostels' executive committee since 1968, though they still attended and voted at the AGM. Regional councils appointed the majority of trustees through the AGM.

Representation was biased heavily towards walkers and cyclists, to people much older than many users and to those who had been youth hostel members for a long time. Purkis' review concluded that the AGM preserved these issues and distorted representation. The AGM began taking steps to open elections to the board of trustees to the wider membership.

Roger Clarke had steered youth hostels through a series of crises, including the foot and mouth outbreak, through a round of traumatic closures and into a review of youth hostels' governance arrangements. With a new chairman, Chris Darmon, in place, Clarke resigned in early 2008.

For six months Caroline White held the reins as interim chief executive. She came from a background in charities and housing associations with an understanding of charities that would be vital when the board appointed her as full time chief executive later that year. She was the first woman in youth hostel's most senior paid role. With the board she launched a new strategic plan and an emphasis on increasing the number of young people who experienced YHA, whether staying in a youth hostel or taking part in an activity.

New youth hostels opened. At Castleton in Derbyshire, a new youth hostel replaced the previous one at Castleton Hall in the village, when the Peak District National Park Authority sold Losehill Hall. New youth hostels, at Berwick on Tweed and at Alnwick, both in Northumberland, opened in 2012. In November 2013, the Queen officially opened a new youth hostel, YHA South Downs, in converted farm buildings, near Itford, in England's newest national park.

In 2013 YHA invested £7.2 million in seven youth hostels including Grinton Lodge and the one at Malham, which John Dower had designed. A new youth hostel for Brighton opened in late 2014. By then YHA had invested in almost half the youth hostels it owned in less than ten years. Selling property provided the bulk of funding. YHA was moving towards a network of hostels it could afford, a network in which every youth hostel paid its own "running expenses, for maintaining the building and its equipment," as national council had agreed in 1964.

In 2015 YHA agreed a move to an AGM open to all members. Voting would no longer be restricted to representatives of regional groups and affiliated societies, ending 85 years of regional groups running youth hostels.

YHA recognises that, because of previous decades of under investment, the number of youth hostels will reduce further. At some youth hostels the level of investment required to meet customer expectations will never give a return. YHA says it will dispose of hostels, that are not critical to the delivery of its plan, to allow investment in others, as the work of modernising youth hostels, begun more than 50 years ago during John Parfitt's time, continues.

Youth hostels aim to be profitable and successful. Achieving this has been difficult. The number of youth hostels YHA owns has fallen though the total overnights recorded remain as high as they ever were. Professional managers have replaced democracy but volunteers work with paid staff. The voluntary tradition of youth hostels, so important to Jack Catchpool, continues.

Youth hostels remain open to all and bring together as friends "all sorts and conditions of men and women", as Herbert Gatliff wanted. They preserve something special in that open easy atmosphere, something that Gatliff might have recognised. We can no longer get a view from David Kingsley on whether he believes the changes he introduced to youth hostels, in the early 1980s, have been successful or not. He died on 13 April 2014.

Travel is easier and more widespread than Tom Fairclough and his friends might ever have dreamed when they set off to Germany in the summer of 1929. The idea of youth hostels they found in Germany and brought back to England has prospered, expanded and changed the world. The 1950s and 1960s saw youth hostels become established institutions, a part of mainstream society. By the 1970s it might have looked as if the idea had become outdated and in the 1980s youth hostels looked as if they might become extinct. Survival seemed impossible. But youth hostels did not go under. They have adapted to the internet and social media. They have abandoned their reliance on a paper guide and handbook. They have dropped their rules and restrictions. They have opened bars. They are open

24 hours of the day. They have changed themselves to meet the world they created.

Notes and references

This chapter covers the period when I was YHA's head of corporate affairs and includes personal recollections of surveys and reports from the time. I refreshed my recollections using *Annual Reports* and the media particularly for coverage of controversial closures. John Martin's catalogue of all youth hostels was essential reading for all the many town and city youth hostels YHA has had. Quotes from *The Road to Wigan Pier* reproduced by permission of Penguin Books Ltd and reprinted by permission of Bill Hamilton as the Literary Executor of the Estate of the Late Sonia Brownell Orwell.

"hostels in Central London..." *The Youth Hosteller*, March 1963, p13
"London has the discredit..." *YHA Rucksack*, Summer 1932, p42
"a lunar landscape of slag-heaps..." Orwell, George, *The Road To Wigan Pier*, p94
"a world from which vegetation..." ibid

EPILOGUE

-30-

Coniston

I first came to the youth hostel at Coppermines nearly 40 years ago. In warm sunny spring weather its isolation above the village and the darkness surrounding it at night reminded me of remote places I had loved and thought I had lost.

Since then I've been back many times, to visit friends who ran the hostel, on work visits and, for the last three years since I retired, with Caroline as a volunteer. We run the youth hostel for a week at a time. We greet guests. We clean. We chat and remind ourselves what makes youth hostels special. In the quiet at night we read a lot. If we're lucky and available time and weather coincide we walk in the surrounding hills. This year we've been here through the first heavy snow of 2016.

The youth hostel is a mile and a half from the village of Coniston and the lake where Donald Campbell died trying to become the fastest man on water in 1967. The lake inspired Arthur Ransome when he wrote *Swallows and Amazons*. Wild Cat Island, where the Walker children camped, is at the south end of Coniston Water.

The walk from Coniston village is a fine way to reach a youth hostel. Out of the village, passing a clutch of houses among Scots pines, the road turns and climbs steeply through a gate beside a stone wall. The damp scent of water, bracken and the fells greets you. The wall drops suddenly and reveals a steep sided gulley and a rushing stream. Water that has hurled itself from the fells above is loud, sparkling and clean, green with the colour of slate. As we climb we crest a rise into the wide flat bottomed valley hemmed about with hills with everywhere old mine workings and the rubble the miners have left. The track goes on beside the stream which here is wide and shallow. It meanders, winds and snakes. The small white building at the head of the valley is the youth hostel. Walking closer I can see the doorway where I sat and soaked in sunshine on a spring day when I first came here and discovered that in England I could find remote, wild landscapes.

The valley has changed since then. Trees have grown where once there were none. The land around has a new owner. He has built a house and a large block, like an Alpine hotel, where once there were only ruins. Cars come up and down the track, proving how wedded we have become to the car and its infernal combustion engine. We think we must drive wherever we can, wherever we please and wherever a rough track can take us. We do anything rather than walk even when we go out to walk.

It is great to be back here, back in the rough readiness of a mountain hostel. The location is a delight, tucked under the hills and facing down the valley to hills in the faraway blue distance. The hostel is small, like the other small hostels of the Lake District, like the one at Honister and the one at Black Sail. The people staying while we are here remind me of the first group who set up youth hostels on Merseyside, of Connie Alexander and her friends. They have come here to be together, to climb the hills. I don't know if they have bought a recipe book.

In the evening, they gather to cook in the little kitchen. They eat and chat. They sit around the fire in the small lounge late into the night. They are there when I go to bed and I leave them to it. I am no longer responsible for hustling them off to bed. They can do that when they wish. They drink wine, beer and gin with the approval of YHA. When they arrived, they found their beds already made with fitted sheets, pillows and duvets in YHA's fresh green colours. Sheets, pillowcases and duvets are changed for each new guest. There are no more sheet sleeping bags. The beds and bedding are cleaner than they used to be. People come and go as they please. No rules, no curfew. They're free to enjoy themselves as they please and my job is easier too without that need to nag and enforce rules.

My job is easier in other ways. The telephone doesn't ring incessantly. Neither does the postman bring bundles of letters that have to be opened and responded to one by one laboriously. People book on line or call a centre in Derbyshire. The hostel no longer has a shop selling basic supplies. It sells no baked beans, no spaghetti in cans, no packets of dried potato, no sweets and no sachets of instant coffee. Tins of rice pudding have gone completely. People bring all they need from supermarkets in their cars.

Further afield even more has changed. The youth hostel at Ambleside has a bar, a lakeside restaurant and meeting rooms. During the summer young people taking part in the national citizen service scheme stay there. Families, visiting the Beatrix Potter Experience or taking their children rambling, stay. Outdoor enthusiasts of all ages and overseas backpackers still stay. The backpackers haven't changed except they now want wi-fi. They no longer queue for the payphone to call home when the hours somewhere else in the world coincide with our time zone. They skype and use Facetime.

The views across Windermere are still fantastic and many of the rooms have en-suite showers. The old bathrooms I used to clean are gone. Staff no longer cook, clean, serve meals, work on reception and mow lawns. They have one responsibility and work in teams of specialists in the kitchens, reception or housekeeping. They tell me they still love the work the way I did. It is still more of a lifestyle, less of a job.

Youth hostels are having a renaissance. Youth hostels record numbers staying that are well above the numbers that stayed in the 1950s which many regard as the golden days of youth hostels. Each year, on average, a million people have stayed in youth hostels since they began.

They stay for the same reason people have always stayed in youth hostels. They stay because prices are low. They stay because youth hostels accommodate groups of all sizes, from groups of friends to families to entire school classes. They stay because they like the style, because they like the informal sociability, that friendliness descended of the social mixing and easy democratic ways of the first youth hostels.

Even Hilton hotels are thinking of opening hostels. Their chief executive reckoned a new chain could offer younger customers "urban flair" and stripped-back services for lower prices. Marriott hotels have linked with Ikea to launch a budget chain for young people with style, service and affordable prices. Everyone wants to get across youth hostels.

The voluntary, democratic organisation of members is now professionally run but the people using youth hostels have changed very little. Young men make up the group staying at Coppermines. They have about them the air of those who first started youth hostels. Outdoor adventure calls them. Snow on the hills excites them.

I started this book because I wanted to find out why youth hostels excited such passion amongst their users. Now I am sure youth hostels excite passion like no other kinds of accommodation because they can give those who stay in them freedom. Youth hostels set people free to travel and in youth hostels people are free to make their own experience. Like the first experience of anything, the first taste of beer, first love, first sex, we don't forget them.

As Gatliff would have wanted, bishop and blacksmith are still equally welcome. Youth hostels bring travellers of all ages, interests, faiths and nationalities to live together side by side, to eat together, to talk and walk together and that as Katie Dawes, a blogger, writes is "a beautiful thing in a world full of war and turmoil mostly brought about by a lack of understanding of other cultures."

We love youth hostels because in them we organise and arrange things for ourselves. We plan our own routes. We take our own freedom. Youth hostels changed the world by introducing that freedom to travel for everyone. That is how they changed the world. They succeeded in that endeavour by remaining open to all. So long as they were open to everyone they have succeeded.

In the morning at Coppermines excitement takes hold. People prepare. They get out boots, check straps. They call to each other, hurrying stragglers. Hostels are always like this as departure approaches. The world and the purpose of travel calls and they want to get out and get going.

I wish youth hostels well. They have survived their long history well. Whenever they have threatened to shut themselves off they have failed. They have failed when they push people away. They failed when they said some people were unsuitable because of the way they travelled, because of the way they behaved. They have succeeded most when they are open to all. I hope they will remain true to that.

Having changed the world they have had to hurry to catch up and change themselves. Having caught up they are now recapturing the idealism from which they leaped. I hope they will rediscover their radical roots and once again, set the way for the young people of the future to change the world.

Acknowledgements

This book was a journey, taken with the help and support of many people, the guests, colleagues, staff and volunteers whom I met along the way, in youth hostels and offices, in meetings, at events, in pubs and restaurants after work, on hills, beaches and cricket fields, in this country and abroad, who shared the time I worked in and for youth hostels. Particular thanks to Graham and Betty Ives. If they had not given me a job, I never could have set out.

Thanks to Dave Allison for arranging bike rides when I was first considering writing this book; to Ken Rome, Jon Cant and Dave Allen, walking companions along the way, and Caroline White who read an early draft and listened with a critical ear to my thoughts when I sometimes stopped to reflect.

Thanks to my brother-in-law, Iain Taylor, who helped me see the wider world of outdoor education in which youth hostels sat. Mills Prudhomme and Ben Butler studied maps to determine routes by which Schirrmann and Fairclough may have travelled.

When I first wrote my reflections of the journey, Helen Maurice-Jones, Katherine Ward, Margaret Howard, Mark Freeman and Sheila Buddell read an early draft and made helpful comments.

Chris Cross assisted my architectural research. He ushered me towards RIBA, a portal I never would have considered entering if Sasha Devas had not introduced Chris to me after an afternoon pause in her garden. Simon Ashworth refreshed my memory of research he undertook while I was still working for YHA.

Staff at various archives helped along the way, at the British Architectural Library, RIBA, at the London Metropolitan Archives and at the Friends Central Library. Thanks to the Carnegie UK Trust for making available their minutes online. They set a standard for accessibility I have not found others reaching. I could not have completed the journey without support, advice and assistance from Sue Worrall, Mark Eccleston and all at the Cadbury Research Library, University of Birmingham.

At a time of cuts to public libraries I am grateful to Derbyshire County Council Libraries for assistance and support and particularly the staff at Matlock library.

Thanks to YHA for permission to quote from its archive; Carol Holding for permission to quote from her father's autobiography; Ian Shaw for permission to quote from his transcript of Bertha Gough's diary; to Jon Rabbett and Hi Hostels for permission to quote from *The Magic Triangle* and Graham Heath's biography of Richard Schirrmann; the Lutterworth Press for permission to quote from *The Hike Book*; The Friends Quarterly for permission to quote from the article by Cynthia Hill. The extract from *The Road To Wigan Pier* by George Orwell (Copyright © George Orwell, 1937) is reprinted by permission of Bill Hamilton as the Literary Executor of the Estate of the Late Sonia Brownell Orwell and Penguin Books Ltd. Every effort has been made to contact copyright holders. I'll be happy to make good in future editions any omissions and errors brought to my attention.

Like walking, I sometimes thought only older people had an interest in youth hostels and their history until I read Katie Dawes' blog, *The Hostel Girl*. I love it that Katie takes the wide view of hostels and their ethos. If you have never come across her blog and have an interest in youth hostels, I recommend it. Thanks to Katie for permission to quote from her blog.

Special thanks to Len Clark for reading an early muddled draft, for his comments and encouragement and for permission to quote from his biography of Gatliff. This might not be the history he wanted but it is nevertheless a book about youth hostels for him. Special thanks also to Caroline White for encouraging this venture.

I could not have written this book without the support of John Martin, YHA's honorary archivist, at every step. He read a draft manuscript not once but twice. He answered questions, offered comments and pointed me towards invaluable materials. Without his efforts YHA's archive would have sat neglected and disheveled in a dusty cage in Trevelyan House, unavailable to anyone. John prompted and nudged me to greater interest in youth hostel history. He and Crewenna Dymond, YHA's head of volunteering, decided that as head of corporate affairs the archive should be my concern. The rest is history.

Caroline and our daughters, Fiona and Anna, shared the journey too much and too often. I missed concerts, prize givings and other events of family life. I was away because youth hostel travels had my attention but they always supported me, even in this when I was supposed to have left youth hostels behind. Thanks to them and especially Caroline who shared every step along the way, its repose, its babbling speech, its sleeping time and waking time.

Glossary

An Óige, the Irish youth hostels association
Board of Trustees, the board replaced the National Executive Committee from the 90s onward
Hostelling News, magazine 1972 - 1985
IYHF, International Youth Hostel Federation
IYHF President, chairman of the international federation
National Chairman, elected by National Council and chairman of the Executive
National Council, YHA's governing body made up of representatives of the regional groups and affiliated societies, the president and vice presidents.
National Executive Committee, executive made up of representatives of the regional groups and co-opted members, ran YHA nationally between national council meetings - throughout I use executive for YHA's executive committees until the arrival of a chief executive
National Secretary, secretary to the National Executive Committee, equivalent of today's chief executive though with less autonomy
NAYHW, National Association of Youth Hostel Wardens
NCSS, National Council of Social Services, forerunner of NCVO, assisted social services to get started in Britain
Regional Chairman, chaired each regional council and was the senior figure in each regional group
Regional Council, governing body for a YHA regional group elected by members from within a geographic area
Regional secretary, executive who carried out the instructions of a regional council
SYHA, Scottish Youth Hostels Association
YHANI, Youth Hostel Association of Northern Ireland
The Rucksack, magazine 1938 - 1956, formerly *YHA Rucksack*, 1932 -

1938

The Youth Hosteller, magazine 1957 - 1972

Triangle, magazine 1990 - 2006 (not to be mistaken for Triangle, YHA's house magazine 1982 – 1988)

YHA Magazine, magazine 1985 - 1990

Bibliography

Archives

From the Carnegie Trust UK:

Carnegie Trust UK, Reports and Minutes

From the National Council of Social Services at the London Metropolitan Archives:

Executive Committee 1930-1933 (1 volume), Annual General Meetings 1925-1943

National Council of Social Service History 1919-1940: five papers by HA Mess

From the YHA Archive held at the Cadbury Research Library, University of Birmingham:

Trevelyan, GM, *Address by Prof GM Trevelyan, OM, The President of the Association, on the wireless January 21st, 1931* Y400004-01

Annual Reports, Y440001

Clark, Len, *Herbert Gatliff, an English Eccentric*, The Gatliff Trust, 1995, Y410101

Concerning Youth Hostels in England and Wales, Y400103

Gough, Bertha, *A Diary of Seven Years with the YHA*, 1937, Y610041

Gummerson, Robert, *The Quick and the Dead, 21 Years a Youth Hostel Warden*, Y630019

Hostelling News Magazine, 1972-85, Y510001

Instructions for Youth Hostel Wardens, Y740001

Martin, John, *Historical Listing of All Youth Hostels and Associated Accommodation* Y900003 (digital)

National Minutes, Y700003

Rowe, Courtney, *Kennack Sands Youth Hostel* account by the wardens' son Y050001-Kennack 701

Rucksack, later *Youth Hosteller* Magazine 1939-72, Y500001

Smith, Geoff, *Caveat Nostalgia: The Personal Reminiscences and Reflections of a*

Hosteller 1937–1990, Y410007

Taylor, Reg, *The Pioneering Years*, Y247001

The National Policy Report (as approved by National Council) 1968, Y716002

The Kingsley Report, Y718001

The Story of the Southern Pathfinders, We Won't Go Cosy, Y650002

Tighe, Michael, *Working party records*, Y610027

Triangle (in-house magazine) 1982-1988, Y520001

Vincent, Noel, *The Tanners Hatch Story*, Y630001

YHA Magazine, later *Triangle*, 1985-2006, Y520101

YHA News, 1992-2006, Y521001

Books

Barton, Susan, *Working-class Organisations and Popular Tourism, 1840-1970*, Manchester University Press, Manchester, 2005

Bloch, Michael, *James Lees-Milne, The Life*, John Murray, 2009

Cannadine, David, *GM Trevelyan A Life in History*, Fontana Press, 1992

Catchpool, E St John, *Candles in the Darkness*, The Bannisdale Press, London, 1966

Coburn, Oliver, *Youth Hostel Story, the First Twenty years in England and Wales*, The National Council of Social Service, London, 1950

Cox, Jack, *The Hike Book*, Lutterworth Press, 1960

Foot and Mouth Disease 2001: Lessons to be Learned Inquiry Report, The Stationery Office, London, 2002

Gillis, John R, *Youth and History, Tradition and Change in European Age Relations 1770-Present*, Academic Press, New York, 1974

Grassl, Anton, and Heath, Graham, *The Magic Triangle, a Short History of the World Youth Hostel Movement*, International Youth Hostel Federation, 1982

Hardy, Dennis, and Ward, Colin, *Arcadia for All, The Legacy of a Makeshift Landscape*, Mansell Publishing Ltd, 1984

Heath, Graham, *Richard Schirrmann, the First Youth Hosteller, A biographical sketch*, International Youth Hostel Federation, Copenhagen, 1962

Hill, Howard, *Freedom to Roam: The Struggle for Access to Britain's Moors and Mountains*, Moorland Publishing, 1980

Leonard, T Arthur, *Adventures in Holiday Making*, Holiday Fellowship, 1934

Maurice-Jones, Helen, and Porter, Lindsey,
  Spirit of YHA, published privately by the authors, 2008
  Eighty Years of Hostelling, YHA, 2010

Matless, David, *Landscape and Englishness*, Reaktion Books, 2001

Moffat, Gwen, *Space Below My Feet*, Hodder & Stoughton, Great Britain, 1961

Morris, AJA, *CP Trevelyan 1870-1958 Portrait of a Radical*, Blackstaff Press, 1977

Ogilvie, Ken C, *Roots and Wings: a History of Outdoor Education and Outdoor Learning in the UK*, Russell House Publishing, 2013

Orwell, George,
>   *The Road to Wigan Pier*, Penguin Books, 1970
>
>   *Collected Essays and Journalism, Volume 1*, Penguin Books, 1970

Report to Natural England on Childhood and Nature: A Survey on Changing Relationships with Nature across Generations, March, 2009

Snape, Michael, *The Back Parts of War, the YMCA Memoirs and Letters of Barclay Baron, 1915-1919*, The Boydell Press, 2009

Smith, Daniel, *Isabel Bacheler Smith: Artist, Teacher, Mother, & Peacemaker*, Living Legacy Productions, 2012

Stachura, *The German Youth Movement 1900 – 1945*, Macmillan Press, London 1981

Tatham, Meaburn, and Miles, James E, *The Friends Ambulance Unit 1914 - 1919, A Record*, The Swarthmore Press, 1920

Trench, Terry, *Fifty Years Young, The story of An Óige*, Irish Youth Hostels Association, Dublin, 1981

Trevelyan, G M, *An Autobiography and other essays*, Longman, Green and Co, 1949

Trevelyan, Laura, *A Very British Family*, IB Tauris & Co Ltd, London, 2012

Williams-Ellis, Clough, *Britain and the Beast*, JM Dent and Sons, London, 1937

Articles

Biesanz, John, *Nazi influences on German Youth Hostels*, Social Forces Vol 19 No 4, May 1941

Biesanz, John and Mavis, *The School and the Youth Hostel*, Journal of Educational Sociology Vol 15, No 1 Sep 1941

Dickinson, AEF, *Rev HH Symonds Appreciations*, the Guardian Dec 31 1958

A Champion of Natural Beauty (Rev HH Symonds) the Guardian Dec 29 1958

Freeman, M, *Fellowship, Service and the "Spirit of Adventure"* 2002

Harris, Cynthia, *E St John (Jack) Catchpool*, the Friends Quarterly, July 1971

Hodgson, Geoffrey M, *What are Institutions* in JOURNAL OF ECONOMIC ISSUES March 2006

McCulloch, John, *Background Information Brief No 21*, Queensland Parliamentary Library, Brisbane, 1991

McCulloch, John, *The Youth Hostels Association: Precursors and Contemporary Achievements*, The Journal of Tourism Studies Vol 3, No 1, (Australia) May 1992

Smith, MK, and Doyle, ME, *The Albemarle Report and the Development of Youth Work in England and Wales*, the Encyclopaedia of Informal Education

Stevenson, *John, The Countryside, Planning, and Civil Society in Britain 1926 - 1947*

Youth and Peace, Derbyshire Countryside Magazine, January 1953

Index

read more

DUNCAN M SIMPSON

RICHARD SCHIRRMANN – THE MAN WHO INVENTED YOUTH HOSTELS

Richard Schirrmann invented youth hostels. Today they cover the world.

Taken up in Germany, then in Europe and then around the world, they survived the rise of the Nazis, two world wars and an economic depression. Schirrmann never gave up. He never copyrighted his idea, never built it into a brand, never sold it to anyone. He was a volunteer and an amateur in the best sense of the word. He wanted the best for young people.

Working from previous biographies and original records in English, *Richard Schirrmann – the man who invented youth hostels* reveals the life of the man who invented youth hostels and of those who worked with him like Jack Catchpool and Isabel and Monroe Smith, the young couple who took youth hostels to the USA.

---

www.duncanmsimpsonwriting.com

Lightning Source UK Ltd.
Milton Keynes UK
UKOW02f0846280916

283989UK00001B/107/P

9 781786 972330